Measures
of the Mission

Measures of the Mission
A Survey of the Bible, Church, and Family

Copyright © 2023 by Rich Lusk

Athanasius Press
715 Cypress Street
West Monroe, Louisiana, 71291
athanasiuspress.org | (318) 323-3061

Cover design and typesetting: Rachel Rosales

ISBN: 978-1-957726-08-3

Printed in the United States of America.

Measures of the Mission

A SURVEY OF THE BIBLE, CHURCH, AND FAMILY

RICH LUSK

Table of Contents

Preface

My friend Kevin Fox has done the church a great favor by helping put this book together. Kevin came to my church, Trinity Presbyterian (Communion of Reformed Evangelical Churches, or CREC) in Birmingham, AL years ago because we offered some things he had found missing in previous churches. But when Kevin made the transition, he received a lot of questions from his friends about his ecclesiastical shift. As he tried to field their questions, he realized it would be great to have a book to place in their hands. The problem is that such a book did not exist.

Around that same time, Kevin was jotting down notes from sermons I preached. Anytime I said something in a sermon that made him think, "That's why I'm here. That's what was missing!" he would transcribe that part of the sermon and file it away. Eventually Kevin showed me what he had and I told him, "Kevin, I think you have the book you said you wanted to give to people."

Of course, it is a long way from some sermon notes to a finished book, and the journey has been quite slow for us. Like any book, it is hard for the writer—or in this case writers plural—to let go because it could always be made better in both form and content. But the time has come for us to release this work to the public with the goal of bringing people to a deeper and broader understanding of the gospel, the Scriptures, liturgy, and the church.

I often consider myself to be a patchwork of those people who have influenced me in various ways. This book is no different. It would be impossible to thank, much less footnote, all those who have contributed to making this book what it is. Kevin might have used sermons I preached as the original basis for this material, but his own finger-prints are all over it. Kevin is a sharp, well-read, and in-sightful churchman. In addition, several friends read ear-ly versions of this work and provided helpful input. Of course, I bear full responsibility for the final product. But very little presented here can claim to be original. Do not let the shortage of footnotes fool you; we are channeling things we have both learned from other Spiritual giants who have influenced us deeply.

Our hope is to especially help evangelical and re-formed Christians discover biblical and liturgical riches that are often missing from our churches. Why do so many Christians in American seem to make so little difference? What if the biggest problem our churches face is not op-position from the world, but our own spiritual laziness and indifference to the great inheritance that could be ours, if only we would claim it? What if the church is all too often her own worst enemy? What if our churches are trying too hard to entertain bored Christians, instead of challenging Christians to live as the royal priesthood God has made them to be? What if our version of the gospel is too small and too thin? The point of this project is to prod readers to find that bigger, thicker gospel that Scripture offers. The church in our day is a mess. Even if we confine our assessment to more conservative/traditional evangelical and reformed Christians, we are still divided against one another. We are weak and impotent when we ought to be strong, going forth conquering and to conquer. We tend to either naively ignore the culture war or try to fight the culture war using the culture's weapons. Our hope is that this book will be one of many resources that can aid in bringing reformation to the church, that she might be strengthened, renewed, and able to claim the inheritance that God has promised to her through Jesus Christ, her savior.

Just as we have shrunk the gospel, we have tended to shrink the mission of the church. A gospel that is only concerned with saving souls will produce a church only concerned with saving souls. But what if the goal God wants us to pursue is not just getting souls to heaven but creating Christendom—a Christian civilization—on earth? Is the church up to the task? Can the gospel we profess to believe in produce such a result? We are convinced the gospel revealed in the Scripture is comprehensive and world-changing. Through the gospel, God not only forgives our sins and makes us new; through the gospel, God promises to fulfill the original mandate He gave to the human race. In and through the new Adam, Jesus, united to His bride, the church, the earth will come to be filled with image bearers who worship and serve the triune God. Christ and His church will rule and subdue the earth in wisdom and righteousness. The kingdom will come, and God's will shall be done on earth as in heaven.

As noted already, much of this book is based on sermons that were preached at Trinity Presbyterian Church, mostly in the early 2010s. This means the material was developed before "wokeness," social justice, critical race theory, and transgender ideology got mainstreamed and infiltrated ostensibly conservative churches. We have updated the material to touch on some of these issues in passing along the way, but our main goal is not to address the theological and cultural fads that are changing faster than most of us can keep up. Our goal is to call the church back to the "old paths" found in Scripture and best represented in the Reformation/post-Reformation era of church history.

Obviously no book can be comprehensive but we are seeking to give our readers a "taste" of God's whole menu. Too often, Christians who are so quick to show they are "grace centered" really do not pay attention to God's foundational work of creation. This book is certainly grace based—we believe our whole salvation is found in the crucified and risen and reigning Christ, whom we receive and are united to by faith alone—but God's saving grace restores and ultimately glorifies His original work of creation. To be truly grace-centered is to be creation-based. When God made the world, He not only made it good; He set it on a particular trajectory. The goal from the beginning was for man, as God's vice regent, to transform the garden into the garden-city. Sin derailed that trajectory; grace restores that trajectory. That's what this book is about, in a nutshell: Creation, creation lost, creation regained, creation consummated.

The biggest area of controversy in our day is sexuality. This is where Satan is especially attacking us, and so it is important for us to especially fortify our understanding of God's design in this area. While it is necessary for us to understand the more extreme perversions of God's sexual design—homosexuality, pornography, and transgenderism come to mind as the worst distortions right now—we have chosen to focus on the basics of men, women, marriage, and children. The chapter on marriage is considerably longer than others in the book for a reason. If we do not get marriage right, we are going to get everything else wrong. But if we properly understand marriage, including the meaning of male and female, we are going to be pretty well safeguarded against almost every form of sexual chaos and confusion that comes down the pike.

We are writing as convinced ecclesiocentrists because we believe the church is the body and bride of Christ. Church history is central to world history. God created the world for the sake of the church, that He might have a bride for His Son. The church is our first family and our first nation and our first city. But this does not mean the church is our only family and nation. The church is tasked not with absorbing these other spheres but with discipling these other spheres. The means of grace have been entrusted to the church, which means she applies the Word of God, in principle, to all of life; by exercising the keys of the kingdom she admits and excludes sinners for the realm of God's forgiveness and new life; as citizens of a heaven, she manifests resurrection life in ways appropriate to the pre-resurrection age.

While the church is central to the identity of the Christian, Christians are more than just members. And the church has (or should have) a mutually beneficial relationship with other God-ordained spheres. Thus, we insist, the family is also vital to God's purposes in the world. The church is central and the family is foundational, as God's purposes center on the church, in history and eternity. But those purposes cannot be fulfilled without faithful families. The church trains people in the meaning and purpose of the creation mandate, but the family is largely responsible for executing that mandate by multiplying and taking dominion. Some have said, "As the church goes, so the society goes." Others say, "As the family goes, so the nation goes," or even, "As men go, so the family goes, and as the family goes, so society goes." In reality, it is possible for all of these to be true at the same time, albeit in differing ways. It is true that families depend on the men who lead them and when there is a shortage of good men, society as whole will suffer. But where are we going to find good men? How shall we form men into reliable and trustworthy patriarchs who establish and lead families wisely? The church is given the task of discipling men and their families. Thus, the family depends on the church. Psalm 128 celebrates the blessed man who leads his family in fulfilling God's design, but note that the blessing comes out of Zion (Ps. 128:5), which must be understood as the church (Heb. 12:22ff). But, again, the church/family relationship at its best is highly symbiotic. The church needs good men to serve as pastors and elders. Where will these men come from? Where does the church get her supply of well-equipped, proven men who are qualified for leadership? Paul says in

1 Timothy 3:4-5 that a man should only be considered for these offices if he has proven to be a competent and faithful ruler of his own household; if his ministry does not bear fruit in his own household, why should we expect it to bear fruit in God's household of the church? Family and church are thus interdependent. To be sure, the church has a kind of ultimacy that does not belong to the family because the church is our primary and eternal family, city, and nation. But the church is not our *only* family, city, and nation. We need these other institutions to play their roles as well.

Further, it is not our purpose in this book to develop a comprehensive political theology, though we will certainly touch on the big picture politically. Of the four basic governmental spheres God has established—self-government, church government, family government, and civil government—the civil sphere is probably the most neglected or misunderstood by Christians in our day. While we do not go into great detail addressing the political ills of the modern West here, the ultimate solution to our political problems will be found in the gospel. The foundation of any Christian political platform must be the confession "Jesus is Lord." Attempts to privatize Jesus' lordship end up truncating the Gospel in precisely the ways we are seeking to refute in this book. Jesus is Caesar's Lord. Caesar is called upon to render to God the things that belong to God. Christians living under a secular or humanistic government should call upon their leaders to "kiss the Son lest He be angry," as David put in in Psalm 2. There is no neutrality. There is nothing outside the scope of Christ's reign. Discipling the nations requires teaching nations, as nations, as political and governmental entities, to conform to God's law. Anything less falls short of the mission Jesus gave us. Francis Schaeffer warned a generation ago that statism would be the great threat to the church. We are seeing that threat play out before our eyes. Far too many Christians today are drifting into various forms of socialism, woke-ism, and progressivism, all of which are variations of statism. Even movements like feminism and LGBTQism ultimately trace back to statism; these movements are unnatural and so can only be sustained by the force of the state.

A lot of evangelical Christians today do all the right things, but do them in the wrong way. We worship, we evangelize, we engage the culture. But our worship is shallow and trite rather than full of reverent joy. We evangelize, but we focus on saving individual souls rather than discipling nations. We engage the culture but we do not use the Spiritual weapons God has given us, so the culture ends up influencing us a lot more than we influence the culture. We need nothing less than a comprehensive reformation of the church. Reformation 2.0 will have to be as deep and as thorough as the work God did in the sixteenth and seventeenth centuries—perhaps more so since in the previous Reformation, it was a largely Christianized-but-dilapidated society that needing reforming, whereas in our day it is a full-blown secular society that needs reforming.

This book is not intended to be a scholarly tome but neither is it an entry level work that reinforces what has become the status quo in evangelicalism. Evangelical culture has become addicted to mediocrity, seen in all kinds of ways, including our anti-intellectualism. We can do better. We need to be pushed. This volume was written out of the conviction that the kind of church needed to fulfill the mission God has given us does not really exist in the present moment, at least not in the form she needs to exist. We want to beckon evangelical Christians into the future, into a different kind of church than most have experienced. We want to help form the kind of church we see described and called for in Scripture: A church that preaches the whole counsel of God, applying the word of God not only to personal matters but also public and political issues, a church that pursues unity and truth with zeal and courage, a church that worships faithfully and according to the fullness of Scripture, with a deep appreciation for the sacraments, symbolic beauty, rituals, and liturgical patterns given to us in Scripture, a church that ministers not only in word but also in deed, by showing compassion in Jesus' name to the needy, rather than relying on a secular state to be the primary agent of charity, a church that is rooted in the creational norms God established in the beginning but is empowered by the new creation life of the risen Christ and His Spirit; a church that embraces God's design for sex, marriage, and family life in robustly counter-cultural ways; a church that trains her members in how to live out the faith in every legitimate vocation under the sun; a church that is filled with confident hope in the triumph of the gospel in and over all nations, according to the promises of Scripture—such a church does not yet exist, at least not on a wide scale. But that is the kind of church we want to see come into existence. It is the kind of church we pray for. And it is the kind of church we aim to help create by putting forward this book. May God show us His mercy.

Introduction

Jesus did *not* preach the gospel. Rather, "Jesus came to Galilee, preaching the gospel *of the kingdom of God*" (Mark 1:14). What difference does "the kingdom" part make? In truth, it makes a huge difference. Indeed, one of the biggest problems in the church today is that we preach the gospel rather than *the gospel of the kingdom*.

So often in the church today, our presentations of the gospel, whether in evangelism or from the pulpit, really focus on just one thing: How to make sure your soul will go to heaven when you die. The gospel is often shrink-wrapped to this: "You're a sinner. Jesus died for sins. Trust Him and you'll have a blissful life after death." And there is no doubt that all of that is true. But if that's presented as the whole truth, it leaves us with a lot of questions. If that's the gospel, where is this kingdom that Jesus talked about so much? If that's the gospel, what is the church for? If that is the gospel, what is most of the Bible for? Why do we have so much in the Bible about history, about the nations, and especially about the people of Israel? If the thrust of the Scriptures is the salvation of the individual soul, why so much extraneous material? Shouldn't the Bible be a lot shorter?

If the gospel is just about how to get your soul into heaven when you die, let's face it, that gospel is irrelevant to most of life. If the gospel is just a me-and-Jesus message, the church isn't really necessary and the kingdom isn't really here. That gospel is really just fire insurance and a get-out-of-hell-free card.

Some gospel presentations start out this way: "If you were to die tonight, do you know your soul would go to heaven?" That is an important question, and it is vital that we know how to answer that question. Many people have been genuinely converted because someone posed that question to them and then showed how Jesus is the answer. But what if you *don't* die tonight? What if you live? Then what does the gospel do for you? Does the gospel have anything to say to that? We all know the gospel gives us hope in the moment of our dying breath, but does it provide us with direction and purpose while we still live and breathe?

Certainly the gospel does promise forgiveness, it does promise us heaven after death, and all of that is glorious. But a gospel that leaves our lives and the world unchanged, a gospel that leaves us to wallow in our sin, a gospel that says nothing about poverty and war and broken families and disabled bodies—is that good news really good enough?

The gospel of the kingdom that Jesus preached isn't just for death, it's for life. His Good News isn't just about forgiveness, as glorious as that is. It's also about the restoration and the re-shaping of how we live in this world. This gospel of the kingdom promises to transform the whole of our life. It promises to us a renewed and transfigured creation, and in the end, nothing short of a new heavens and a new earth. This gospel of the kingdom makes us truly and fully human.

An Americanized gospel, an individualized and privatized gospel, a me-and-Jesus gospel, doesn't do that. It basically leaves my life in this world unchanged. With that kind of gospel, I can pretty much go on living for myself now, and then go to heaven when I die. But what if the gospel is bigger than that? What if it is not just your soul going to heaven when you die, but the coming of the Kingdom, the inbreaking of the reign of God in the present? What if the Gospel isn't just about our souls going to heaven when we die, but heaven coming to earth through how we live in our callings here and now?

One reason so much of the evangelical church has been susceptible to wokeness and progressivism the last few years is due to ways we have truncated the gospel. Because so many evangelicals have privatized the gospel to a "me and Jesus" salvation, most preachers have failed to apply the Bible broadly. Even if we insist on personal piety and law-keeping, many have drifted into public and social antinomianism. Because it is thought that the Word of God is not comprehensive in scope and authority, there is a void of application that must be filled. After all, even if we say the Bible does not apply to public and political issues, we are still public and political creatures. Because we have not taught how the Word of God governs all of life, that void of application has been filled by progressive forms of "social justice," by wokeness, by whatever the state or celebrity influencers tell us to do. This is why so many evangelical Christians—who should know better!—have so easily caved to COVID tyranny, climate change hysteria, socialist economic policies, and so on. Wokeness is a counterfeit of the kingdom of God, counterfeit Torah, counterfeit wisdom; as G.K. Chesterton pointed out even a century ago, progressivism is just the old Christian virtues gone mad. The church today is in desperate need of an "all of the Bible for all of life" program. That's what this book is about—though it is only a start.

The gospel is the announcement that the kingdom has come, because the king has come. The gospel of the kingdom is not just about how the story of your individual life can have a happy ending. It's about how God is bringing in a new heavens and a new earth, filled with His glory, so that the story of the whole cosmos has a happy ending. Yes, the unrepentant will be thrown into the lake of fire for their wickedness, to the praise of God's glorious justice. But the overwhelming emphasis of Scripture is on the redemption of a great multitude no man can number, to the praise of His glorious grace. God's original purpose for the creation will be fulfilled. The world will be saved. Grace restores and glorifies the fallen creation.

To understand the Kingdom, we have to move in two directions: back to the beginning and forward to the end. We have to go back to the beginning of the book of Genesis, where we find God made the world, and made it good. In the beginning, there was no sadness, no sickness, no suffering. All was love and light and laughter. In the beginning, God made mankind in His image, male and female, a complementary pair. He placed them in a glorious garden, and He gave them a commission. This commission was to rule over the earth as king and queen, to transform the world from one degree of glory to an even greater degree of glory, to transform the garden into a city.

But then tragedy struck. Our first parents in the garden chose to listen to the lies of the evil one, rather than the words of truth from God Himself. They rebelled against their creator, overthrowing His order for the world and poisoning the creation.

You might think that should have been the end of it. Shouldn't God have just scrapped everything at that point? But that's not what God did. The Father, Son, and Spirit promised together to act to undo the work of the evil one, to renew humanity, to put creation back on track so the original plan would be fulfilled, albeit now with a detour to deal with sin and death.

Fast-forward to the end of the Bible, and how does it all end? In Revelation 21-22, it ends with a glorious vision of the garden now transformed into a garden-city. Eden has become the New Jerusalem. What do we find in Revelation 21-22? It's the same garden, just as in the beginning, with the same Tree of Life, the same river running through it, and the same precious metals are found there. But the garden has been glorified, transformed, transfigured, and matured into the glorious city of God. That's the trajectory of the Biblical story: from garden to garden-city.

When Adam and Eve sinned, what happened? Death, decay, disorder, and disease came into the world, marring and disfiguring God's good creation. But what does God promise right away after the fall? Even in the midst of passing judgment on sin, He promises to send a seed of the woman, a new Adam, who will set things right, who will take what is twisted and untwist it, who will roll back the curse so creation can again know God's blessing.

As the historical story of Scripture continues, God forms Israel as a new humanity, a new Adamic race. They will be His treasured possession, His special people. He blesses the nation of Israel, not merely for their own sake, but for the purpose of blessing all the other nations, so that the blessing God has given them can flow out to all the other peoples of the earth (Gen. 12). But sadly, Israel ends up being just like Adam. She fails more often than she succeeds; instead of blessing the nations, she becomes just like the nations.

Israel was supposed to be the solution to Adam's sin but becomes part of the problem. What is needed? A new Adam who will be true and faithful, who will undo the lies of the evil one. A new and faithful Israel is needed who will carry the blessing of God to the nations.

When Jesus announces the kingdom is at hand, preaching the good news of the kingdom, He is claiming that the new Adam and the new Israel are here. He is claiming to be in Himself the answer to the curse, the answer to all of the world's evils. He is the answer to wars, terrorist bombings, cancer, crime, gossip, and godlessness. Whatever the problem is in this fallen world, Jesus and His kingdom are the solution. When He says, "The kingdom is here," He is saying, "I am the cure for sin, I am the remedy for death." When Jesus begins preaching by saying, "The time is fulfilled," He is saying, "All that God has promised about reclaiming and restoring His world is beginning to happen through me." The kingdom has arrived because the king has arrived.

God's purposes for the creation are coming full circle and they are going to be completed. Jesus is saying, "In me, dominion is going to be restored to one who is truly human." When Jesus says, "The time is fulfilled," it is like those whispers through the pages of *The Lion, the Witch, and the Wardrobe*: "Aslan is on the move!" Yes, the gospel announces Jesus is on the move. The great event, that great history-altering event that will break the spell of the evil one, that will free us from perpetual winter and bring in the bright colors and the new life of spring—that is all about to happen. The evil empire is about to be overthrown and a new empire of great grace, glory, joy and blessing is about to dawn. The gospel is the arrival of the king and His kingdom.

Why does the gospel of the kingdom sound so foreign to so many Christians in our culture? Even though we have large numerical significance in America, why does the church have such a relatively small impact on our culture? This book was written to tackle these very questions. The real problem lies with the church. The problem is not merely the liberal, unbelieving, watered-down gospel church (which, to be honest, is more the synagogue of Satan than a real church). There are also issues within the earnest, Bible-believing, evangelical church. As the church goes, so goes the culture. But instead of leading the culture in God's righteousness and wisdom, the salt has lost its saltiness and is being trampled underfoot.

For some time now, the evangelical church has been focused on short-term success in which we seek to win large numbers through planned revival events, altering the worship service, and evangelistic methods that aren't too different from selling fire insurance. We have separated Christ from culture, and the predictable result is an increasingly Christ-less culture. However, this book is not another call for individuals in the church to look inside themselves and dig deeper to foster individual evangelical activism, but a plea with the church to reform her ways.

The book is divided into three sections, revolving around this theme of the kingdom of God: the kingdom story (the Bible), kingdom central (the church), and kingdom living (culture/vocation). In order to recover the kingdom, we must understand what our story is. In order to live out the kingdom, we must see the church's place at the center of the kingdom. And if we are going to (by grace) transform the kingdoms of this world into the kingdom of God, we must understand how to live out our kingdom citizenship in everyday life. Faithful kingdom living in our vocations brings us full circle, back to God's original purposes for creation and humanity.

Section 1

The Kingdom Story

Chapter 1

Recovering the Kingdom Story

Have you ever noticed that the Bible does not read like a systematic theology textbook? Systematic theology, done in submission to Scripture, is good and necessary. But it is not the only or even most obvious way to look at the Scriptures. Rather than moving along topic by topic in an organized, scientific method, the Bible unfolds as a story. The study of the narrative of Scripture is known as biblical theology. When we look at how the apostles used the Old Testament in their writing of the New Testament, we find some things that strike us as odd. The apostles read the Old Testament very differently than most Christians today. The apostle Peter can move from the Flood and Noah's ark to the claim that "baptism now saves you" (1 Peter 3). What? Paul can make an argument for paying pastors from Deuteronomy 25:4: "You shall not muzzle an ox when it treads out the grain" (1 Tim. 5:18). How exactly does the prooftext make Paul's case? It's been pointed out that the apostles would likely fail a modern day seminary class on biblical interpretation. But if that is the case, isn't there something wrong with the way *we* read the Bible and not with the way the apostles read the Bible? Biblical theology looks at the Bible "through time," treating the Bible as a book with a history. It reads the Bible as a typological book, in which earlier persons and events foreshadow what is to come later. The Bible has a promise-fulfillment structure. If we are going to understand the Bible, we have to learn to read the Bible like the apostles, which means we have to learn typology.

Essentially, biblical theology is story theology. The Bible tells a story, and biblical theology seeks to understand that story on its own terms. Biblical theology looks at what the Bible actually says and how it says it, examining the patterns and symbols within Scripture.

Before examining the nature of the biblical story itself, we need to examine what we mean by "story." Foundational stories allow us to interpret and organize our experience, both corporately and individually. These basic stories define our past and provide a grid for mapping out future courses of action. Shared stories create social cohesion and give rise to community. Stories also embody an ethic, a particular way of "being in the world." The question "Who am I?" is essentially the question, "What's my story?" As image bearers of the story-creating, story-telling God, we inevitably give our life experiences narrative shape. Or perhaps we should say we seek to discern the shape given to our lives by the divine storyteller (Ps. 139:16).

Every identifiable civilization in history has been held together by some overarching story, or metanarrative. We see this with the ancient Hebrews. Israel understood herself in terms of several basic narratives—the creation account, the fall of Adam and Eve into sin, the call of Abraham, and most especially the exodus. Ancient Greek culture was formed by narrative, first by the stories of Homer and Hesiod, and later by the stories of the philosophers (for example, Plato's allegory of the cave). Augustine shaped medieval Christendom by re-telling the world's story in *The City of God*. In the modern West, the Augustinian story has been replaced by the stories of Locke, Darwin, Marx, and Freud. In step with these stories, the cultural stories of Western civilization have moved away from the God of the Bible.

Part of our present cultural crisis is our loss of story. People no longer believe they inhabit a "narratable world," that is, a world in which the flow of events have meaning and direction. People no longer sense history has a *plot*. It does not seem like history is *going somewhere* to moderns. In rejecting Christ, our culture rejected creation's ultimate purpose (*telos*). Robert Jenson explains the implications of this for the church and her mission:

> If there is little mystery about where the West got its faith in a narratable world, neither is there much mystery about how the West has lost this faith. The entire project of the Enlightenment was to maintain realist faith while declaring disallegiance from the God who was that faith's object. The story the Bible tells is asserted to be the story of God with His creatures; that is, it is both assumed and ex-

plicitly asserted that there is a true story about the universe because there is a universal novelist/historian. Modernity was defined by the attempt to live in a universal story without a universal storyteller.

The experiment has failed. It is, after the fact, obvious that it had to: if there is no universal storyteller, then the universe can have no story line. Neither you nor I nor all of us together can so shape the world that it can make narrative sense; if God does not invent the world's story, then it has none, then the world has no narrative that is its own. If there is no God, or indeed if there is some other God than the God of the Bible, there is no narratable world.[1]

Biblical theology enables the church to recover her sense of story, and therefore her sense of identity and mission in the world. Thus, it is crucial to the church's vitality and fidelity.

The Bible uses stories to expose sin, encourage faith, and build community among God's covenant people. We learn that the story of Israel and Jesus is now the church's story. The gospel, enacted in the liturgy and proclaimed in preaching, transforms our fallen Adamic identity by telling us the true story about the world and ourselves.

Biblical theology requires us to learn to read the biblical narrative *from within*. We are *insiders* to the story of Scripture. It's *our* story. We should read the Bible the

---

1. Robert Jenson, "How the World Lost Its Story," *First Things* March 2010, https://www.firstthings.com/article/2010/03/how-the-world-lost-its-story.

same way Peter, Susan, Lucy, and Edmund would read *The Chronicles of Narnia*—as a story not only *for us*, but *about us*. The Bible tells *our* history. We have to allow the Word to absorb the world rather than allowing the world to absorb the Word. We have to take Scripture's outlook as normative rather than imposing another worldview on our reading of Scripture. We must learn to read the Bible organically, in terms of itself. This is an *authoritative* story.

The biblical story is given its shape by the various covenant renewals God makes with His people. Ultimately, there is one foundational covenant—the triune God Himself: Father, Son, and Spirit. The one God exists eternally in three persons, who share the same attributes, the same life, the same glory. The trinitarian life of God can be described as covenantal, as each of the persons is faithful to the others. In creation and redemption, the triune God has opened up His life to humanity (John 17:20-24). Thus, the various covenants and covenant renewals we find in Scripture (Adam, Noah, Abraham, etc.) are ultimately all manifestations of man's covenantal relationship with the Trinity. The covenant between God and man matures through the course of history, moving from glory to ever greater glory, culminating in the New Covenant of Christ. Yet, the various covenants of history, while partaking in a basic unity, also have diversity, with each covenantal administration having its own unique features. Each covenant renewal event includes the previous history but also transforms that previous history into something new. Thus, history spirals upward.

The Trajectory of Creation

Looking at the Bible as a narrative means that we always keep in mind the goal of the story. God always intended for the creation, and especially humanity as the crown and representative of creation, to grow and mature. Adam's fall sent the story off course, but in His eternal plan, God used that sinful twist in the plot to manifest His glory to an even greater degree. In redemption, God restores the created order to the plan that He intended for it all along. In the incarnation, the storyteller writes Himself into the script to set the story straight. The unfolding story of Scripture cannot be understood apart from its promised end.

The happy ending of world history has broken into the middle of history through the death and resurrection of Jesus. His cross and exaltation were the beginning of the end, but there is a final end still to come. This is the narrative dynamic of the biblical story and, indeed, of the Christian life. Christians believe in a sort of time travel— the future has traveled back into the present. We are called to live now as we shall live then. We are already resurrected; we shall be resurrected. Just as we live from back to front, so we have to read the Bible from end to beginning.

A note of caution is in order here, lest we fall into an over-realized eschatology. If the life of the future has broken into the present, someone might wonder, for example, why we still marry, given what Jesus teaches about the resurrection in Matthew 22:30. Scripture is clear that the eschaton has broken into the present (e.g., Eph. 1:19-20), but it is only here in principle, not in fullness. We experience the power of the resurrection even though we are not yet resurrected. In this age, the grace of the gospel restores the original creation in such a way that God's design can be fulfilled. So, for example, in marriage, redemptive grace helps us to fulfill our natural, creational roles as husbands and wives. When Jesus returns to wrap up history and bring us into the final form of the new creation, our marriages will give way to only eternal marriage, that of Christ to His church. In the meantime, marriage must endure as symbol of what is to come.

Dorothy Sayers once said, "The dogma is the drama." Or perhaps we should say, "The drama—the story—is our dogma." Biblical religion is not reducible to a philosophy or ideology. Rather, it is a history—a story with a happy ending. It is the story of stories. It is the true story of the world. Like any good story, it has good and bad characters. It has conflict and resolution. It has a hero—Jesus—and heroine—His church.

This whole story, from creation, to the Fall of man into sin, to redemption in Christ, to the glorious end of resurrection life has been truncated by many modern evangelicals. Rather than beginning our story with creation and the trajectory God built into the world from the beginning, many have essentially shifted the starting place of our story to the Fall of man. And rather than ending our story with the resurrection and restoration of this physical world, as the Bible describes, many have tended to end the story with a disembodied existence in heaven. By this, we do not mean to imply that evangelicals are denying the fact of creation, but that many fail to connect the creation account to the rest of Scripture. And we do not mean that evangelicals are actually denying the bodily resurrection, but rather they are not giving it sufficient prominence in

their eschatology. Creation and redemption are woven together. A simple way to diagnose this issue: Do we see a
clear connection between the Great Commission Jesus gave
the disciples (Matt. 28:18-20) and the Dominion Mandate
given by God to Adam and the woman (Gen. 1:26ff)?

Our culture needs to recapture this more complete
story, the gospel of the kingdom, which gives meaning to
both individuals and society as a whole. Jesus preached the
kingdom and established the kingdom through His life,
death, resurrection, ascension and the formation of His
church, with the outpouring of the Holy Spirit at Pentecost. This gospel of the kingdom story begins at creation
in the Garden of Eden and ends with the heavenly city
descending to earth. It is a divine comedy, with a happy
ending in which Christ and His bride (the church) "live
happily ever after."

Of course, in between the bookends of creation and
glory, there is the rest of the story, including the part that
modern evangelicalism gets right. We are fallen sinners,
and Christ died for us so that when we die, we get to go
to heaven. But this "gospel of the kingdom" story includes
much more fits into typical evangelistic tracts. We cannot
end the story at the death of Christ but must preach the
resurrection, ascension, and Pentecost with zeal. These
events and their meanings are included in the gospel.

In the gospel of the kingdom, the church as Christ's
bride is not just an afterthought, but front and center. In
the classic hermeneutics text, *On Christian Doctrine*, Augustine starts with the basic principle of *Totus Christus*: the
whole Christ, head and body. To find Christ in the story
is to find the church, and vice versa. Christ cannot be sep-

arated from His people. The story of Scripture is not just about Jesus; it is also about His bride, the "damsel in distress" whom He comes to rescue from the clutches of the dragon. In Old Testament narratives, we not only have to find "Christ figures" but also "church figures."[2] We have to learn to find ourselves in the biblical narrative. The biblical story is our story. We must locate the place of the church within the biblical storyline as a whole, as well as in the Bible's individual stories.

God's Plan for History

Jesus Christ is the heart of God's plan for creation and history. The entire message of Scripture is about Jesus Christ: His person, His sufferings, and His glory (Luke 24:27). There is no "hidden plan" or "hidden God" lurking behind Christ; rather, in and through Christ, God has revealed Himself and His intentions toward the world. In Christ, the Father has *made known* the mystery of His will, which is to gather up all things into a gift for His Son (Eph. 1:3-14). Jesus is God's Plan A and there is no Plan B.

To understand why a Christ-centered reading of Scripture is so important, we need to understand why a Christ-centered view of God is important. It is not enough to read the Bible as a book about God. We must learn to read it as a book about God-in-Christ, lest we fall into

---

2. Of course, this means reading Scripture *typologically*. Typology properly done arises from within the biblical narrative itself; it is not imposed from the outside. We are looking for patterns *within* the Bible's story. Typology cannot be done piecemeal; it must be organic and holistic.

moralizing or doctrinalizing patterns of interpretation.[3] Yes, the whole Bible teaches ethics and the whole Bible teaches doctrine. But the whole Bible is also a history, a story, and that history centers on Jesus Christ. He reveals the very character and nature of God. To see Jesus is to see what the Father is like. In the incarnation and the cross, God is not acting out of character; rather, this is what He's really like from the inside. Jesus is the revelation of God in human form.

All of this means we must not contemplate God apart from Jesus. In a certain sense, *all theology is Christology*. The Father creates and redeems through His Son. But this means we must read the Bible as a book about Jesus— or more pointedly, as God's revelation of Himself in and through Jesus. A Christ-centered theology feeds into a Christ-centered reading of the Bible. Jesus is the "leading man" in this story. He is the hero of the story the Bible tells.

All of Scripture is held together by its testimony to Christ. The Old Covenant Scriptures foreshadow His coming, often in puzzling and paradoxical ways. The New Covenant records His coming and unpacks its meaning. All the types and shadows of the old aeon converge upon Him; from Him emerges a new creation and a transformed Israel. The New Testament writers essentially retell the story of the world and Israel in light of Christ. They draw out what was implicit but hidden in the Old Covenant Scriptures all along, only coming to full light in Christ.

---

3. Fundamentalists are usually guilty of moralizing Old Testament narratives, while Reformed preachers are more likely to preach them as vehicles of doctrine.

Like a prism breaking light up into a beautiful spectrum of colors, the Old Testament presents Christ to us in a wide range of shapes, hues, and tones. The death and resurrection of Christ complete the Old Testament story, just as the Old Testament story prepares the way for the story of Christ. The Old Testament was a story in search of an ending; that ending is found in Christ. The Bible is like the prongs of a ring holding the diamond—Christ—in place so we can gaze at His perfect glory and beauty.

It is not enough to end at a Christ-centered reading of the Bible. We must also have a Christ-centered view of human history. Scripture is a narrative that is *going somewhere*—and that goal, is Christ himself. The whole of Scripture is to be read through an eschatological lens. As already noted this story ends not with a "loner Christ." It does not end with Christ as a confirmed bachelor. It ends with a marriage. Christ cannot be separated from the people He came to save, and so if the story of the Bible is about him, it is about them as well. The *Totus Christus*, Christ and the church, are at the center of history. In Christ and through the church, the kingdom will spread to fill the whole earth (Ps. 72:8). The church is Christ's helper, His bride, His body, His dwelling place. As Jesus fulfills the Great Commission (Matt. 28) through His church, He also fulfills the original creation mandate (Gen. 1).

In a society in which the narrative has been lost, the church must recapture the divine story of Scripture. Our culture has no coherent way of looking at history; it is all sound and fury signifying nothing. Since the world has lost its story, we must re-narrate the world for the world. We must proclaim Christ as the center of the Scriptures and God's plan for humanity. He is the one in whom all things hold together. Where do we begin? At the beginning. Let's turn to the creation account.

Chapter 2

Creation: The History and Trajectory of God's World

Every good story has a good beginning, including the true story of Scripture. Genesis, the book of beginnings, is the proper starting place for proclaiming the wonderful true story of God's mighty acts. The goodness of creation is the foundation for everything that follows.

The first two chapters of Scripture, before the Fall of mankind into sin, set the trajectory for mankind's purpose. The creation account in Genesis shows us the goodness of the physical creation, the uniqueness of mankind in God's world, the division of mankind into male and female sexes, and the original task of mankind in developing dominion over God's world. When these are properly understood and applied, we have a pathway for understanding God's unfolding story of redemption throughout the Scriptures and our place in God's mission today. Like a good piece of music, the key themes are present in the beginning of Genesis and repeat with variations along the way, and brought to full fruition as the story unfolds, finally reaching a crescendo in the new creation.

The Goodness of Creation

"In the beginning, God created the heavens and the earth," says the first verse of the Holy Bible, in Genesis 1:1. The very existence of God is challenged these days by modern scientists, but according to the Scriptures, the creation constantly displays the majesty and glory of the Creator throughout the earth. What is made reveals its Maker. Psalm 19:1-4 says:

> The heavens declare the glory of God;
> And the firmament shows His handiwork.
> Day unto day utters speech,
> And night unto night reveals knowledge.
> There is no speech nor language
> Where their voice is not heard.
> Their line has gone out through all the earth,
> And their words to the end of the world.

On account of God's act of creation, all people everywhere are obligated to worship Him. This is the real rub for modern atheistic scientists; the whole theory of evolution is merely a way to escape the obligation to obey and worship the Creator God. Aldous Huxley, grandson of evolutionist Thomas Huxley had this to say:

I had motives for not wanting the world to have meaning; consequently assumed it had none, and was able without any difficulty to find satisfying reasons for this assumption….The philosopher who finds no meaning in the world is not concerned exclusively with a problem in pure metaphysics; he is also concerned to prove there is no valid reason why he personally should not do as he wants to do. . . . For myself, as no doubt for most of my contemporaries, the philosophy of meaninglessness was essentially an instrument of liberation. The liberation we desired was simultaneously liberation from a certain political and economic system and liberation from a certain system of morality. We objected to the morality because it interfered with our sexual freedom. . . . yet I found that, whatever route I took, before long I came to a tall formidable-looking fence. Confident as I might be in the existence of an ancient and indefeasible right of way, before me stood the thorny barrier with its comminatory notice board—"No thoroughfare— By order, Moses." . . . The only alternatives were to give up on my journey which I was not minded to do—or to break the fence down and go through it.[4]

Darwin, Huxley, and others were seeking to escape God because they wanted to live autonomous lives. But there is no escape from God, "For since the creation of the

---

4. Aldous Huxley, "Confessions of a Professed Atheist," *Report: Perspective on the News*, Vol. 3, June, 1966, 19.

world His invisible attributes are clearly seen, being under-stood by the things that are made, even His eternal power and Godhead, so that they are without excuse" (Rom.1:20). Scripture is clear: God made the world in the space of six days. Here is a summary of God's acts of creation in the Genesis account of the first week of history:[5]

- First Day: God created heaven and the earth.[6] God said, "Let there be light," separating the darkness from light (1:3-5). He saw that it was good.

- Second Day: God separated the heavens and earth (1:6-8). God does not declare the separation of heaven and earth good because it is not meant to be permanent; God's ultimate aim is to unite heaven and earth so the veil between them is only temporary.

- Third Day: God separated the land and sea (1:9-10) and created vegetation (1:11-13). God saw that it was good.

---

5. James B. Jordan, *Creation in Six Days* (Moscow, Idaho: Canon Press, 1999), 19. James Jordan says, "Genesis 1 presents God as creating the world and building it up over the course of a normal week of 24-hour days." This is an excellent book for a defense of the traditional reading of Genesis 1, showing that various theories such as the framework interpretation, anthropomorphic days, and limited geography interpretation are inconsistent with the text.

6. This heaven is the throne room of God, not the heavens of what we would call the sky and outer space.

- Fourth Day: God created lights in the heavens, the sun, moon, and stars (1:14-19). God saw that it was good.

- Fifth Day: God created the winged creatures and sea creatures (1:20-23). God saw that it was good.

- Sixth Day: God created land animals (1:24-25) and saw that it was good. He also created man (1:26-31) and saw that it was good. The second angle of the account given in Genesis 2 reveals that though His creation of man was good, it was not good for man to be alone, so God made a woman for him.

- Seven Day: God rested, enthroned over His creation, enjoying the beauty of His work and establishing the principle of the Sabbath refreshment on the seventh day (2:1-3).

At the beginning of the creation week, the creation is formless, empty, and dark. Over the course of the six days, God forms, fills, and glorifies (brightens) His creation. In doing so, He establishes a pattern for man to follow.

We should note that on nearly every day of creation, God repeatedly called the material world that He created good. The physical, material world as created by God is good. We must move away from any over-spiritualizing view that denigrates the physical world. We must beware of any Platonic and Gnostic tendencies which elevate the spiritual above the physical. Later on, in the fullness of time, this same Creator God would become part of His creation, taking on human flesh in the incarnation of Christ. Clearly, we cannot associate physicality with sinfulness in any way.

While Darwin's story has been set up as a rival to the creation story, the Darwinian account is completely bankrupt. By faith, we know God created (Heb. 11:6), but only faith in God as Creator provides a framework within which reason, morality, and purpose all make sense. If God is the Creator, we can account for human love and relationships; we can explain why science and the scientific method work, since we live in a world ruled by a God of law and order; we can explain why human life has meaning and purpose. Darwinism, on the other hand, requires a leap of blind faith that can account for absolutely nothing. Think of the questions the theory of evolution simply cannot answer, but which must be answered if we are going to have a coherent view of the world and give an account for how we actually live:

- How did something come from nothing?

- How did life come from non-life?

- How did the personal come from the impersonal?

- How did the moral come from the amoral?

- How did design and order come from chaos and chance?

- Where did love come from?

- Where did language come from?

- Where did rights come from?

- How is irreducible complexity explained? Organs like the eye that require numerous fully developed parts working together in order to provide evolutionary advantage could not possibly have evolved all at once.

The theory of evolution, in any and every form, is fraught with unsolvable problems. On Darwinian principles, there is no way to account for the most basic and inescapable realities of human life. It is impossible for life to have meaning since the universe had no meaning in the beginning and will have no meaning in the end. If matter in motion is all there is, there is no way to distinguish between hitting a child and hugging a child. Might makes right, which means there is no right, just raw power, survival of the strongest. The theory of evolution is a perfect illustration of fallen man's propensity to suppress God's clearly revealed truth in unrighteousness (Rom. 1:18ff).

As Glen Scrivener has said, we must "choose our miracle." Do you believe in the virgin birth of Jesus, when the Creator came into His creation? Or do you believe in the virgin birth of the universe (with no virgin), where the universe popped into existence on its own? True, the Christian story makes claims that go beyond what we can empirically verify; creation cannot be proven scientifically because there was no one there to observe it and it is an unrepeatable event. At the same time, the creation account provides the necessary preconditions for science, by showing us we live in an orderly, structured world that can be investigated (and indeed must be investigated since man was made to rule over it).

But the Darwinian account makes claims that cannot be empirically verified as well. In other words, Darwinism is a faith—an alternative religion. And frankly, the miracles it takes to make Darwinism work are far more difficult to account for than those in Scripture. Given Darwinism, human life becomes unlivable. As already noted, in a Darwinian world, all that exists is matter in motion. Given the Darwinian view of the world, why should we trust our own thought processes to lead us to truth if our brain is nothing but matter in motion? Our thoughts have no more truth value than a piece of granite. If matter in motion is all that exists, love, purpose, morality, and logic/reason do not exist. Of course, Darwinists cannot live this way. They live as if their morality is not merely a matter of personal preference but of absolute authority. Virtually no Darwinist actually lives by the code "might makes right" which is what "survival of the fittest" actually entails. Darwinists still want to use reason, they hug their children as if love were real, and they act as if life had meaning—but in each case, they are failing to be consistent with their own worldview and are smuggling in features of the Christian worldview. While the influence of Darwinism on the modern mind is waning, it still holds sway in academia and public education. Someday it will be exposed as one of the biggest hoaxes ever foisted on humanity.

Creation's Design

The creation reveals the wisdom and power of its Creator. Nature shows unmistakable signs of design. Everything God made reveals His character to us. Because man is made by God, he cannot help but know God. This is what

Paul teaches in Romans 1:18ff—while man might suppress the clearly revealed truth about God in the created order, exchanging the worship of God for an idol and exchanging God's truth for a lie, man is fully accountable for his failure to thank and glorify his Maker. There is no one who has an excuse for not worshipping and serving the true God.

From the beginning God designed His special, verbal revelation of Himself to work together with His creational revelation of Himself. God spoke to Adam at his creation in Genesis 2, and those words from God provided the lens through which Adam was to interpret the world around him. God gave him his job description (to guard and work the Garden of Eden) and his test (to refrain from eating of the Tree of the Knowledge of Good and Evil until granted access). Because God's creation reveals God—indeed, it "speaks" of God. Because we bear God's image, we can learn about God and ourselves by reflecting on the way God designed the world to work. Throughout Scripture, we find biblical authors pointing us to creation or nature (rightly interpreted) as a source of wisdom (1 Cor. 11:14). But we must be careful. Unless we "read" creation through the spectacles of Scripture (to borrow a metaphor from John Calvin) we will misread what it teaches us. There is no need to try to develop a "natural law" based on God's creational revelation of Himself, independent of Scripture. Since God has given us the Bible, we ought to use it. But there are some issues that are not directly addressed by Scripture; in those cases, wise reflection on human nature and the created order can help us. Further, God does not always explain the rationale behind His commandments in Scripture. Again, reflection on the world God made can help us better understand why God commands what He commands.

One example will have to suffice: In Romans 1:26-27, homosexuality is condemned as "unnatural." Scripture has many such condemnations of homosexuality, but even apart from them, Adam and Eve could have figured out that homosexuality would be contrary to God's creational design. Many natural lawyers have developed this sort of argument: It is obvious the fundamental purpose of our sexual powers is procreation; it is also obvious that whereas each human has many systems that are complete (e.g., a complete respiratory system, a complete circulatory system, a complete nervous system, a complete digestive system, a complete skeletal system, etc.), no human has a complete reproductive system. The male reproductive system finds its completion in the female reproductive system and vice versa; the man's reproductive anatomy makes no sense apart from the woman's and vice versa. Same-sex couplings are thus obvious misuses of our reproductive organs because they do not produce completeness and are intrinsically infertile, frustrating their very purpose, which is "to be fruitful and multiply." Thus, we can see why Paul would call homosexuality "unnatural"—it is contrary to the way God designed us to use our bodies. Further, because it is unnatural, those who practice homosexuality receive "in themselves the due penalty for their error" (Rom. 1:27). While political correctness leads our media to suppress the truth about the consequences of homosexuality, it has disastrous health effects, far worse than smoking a pack of cigarettes a day (which we have practically outlawed for health reasons in our culture). Homosexual men cut a decade or more off their life expectancy, the risk for terrible STDs and cancers skyrockets, severe mental illness is common, and so on. It is clear from Scripture and nature that homosexuality is not only a sin that will bring God's judgment; it is a form of confusion, misery, and slow motion suicide that is itself a form of divine judgment.

Mankind: The Pinnacle of Creation

Let's return to the creation narrative. The creation account crescendos from darkness to light, to heavens and earth, land and sea, plant life, the solar system and galaxies, animals, and finally to human beings. It is clear that mankind, male and female created in God's image, is the height of God's creation. Man and woman are both created in glory, albeit with differing glories, and together they are given a glorious mission, called the creation mandate. Genesis 1:26-27 says:

> Then God said, "Let us make man in our image, after our likeness. And let them have dominion over the fish of the sea and over the birds of the heavens and over the livestock and over all the earth and over every creeping thing that creeps on the earth." So God created man in His own image, in the image of God He created him; male and female He created them.

Being created in the image of God is unique to mankind. Unlike the animals, human beings image the Creator in their ability to transform the earth from glory to greater glory in righteousness.

Mankind was created by God to have dominion over the earth, including glorifying God through all aspects of culture. The majesty and dominion endowed upon mankind by his Creator is echoed in Psalm 8:

> When I look at your heavens, the work of your
>   fingers,
> the moon and the stars, which you have set in
>   place,
> what is man that you are mindful of him,
> and the son of man that you care for him?
> Yet you have made him a little lower than the
>   heavenly beings
> and crowned him with glory and honor.
> You have given him dominion over the works of
>   your hands;
> you have put all things under his feet,
> all sheep and oxen, and also the beasts of the field,
> the birds of the heavens, and the fish of the sea,
> whatever passes along the paths of the seas.
> O Lord, our Lord, how majestic is your name in
>   all the earth!

Darwin's story tells us humanity has evolved from the lower creation—microbes evolve into fish, fish into land creatures, and finally we end up with humans a little higher than the apes.[7] In Scripture's creation account, the Psalmist says we are "a little lower than the heavenly beings." Rather

---

7. And some today even go so far as to place us below the animals, preferring to save the whales rather than baby humans.

than being slightly higher on the food chain than gorillas, humans are in fact created a little lower than the angels. And our destiny is to be exalted above angels (1 Cor. 6:3)! In God's design of the world, mankind has dominion over the beasts of the field, birds of the sky, and fish of the sea.[8] In our efforts to shed light on mankind's total depravity after the Fall of man into sin, we cannot neglect mankind's glory as endowed by our Creator. We must begin the story where the Bible begins it: humans have great dignity and worth on account of their being made in the image of God. Therefore, we must cry out with the Psalmist, "O Lord, our Lord, how majestic is your name in all the earth!"

The creation account not only exposes the bankruptcy of Darwinism in all its forms, it also shows us the problems with the radical environmental movement. Radical environmentalists misunderstand man's place in the created order. We are not parasites, raping the earth. We are creation's caretakers and stewards. Creation actually thrives under man's care. For example, sheep do much better with a shepherd than without one. There are more trees in North America today than there were when the first European settlers got here because of the way man has stewarded the land. And so on.

God has given creation to us, with all its vast potentiality, and He expects us to develop it. The radical environmentalists believe that creation should be left alone as much as possible. Christians believe that creation should

---

8. Dominion involves responsibility. Thus, mankind has responsibility to properly take care of the animals and environment that is in their care. In Genesis 2:15, Adam was placed in the Garden of Eden "to dress and keep it."

be developed and used to serve human flourishing and the formation of a godly civilization. Yes, we should care about pollution; we want the earth's beauty to be preserved. Yes, we should care about what we are leaving behind for future generations. But radical environmentalism is a perfect illustration of Proverbs 8:36: "All who hate me love death." Earth worship is a death wish (quite literally, given that some radical environmentalists want to significantly depopulate the earth). It's an idolatrous religion that will cause untold human misery and suffering if allowed to have its way. We must stand against it.

Man's Tasks: Worship and Culture, Transforming the Earth for God's Glory

Worship[9]

Mankind was created with glory and He was created to glorify God by spreading His glory throughout the earth. As the Westminster Catechism says, "The chief end of man is to glorify God and enjoy Him forever." When man was created, he was put in a sanctuary, the Garden of Eden. Man was given a mission, "Be fruitful and multiply; fill the earth and subdue it; have dominion over the fish of the sea, over the birds of the air, and over every living thing that moves on the earth" (Gen. 1:28). Mission flows out of worship; there is a downstream effect from worshipping God in the sanctuary out to God's mission to the world. This is built into the fabric of our being human. We cannot

---

9. Peter J. Leithart, *The Kingdom and the Power* (Phillipsburg, New Jersey: Presbyterian and Reformed Publishing, 1993), 26-28. This section on worship relies upon this portion of Leithart's book.

have dominion and subdue the earth properly if we are not rightly relating to God by worshipping Him. Central to the mission of subduing the earth for God's glory is public worship. This is because Adam was created by God to be a priest (Gen. 2:15; the same verbs used for Adam's task are later used of the priests' work at the tabernacle; the Garden of Eden is the original sanctuary; etc.). In God's ordering of the creation, worship precedes dominion; priesthood precedes kingship.

Subduing the earth is a daunting task. To sustain and empower humanity for this task of worldwide dominion, God met with Adam and his wife regularly in Sabbath worship in the Garden of Eden. In the creation account, Adam and Eve were made on the sixth day, with Eve being created later in the day after Adam had not found "a helper comparable to him" (Gen. 2:20). Therefore, Adam and Eve's first full day together would have been the seventh day of rest and worship, showing that worship precedes our task of cultural dominion.

With God's special presence in the garden, Eden was a sanctuary on a mountain.[10] Hearing God's words and eating from the Tree of Life would strengthen and transform Adam and Eve, so that they could go out and transform the earth. Contrary to popular opinion, there was no restriction on eating from the Tree of Life before the Fall of Man into sin. By worshipping and feasting with God in the

---

10. James B. Jordan, *The Sociology of the Church* (Tyler, Texas: Geneva Ministries, 1986), 86. Out of Eden flowed a single river, which then split into four rivers: Pishon, Gihon, Hiddekel, and Euphrates (Gen. 2:10-14). Water flows downhill, so the Garden must have been on a mountainous plateau.

sanctuary Garden of Eden, Adam and Eve would receive the gifts of God, empowering them to fulfill the task of subduing the earth.

Culture

Before the creation of Eve, one of Adam's first tasks was to name the animals. As he examined the animals, Adam realized there was no helper comparable to him. God had assigned him a great task, to be fruitful and multiply. How could he do that alone? "Man learns from the animals that he lacks something needed for his kingly task. God provides what man lacks: a helper fitted for him, a queen."[11]

Adam's loneliness also depicts an aspect of being created in the image of God. God is eternally three in one; by His very existence He is in relationship. Unlike other gods, given the Trinity, we can say "God is love," because the persons of the Trinity loved one another from all eternity. Mankind, created in His image, is made for community that reflects the reality of the Trinity. At first, Adam would receive community and companionship in marriage, then these gifts would expand to family, and eventually to cities and then civilizations. Adam and Eve were to have children and fill the earth with God's image-bearers.

A garden is nature plus culture (cultivation). Andy Crouch makes the observation that, from the very beginning of creation, mankind was placed not just in raw nature, but culture: "Whatever distortions may arise as the man and the woman carry out their cultural task [after the Fall]…culture begins, just as human beings begin, in the

---

11. Jordan, *The Sociology of the Church*, 46-47.

realm of created blessing. The beginning of culture and the beginning of humanity are one and the same because culture is what we are made to do."[12] Adam had community with Eve, worship of God, and work to do in tending the garden. These are all aspects of culture, our everyday existence. Because God's creation was good from the start, this means that all aspects of civilization and culture—work, childbearing, community, art, economics, politics—were good things built into God's original design for mankind within His creation.

Transforming the Earth for God's Glory

Every good story involves character development. In the case of the Scripture, the overarching theme shows the maturation of mankind. In the beginning, man was placed in a garden with everything around him, basically spoon-fed food like a baby. Yet, mankind was not to remain in the garden, but to go out and subdue the earth. God's intent was for mankind to continue His good yet incomplete creation, to fulfill what Christ would later pray, "Thy Kingdom come, Thy will be done on earth as it is in heaven." God desired for man to mature.

The first tasks for man were to name the animals and to cultivate the garden. Ultimately man was to extend his dominion by building an entire civilization under God's reign. God's plan was that, over time, the man and woman would mature and use the raw materials of creation to imitate Him and make new sub-creations of their own, reflect-

---

12. Andy Crouch, *Culture Making* (Downers Grove, Illinois, 2008), 36-37.

ing back His glory. They were to be fruitful and multiply and fill the earth, taking the creation from glory to greater glory. They were to create a civilization and a culture that reflected God's glory back to Him. Heaven has always been the blueprint for earthly transformation. Reflecting on man's original assignment, Peter Leithart says:

> God commanded two people, a man and a woman, to be king and queen of the whole creation and to produce a worldwide race of kings and queens to rule the creation.... He told Adam and Eve to construct a culture that would glorify Him, and He made them culture-building creatures. The royal task of "ruling and subduing" is, as much as the procreative task of "filling the earth," a "natural" activity for men and women made in the image of God. [13]

The cultural mandate to be fruitful and multiply has never been repealed by God. After the Flood, this mandate was re-issued to Noah in Genesis 9:1, "Be fruitful and multiply, and fill the earth." This is the basis of God's promise to Abraham in Genesis 12:3, "I will bless those who bless you, and I will curse him who curses you; and in you all the families of the earth shall be blessed." And it is the background behind the Great Commission of Jesus in Matthew 28: "Go therefore and make disciples of all the nations, baptizing them in the name of the Father and of the Son and of the Holy Spirit." The Great Commission fits inside

---

13. Leithart, *The Kingdom and the Power*, 25.

of the creation mandate in a fallen world; because of man's idolatry, he must be converted before he can begin building the kind of civilization God desires. But God's plan still stands, despite the fall: From the very beginning, God has planned for His glory to spread over the earth through His image-bearers.

Maturation is built into the fabric of the creation story. God could have created everything in an instant, but instead chose to create the universe over a six day period. In doing so, He is showing His image-bearers that their pathway to dominion will take time. Recall that God declared each day of creation "good," with one exception. On the second day, in which God separated the heavens and the earth, He did not call it good. This suggests that over time, God intended for the heavens and the earth to be joined back together.

Eschatology is built into the fabric of the creation story. By "eschatology," I do not merely mean end-times charts and debates regarding the millennium, but more broadly a view of history which sees God working over time through His people to bring His plans to fulfillment, to a consummation. If we fast forward from the beginning of the Bible to the end of the Bible, we see this intended progression more clearly. Revelation 21 says, "Then I saw a new heaven and a new earth...I saw the Holy City, the new Jerusalem coming down out of heaven from God." The Bible starts in a garden and ends in a city! In the end, God's plan for a culture and a civilization which reflects His glory back to Him is made complete when the new heavens and new earth are joined together. And when heaven and earth are fully re-joined in the new creation, we will rejoice and say, "And it was very good."

Conclusion

The creation account in Genesis is only two chapters long, yet out of this true story flows the rest of history, including the rest of the Scriptures. Creation is the foundation on which the rest of the story of Scripture is built. In order to have greater cultural impact, the church must purposefully begin with creation and all its implications. The gospel of Jesus Christ is not about escape from this world for individuals; it is not about moving from a material realm to a spiritual realm. Rather, it is about the redemption and restoration of the human race through the God-man, Jesus Christ, with the ultimate purpose being a renewed creation in the new heavens and the new earth. God has never repealed the dominion mandate given to Adam and Eve. Only in Christ and through His church can humanity find fulfillment for our original purpose of dominion. The command of Christ to disciple the nations, given in the Great Commission, is a call to transform not just individuals with the gospel but entire nations and cultures.

Beginning with the Genesis account of the Creation and mankind's purpose to build a civilization to reflect God's glory back to Him, our cultural pursuits (those things we do on a daily basis) have meaning in and of themselves rather than just being means to "spiritual" ends. Christians can glorify God and fulfill the Great Commission in their callings rather than feeling guilty about not being "radical" enough in their shunning of the material world. Our work has dignity and purpose for the work itself has eternal value. Our work is not just a means to a paycheck so we are able to tithe; if the work is done with an aim toward God's glory, we can be assured our efforts are going toward the construction of the New Jerusalem. Being fruitful and multiplying, training and discipling our children in God's ways, doing our daily chores and tasks with excellence, become ways to fulfill our created purpose. God does not leave us on this earth merely so we can evangelize the lost; He wants us to disciple the whole planet, meaning every human endeavor is to be reordered under Christ's lordship. Understanding the way creation sets the trajectory for the whole of history, we not only have purpose as individuals, but we also discover the purpose of societies and cultures.

Chapter 3

From the Fall to
the Death of Christ

The Fall

Mankind, made in God's image, was created good. Adam and Eve were to tend the Garden of Eden, meeting with God in the garden sanctuary. As worshippers of God, they were also given the mission to have dominion, subdue the earth, and multiply, thus creating a civilization under the reign of God. But something happened along the way that changed the course of human history.

God had given a command to Adam, "Of every tree of the garden you may freely eat; but of the tree of the knowledge of good and evil you shall not eat." The adversary (Satan), in the form of the serpent, came and twisted God's words: "Has God indeed said, 'You shall not eat of every tree of the garden'?" Eve answered the serpent, most likely with a legitimate outworking of the commands: "God has said, 'You shall not eat it, nor shall you touch it, lest you die.'"

Adam, in his priestly role as guardian of the garden, should have intervened and fought the serpent, but he stood by silently as the woman gave in to the tempter. "So when the woman saw that the tree was good for food, that it was pleasant to the eyes, and a tree desirable to make one wise, she took of its fruit and ate. She also gave to her husband with her, and he ate." When they ate together, in violation of God's command, sin entered the world.

The descent of man from holiness into sin is called the Fall. Before this first sin, Adam and Eve[14] were holy and happy. They had fellowship with God, harmony with one another, and Eden was a pristine environment in which to live. Eating of the forbidden tree was deformative. They became ashamed, realizing their nakedness and sewing fig leaves to cover it up (Gen. 3:7). They lost fellowship with God, hiding from Him when He walked through the garden (Gen. 3:8). They lost their perfect relationship with one another, as Adam blamed both God and Eve for his sin: "The woman whom You gave to be with me, she gave me of the tree, and I ate" (Gen. 3:12). Even humanity's relationship to the rest of creation was marred as God said:

> Cursed is the ground for your sake; in toil you shall
> eat of it all the days of your life. Both thorns and
> thistles it shall bring forth for you, and you shall eat

---

14. She was not named Eve until after the Fall but we call her by this name before the Fall for convenience.

the herb of the field. In the sweat of your face you
shall eat bread till you return to the ground, for out
of it you were taken; for dust you are, and to dust
you shall return (Gen. 3:17-19).

Adam infected the human race with the virus of sin
and death, a virus that has spread to every last one of us.
We are born sinners, brought into the world with sinful in-
clinations, going all the way back to our first father Adam.
Adam's sin didn't just wreck his own life, but had wider implications for the whole world. Because of Adam's sin, we
have war, disease, depression, and poverty. The fall brought
condemnation and misery to the whole of humanity.

God's mandate to subdue and fill the earth didn't get
cancelled by the Fall, but sin now frustrates and perverts
any attempt at dominion. Humanity, created to reflect
God's image and glorify Him across all the earth in every endeavor, is now in rebellion. This rebellion is evident
in our relationship to God, each other, and the creation
(including death). The ruined race and the whole world
became in need of a grand reclamation project, which God
graciously promised to bring about.

The Promised Redeemer

As soon as Adam and Eve fell into sin, God sought them
out in the garden and made a gracious promise of redemption while speaking to the serpent: "And I will put enmity
between you and the woman, and between your offspring
and hers; He will crush your head, and you will strike His
heel" (Gen. 3:15, NIV). God promised to reclaim the woman and her seed for Himself. Throughout the Bible, we see

a theme of the people of God *crushing* the serpent's head. In Judges 4, Jael took the tent peg and drove it through Sisera's skull, crushing his head. In Judges 9, Abimelech wrongfully claimed kingship in Israel. He was a great terror to the people of God, slaughtering the people of Israel. There was a great battle, and a woman dropped a millstone from a tower that landed on his head and crushed his skull. In 1 Samuel 17, we find the story of David versus Goliath. Goliath was dressed in scaley armor, like a snake. David went into battle with just a sling and five stones. When he slung his stone, it hit Goliath in his head. And when Goliath fell to the ground, David cut off his head. Goliath, the serpent figure, was killed by having his head crushed. For his generation, David was the seed of the woman, who went into battle and won the victory. All of those Old Testament stories are *provisional* fulfillments of the promise in Genesis 3:15 with the *definitive* fulfillment of the promise coming in Jesus.

When did Jesus crush the serpent's head? Matthew 27 tells us where Jesus was crucified: at Golgotha, the place of the skull. Some scholars believe Golgotha got its name from the place where David put the skull of Goliath after he had defeated him in battle. Visualize the scene of Jesus's crucifixion: Golgotha was a hill, possibly shaped like a skull. As Jesus hung on the cross, and what was under His feet? The skull. As Jesus was on the cross His heel was being bruised, but the skull of the serpent was being crushed. This tree that was buried in the ground was penetrating the skull, like Jael's tent peg into the skull of Sisera. What looked like defeat was actually Jesus's victory, fulfilling Genesis 3:15.

Jesus died in order to *destroy* Satan (1 John 3:8). This is how Hebrews 2:14-15 puts it:

> Inasmuch then as the children have partaken of flesh and blood, He Himself likewise shared in the same, that through death He might destroy him who had the power of death, that is, the devil, and release those who through fear of death were all their lifetime subject to bondage.

The way that Satan had power over people was by putting them in bondage to the fear of death and the consequences of their sin. Those who are in union with Jesus do not live in that fear anymore. Satan's greatest weapon has been taken from him.

The New Testament epistles continue with the theme of crushing the serpent. In Romans 16:20, Paul says to the church that "the God of peace will crush Satan under your feet shortly." It is not just Jesus who is the skull crusher, but God's people become skull crushers as well, because we are in union with Jesus. Through the church, God continues to work out His victory over Satan the serpent. Genesis 3:15 is the first post-Fall eschatological promise in Scripture. It is the gospel in seed form, a promise of victory. It is a promise which has now been fulfilled in Christ: Jesus has defeated Satan. This means God's purposes for the creation will not be thwarted.

Christ the Priest

Christ Jesus, God in the flesh, is not only our King, He is our High Priest. Ever since man's first sin, God has required sacrifice, for "without shedding of blood there is no remission" of sins (Heb. 9:22). After Adam and Eve ate of the forbidden tree of the knowledge of good and evil, they deserved death (Gen. 2:17). However, God graciously intervened, and Adam and Eve were covered with the garments of an animal (Gen. 3:21). Rather than their own death, an animal substitute died in their place. By the first sin, Adam had failed in his priestly role, and mankind was driven from open access to God in the Garden sanctuary (Gen. 3:24). After the expulsion from Eden, God would provide mediated access to His presence through the sacrificial system and priesthood.

The Old Testament is about the implementation and development of the sacrificial system and finds its fulfillment in the sacrifice of Christ on the cross. Cain and Abel knew that blood sacrifice was required to relate with God, though only Abel offered a proper sacrifice (Gen. 4:3-5). Noah offered a sacrifice with a soothing aroma as his first act of worship after the Flood subsided (Gen. 8:20-21). Abraham set up altars as he traveled the land that God had promised His seed (Gen. 12:8; 13:18; 22:9). With Moses, the sacrificial system was more fully implemented after God led the people of Israel out of Egypt. Moses received the divine blueprint for the tabernacle, which was patterned after heaven itself (Heb. 8:5). Eventually, after David's reign, Solomon built the temple in Jerusalem, which became the central place of the sacrificial system in the Old Testament. But all these continual sacrifices were only shadows of Christ's once-and-for-all sacrifice which came at the cross, "for it is not possible that the blood of bulls and goats could take away sins" (Heb. 10:4).

The old covenant was meant to point to Jesus, the mediator of the new and better covenant. There are far more details in the system than we can cover here, but a broad overview is still useful. Hebrews 7:20-28 discusses the superiority of Christ as priest to the old covenant shadows and types:

> By so much more Jesus has become a surety of a better covenant . . . because He continues forever, has an unchangeable priesthood. Therefore He is also able to save to the uttermost those who come to God through Him, since He always lives to make intercession for them . . . For such a High Priest was fitting for us, who is holy, harmless, undefiled, separate from sinners, and has become higher than the heavens; who does not need daily, as those high priests, to offer up sacrifices, first for His own sins and then for the people's, for this He did once for all when He offered up Himself.

In the temple system, only the high priest could enter the Most Holy Place, the location of God's special presence. The high priest would enter once per year, to offer atonement for himself and for the sins of the people. In Jesus, the sinless God came as a man and was perfectly obedient to His Father. Even though He faced the assaults of the devil, Jesus remained righteous throughout His temptations—"For we do not have a High Priest who cannot sympathize with our weaknesses, but was in all points tempted as we are, yet without sin" (Heb. 4:15). When Jesus died His sacrificial death on the cross, "the veil of the temple was torn in two from top to bottom" (Matt. 27:51). No longer would access to God's special presence be through the Jewish high priest in the temple. Now, the new humanity in Jesus has access to Him in a new way. As Hebrews 10:19-22 teaches, we now have access to the true sanctuary in the heavens:

> Therefore, brethren, having boldness to enter the Holiest by the blood of Jesus, by a new and living way which He consecrated for us, through the veil, that is, His flesh, and having a High Priest over the house of God, let us draw near with a true heart in full assurance of faith, having our hearts sprinkled from an evil conscience and our bodies washed with pure water.

Christ the King

When we look further into the identity of the promised Redeemer of Genesis 3:15, the seed of the woman, we find the astonishing truth of the incarnation. The Creator of the world entered His creation as a man. As John 1:14 says of Jesus, "And the Word became flesh and dwelt among us, and we beheld His glory, the glory as of the only begotten of the Father, full of grace and truth." The Creator has written Himself into the story of His creation, in order to redeem His creation. "For it pleased the Father that in Him all the fullness should dwell, and by Him to reconcile all things to Himself, by Him, whether things on earth or things in heaven, having made peace through the blood of His cross" (Col. 1:19-20).

Jesus Christ did not enter this world in an ordinary manner but was miraculously conceived by the Holy Spirit in the womb of the virgin Mary (the seed of the woman). In Isaiah 7, the prophet announced that a virgin would give birth. Matthew's Gospel tells us that the birth of Jesus to the virgin Mary fulfills what Isaiah foretold (Matt. 1:22-23). The baby laid in the manger on the first Christmas was the Creator of the world (Luke 2:7). Jesus Christ is fully God and fully man, in one person. Because of this, He alone can represent humanity before God and fulfill God's will perfectly on man's behalf: "and you shall call His name Jesus, for He will save His people from their sins" (Matt. 1:21).

When Jesus began His ministry, He "came to Galilee, preaching the gospel of the kingdom of God, and saying, 'The time is fulfilled, and the kingdom of God is at hand. Repent, and believe in the gospel'" (Mark 1:15). Later on in His ministry, Jesus asked His disciples a question concerning His identity: "Who do you say I am?" Simon Peter answered, "You are the Christ, the Son of the living God." Upon proclaiming His true identity, Jesus answered Peter, "Blessed are you…for flesh and blood has not revealed this to you, but My Father who is in heaven" (Matt. 16:15-17).

The title *Christ*, or Messiah, refers to the anointed one, especially God's anointed king. God had promised Israel a Christ, a great Spirit-bearing, Spirit-anointed, Spirit-filled king who would rule over the people in power and wisdom. The Christ would be a descendant of David, rising from Israel's royal family. This was promised in passages like 2 Samuel 7 and Psalm 89 where God made a covenant with David: "I have made a covenant with My chosen, I have sworn to My servant David: 'Your seed I will establish forever, and build up your throne to all generations.'" Jesus is the true Israelite king, and He is Israel's true God. If Jesus was only an earthly figure, He could only have an earthly, human kingdom. But He came to bring the kingdom of God. He is not of this world, and so His kingdom is not of this world.

We must embrace Jesus Christ as the God-man, crucified for our salvation. He did for us what we could not do. First John 2:22 says, "Who is a liar but he who denies that Jesus is the Christ? He is antichrist who denies the Father and the Son." First John 4:2-3 goes on to say, "By this you know the Spirit of God: Every spirit that confesses that Jesus Christ has come in the flesh is of God, and every spirit that does not confess that Jesus Christ has come in the flesh is not of God." The only way to understand the teaching and life of Jesus is to see that He is indeed God in the flesh, King of Kings and Lord of Lords.

Jesus the Bridegroom

Why did Jesus leave His throne above, enter into human flesh, and suffer agony on the cross?[15] The story of salvation is a divine love story. It is a story of God setting His love upon His people and choosing, redeeming, and glorifying them. In every step along the way, from eternity past to eternity future, we see the love of God at work. In Ephesians 1:4-5, the apostle Paul says: "He chose us in Him before the foundation of the world, that we should be holy

---

15. Of course, one could write volumes on this topic, such as John Piper's *Fifty Reasons Why Jesus Came to Die*.

and without blame before Him in love, having predestined us to adoption as sons by Jesus Christ to Himself." Unlike the first Adam, who failed his wife in the garden, the last Adam was willing to face the devil and die for His bride, "the church of God which He purchased with His own blood" (Acts 20:28). God loved us before time began; before we were even created God had already set His love upon us.

It was this same love that in the fullness of time moved the Father to send the Son and moved the Son to take on flesh and dwell on earth. John 3:16 says, "For God so loved the world that He gave His only begotten Son, that whoever believes in Him should not perish but have everlasting life." In love, the Son died for us. Romans 5:6-8 says, "in due time Christ died for the ungodly. For scarcely for a righteous man will one die; yet perhaps for a good man someone would even dare to die. But God demonstrates His own love toward us, in that while we were still sinners, Christ died for us." The death of Christ manifests God's love. In John 15:13, Jesus said, "Greater love has no one than this, than to lay down one's life for his friends." When He went to the cross, it was the ultimate act of love.

The Father gave the Son and the Son willingly died on the cross that we might know the love of God. Then, in love, God gave us the Holy Spirit. Ephesians 2:4-5 says, "But God, who is rich in mercy, because of His great love with which He loved us, even when we were dead in trespasses, made us alive together with Christ (by grace you have been saved)." God, by His Spirit, makes us alive in Him. Romans 5:5 says, "the love of God has been poured out in our hearts by the Holy Spirit who was given to us."

This love never leaves us nor forsakes us. This same love is with us every step of the way, through good times and bad, to the very end. Romans 8:38-39 says, "neither death nor life, nor angels nor principalities nor powers, nor things present nor things to come, nor height nor depth, nor any other created thing, shall be able to separate us from the love of God which is in Christ Jesus our Lord."

Our whole salvation is an act of love. It is a story of love from beginning to end. Christ loves His bride, the church, with the strongest love the universe could ever know. Christ doesn't love us because we are lovable, as if His love for us depended upon our performance in any way. Rather, His love makes us lovable. He doesn't love us because we are beautiful, His love makes us beautiful. God's love is a transformative love.

This redeeming love of God to sinners is extremely counter to our current cancel culture. In today's society, when a supposed offense is made, a Twitter mob will demand that the offending person be canceled. The "sins" are usually not even real sins: guilt for causing climate change, accusations of bigotry for failing to use the right pronouns, or ostracism for holding to the same definition of marriage as first-term President Obama. For "sins" such as these, the mob demands that the person be canceled, including loss of job and reputation. There is no hope of clearing one's name, for even apologies and penance are not enough. Our culture cancels offenders of their progressive orthodoxy with a religious zeal that makes the Pharisees look like lightweights. Indeed, wokeness is just modern day secularized Phariseeism. Yet, while these modern day Pharisees cancel people for non-sins, Jesus cancels real sins and redeems people: "He was wounded for our transgressions, He was bruised for our iniquities; the chastisement for our peace was upon Him, and by His stripes we are healed" (Isa. 53:5). Rather than canceling people, Jesus forgives people; rather than canceling people, He cancels the debt of sin. He brings us into fellowship with God through his sacrificial and substitutionary death on the cross: "For Christ also suffered once for sins, the just for the unjust, that He might bring us to God" (1 Pet. 3:18).

Jesus the Last Adam

Jesus came as a second Adam, the head of a new humanity, inaugurating a new history and a new world. Paul contrasts the first Adam and the Last Adam in Romans 5:19, "For as by one man's disobedience many were made sinners, so also by one Man's obedience many will be made righteous." The first Adam brought sin and death; the second Adam brings righteousness and life. He has turned back the curse and brought blessing to the world.

According to Genesis 1:28, Adam's task was to, "Be fruitful and multiply; fill the earth and subdue it; have dominion over the fish of the sea, over the birds of the air, and over every living thing that moves on the earth." Adam was to develop a culture, taking the resources of the earth to build a civilization that reflected God's glory back to Himself. He was to turn the Garden of Eden into the city of God. Adam and his descendants were to develop technology, science, art, music, business, education, and all the range of righteous human endeavors, all to the glory of God. Adam, with Eve, was to fill the earth with divine image-bearers who would share in this work, with each one contributing his gifts to the maturing and growth of this civilization. Ultimately, they were to fill the whole earth, so that man would have worldwide dominion under the reign of God. After Adam sinned, God never canceled the mandate given in Genesis 1:28. Jesus, the last Adam, has taken over this mandate to build the kingdom of God that will cover the entire world. To paraphrase N. T. Wright, in Christ, the human project—begun in Adam but never completed—is brought to its intended goal.

This is what it means for Jesus to be the new Adam. All that Adam should have done but failed to accomplish, Jesus is now doing. When Satan came to Adam and Eve in the garden, Adam should have crushed the serpent's head and driven Satan out of the garden. In the gospel accounts, Jesus goes around exorcizing demons, casting them out. Jesus says in John 12:31-32, "Now is the judgment of this world; now the ruler of this world will be cast out. And I, if I am lifted up from the earth, will draw all peoples to Myself." That is Jesus's mission, accomplished through His death: to cast out Satan and draw all peoples to Himself. This is what history is about now. Jesus is taking dominion, filling the earth with those who bear God's image truthfully. Jesus is driving out Satan and drawing the nations to Himself through His church. The scope of Christ's redemption is large enough to reverse the curse that Adam put on us all. As we sing at Christmas time, in the hymn *Joy to the World*:

> Joy to the world, the Lord is come!
> Let earth receive her King...

No more let sins and sorrows grow,
Nor thorns infest the ground;
He comes to make His blessings flow
Far as the curse is found,
Far as the curse is found,
Far as, far as, the curse is found.

He rules the world with truth and grace,
And makes the nations prove
The glories of His righteousness,
And wonders of His love,
And wonders of His love,
And wonders, wonders, of His love.

If we really understand what Jesus came to accomplish, it cannot but make us optimistic and hopeful. But many American Christians, despite living in the most prosperous nation in history, have been pessimistic about the prospects of the kingdom of Christ. It was not always so: Christians in other eras, often in periods of much greater hardship and even persecution, have been much more confident in Christ's triumph in history. Jesus came to undo and overturn the fall of Adam. If Adam's sin drags more of humanity to hell than Jesus raises up to heaven, can we really say that Jesus is the Greater Adam? Can we really say that He won?

We are convinced that the Bible not only warrants optimism about what will happen at the last day when Jesus returns in glory to raise the dead and carry out the final judgment, but it also warrants optimism about the direction and trajectory of history before that last day. We have not only an eternal hope, fulfilled at Jesus's final coming, but also an historical hope, fulfilled between the first and final comings of Jesus. Jesus will fulfill the Great Commission and the creation mandate. Jesus will inherit the nations. Jesus will save the world. Jesus will undo the Fall. Jesus's blessing will overwhelm sin's curse. All nations, races, and people groups will be converted. Jesus is going to baptize and disciple all nations. In the chapters to follow, we will see more fully how this dual hope for history and eternity shapes the life and mission of the church.

Chapter 4

Resurrection Victory

A commendable aspect of modern evangelicalism is an un-wavering commitment to preaching the cross. But if the cross of Jesus is separated from the resurrection of Jesus, or if the resurrection is underemphasized, we dilute the good-ness and force of the good news. To put it simply, *the resurrection of Jesus Christ is the gospel*. If Jesus had died on Good Friday but not been raised to life, it would have been a tragic ending to the story, not good news. In the very book where Paul says he will know nothing but Christ and Him crucified, he also argues that the resurrection is absolutely integral to the gospel (1 Corinthians 2 and 15).

The resurrection transforms our understanding of the cross from a senseless act of injustice into our very hope of justification. Romans 4:25 says that Jesus "was delivered up because of our offenses, and was raised because of our justification." The resurrection means the debt Jesus paid on our behalf has been accepted. The check has cleared; payment for our sins has been made and approved. But the resurrection is more than a receipt. It is inseparable from the cross and is necessary to our salvation. As Paul says in 1 Corinthians 15:17, "if Christ is not risen, your faith is futile; you are still in your sins!" A dead Christ cannot save. A Christ still in the grave, and therefore still under the condemnation and curse of death, could not give us forgiveness or blessing. The resurrection is our salvation; without it, we have no hope. The resurrection is life; without it, we are dead.

The resurrection of Jesus Christ occurred in our space-time world, *within* history. It is an historical fact. Unlike other religions which are often based upon visions received in private by their originators, the Christian faith is based upon the *facts* of history. The resurrection is not something that can be true for one person, and not for another. It is *public truth.* The apostles witnessed this event and pointed to this public fact as witnesses (1 John 1:1). A resurrected Jesus is a public Jesus, and this public reality means that God cannot be confined to an "upstairs" heavenly realm, far away. God has come "downstairs" and has entered into our world as one of us. The resurrection means the whole Christian faith is based on what God has done "down here," among us, in our public square: He has made His Son the king over all by raising him from the dead. All authority in heaven and earth belongs to him.

The bodily resurrection of Jesus Christ on the third day after His crucifixion is the heart and center of our faith. If the tomb was not empty, there would be no Gospel and our faith would come unglued. The gospel, at its heart, is about

God defeating evil and His triumph over the corrupting power of sin and death that has defaced and deformed His good creation. The resurrection is about God launching His new creation. God is redeeming and reclaiming and renewing His whole creation, "For the earth will be filled with the knowledge of the glory of the Lord, as the waters cover the sea" (Hab. 2:14). The last enemy to be defeated will be death, and until then, all Christ's enemies will come under His feet (1 Cor. 15:24-26). As followers of Christ, by grace, we have the privilege to participate in the mission of the resurrected Jesus, transforming this present world as signposts of the new heavens and new earth to come.

The Resurrection: New Creation Invasion

Jesus died on the cross for His people's sins. This means that when those who believe in Him die, their souls go to heaven. However, that is *not* the final state of things, according to the Scriptures. Biblically, there is a twofold expectation for life after death. It is true to say that when the Christian's body dies, his soul goes to heaven and that this is a place of great joy. Paul refers to this in Philippians 1:21, "For to me, to live is Christ, and to die is gain." Paul's expectation is that at the very moment a believer dies, his soul goes to be with the Lord. At death, the Christian is immediately promoted into the very heavenly presence of God. It's a place Jesus referred to as paradise in the conversation He had with the thieves on the cross. But while the saints in heaven are joyous, they are also expectant. They are still looking for *more* to come. They are looking forward to the resurrection of the body and the renewal of the whole creation. Because there is this further expectation beyond going to heaven at death, theologians refer to heaven as the *intermediate* state—intermediate because it comes between this life and resurrection life.

Heaven is a stopping point on our way to the new creation and resurrection of the body. Heaven is a resting place before the final destination of the new heavens and new earth. There is an old folk song by Jim Reeves that goes, "This world is not my home. I'm just a-passing through." This is the inverse of Biblical truth. This world, remade as the new heavens and new earth, *is* our eternal home. The souls of the saints in heaven are enjoying bliss right now, but they are also longing to reunite with their bodies in a renewed physical creation. Just as body and soul will be reunited in the resurrection, so it will be with heaven and earth.

In His resurrection, Jesus Himself points to this. He is the firstfruits and already has His resurrection body, but He will return to earth. That is why we talk about a final coming. And when Jesus returns at the last day, what will happen? He will make all things new. Jesus will give His people new resurrection bodies, fit for eternal life in this eternal home of the new creation.

Jesus told His disciples in John 14 that He was going to prepare a place for them. In John 14:2, He says, "In my Father's house are many rooms." The word used for "rooms" is a Greek term that refers to temporary lodging, like a hotel room. Heaven is a temporary lodging place for the souls of God's saints until the last day when our souls are reunited with our bodies. At the last day, whatever barrier there is between heaven and earth will be done away with. Heaven and earth will be merged into one renewed creation for the resurrected people of God. Scripture gives us a two-step view of the future for Christians who die. We go to heaven one by one, but we will all enter into the resurrection and the new creation at the last day. There is life after death. But there is also *life after life after death.*[16]

God's salvation and redemption must include not just the soul, but also the body. If your soul lives on forever without your body, you are only half-redeemed, and a half-redemption is no redemption at all. Functionally, an eternal bodiless existence is what many Christians in our time seem to believe. This is evident in American folk music and hymnody such as "I'll Fly Away": "When the shadows of this life have gone, I'll fly away to home on God's celestial shore." Though it sounds great when Alison Krauss sings it, this song is incomplete theology because it leaves the resurrection of the dead out of the picture. The Christian hope is not that the soul will fly away. The Christian hope is an embodied hope. We will be raised body and soul, even as Christ was raised, and we will share the glory of His resurrection life in a new creation.

The Scriptures are clear: we are going to have resurrection bodies. Therefore, there must be a resurrected and renewed creation, a physical world for our bodies to inhabit. The gospels are very clear: when Jesus was raised, He was not raised as a ghost (Luke 24:34, John 21:12-14). He could eat and drink. He clearly interacted with the physical world, as Thomas touched His side (John 20:27-28). When God transforms our bodies at the last day, He will

---

16. N. T. Wright, *Surprised by Hope* (New York: HarperCollins Publishers, 2008), 151. This section on the resurrection is indebted to Wright's scholarship.

transform our whole environment as well. The whole material world will be re-made, perfected, and glorified.

In the creation account in Genesis 1, God declared this material world to be good. The material world is not an illusion as in the Eastern religions, nor is the material world evil as in the Western philosophical tradition. This material world is the work of God, and it is good. C. S. Lewis said that God must like matter, for after all, He invented it.[17]

When God made man, He got His hands dirty, so to speak, forming the first man Adam out of the dirt. From that point on, there is a connection between man and the earth that plays out through the rest of Scripture. The destiny of man and the destiny of the rest of creation are tied together. When man fell, creation as a whole fell. When man was cursed, creation as a whole was cursed. In Genesis 3 when man is cursed, God also says, "Cursed is the ground because of you." God has tied the fate of creation as a whole to the fate of His most glorious and cherished creature: human beings. We're made from the earth and the earth shares in our Fall. But does it share in our redemption? In Romans 8:19-23, Paul says:

> For the creation waits with eager longing for the revealing of the sons of God. For the creation was subjected to futility, not willingly, but because of him who subjected it, in hope that the creation itself will be set free from its bondage to corruption and obtain the freedom of the glory of the children

---

17. C. S. Lewis, *Mere Christianity* (New York: Simon & Schuster, 1996), 65.

of God. For we know that the whole creation has been groaning together in the pains of childbirth until now. And not only the creation, but we ourselves, who have the firstfruits of the Spirit, groan inwardly as we wait eagerly for adoption as sons, the redemption of our bodies.

Our resurrection will be the moment of creation's liberation. When we are raised, when our redemption is complete, the creation itself will be liberated from bondage. So Paul says that creation right now is yearning for redemption, a redemption that will be completed when our redemption is completed.

God did for Jesus in the middle of history what He intends to do for the whole of creation at the end of history. This world that God made is not going to be scrapped. It's not headed for the cosmic incinerator. God is not going to just crumple it and throw it away. This world is headed for renewal. This world is going to be reborn. Paul shows us in Romans 8 that redemption is cosmic in scope. The creation itself can hardly wait for what is coming: it's standing on its tiptoes, peering out into the future, eagerly awaiting the final coming of Jesus and the redemption of our bodies.

In the resurrection of Christ, the new creation has broken into the old and is now growing to fill the earth. God has not abandoned the creation; He has not left humanity to its own devices. He has promised to bring His people into a renewed world. A transformed world is coming in which God's people will dwell with transformed bodies.

Resurrection: Perspective on the Kingdom

Christ's resurrection on that first Easter Sunday was the genesis of a new creation. What began when the stone rolled away and Christ came out of the tomb will continue to grow until Jesus returns. This is the New Testament's teaching on the outlook of the kingdom within history, before Christ comes again. Ever since the resurrection of Jesus two thousand years ago, the story of history is the story of the progress of Christ's kingdom.

Perhaps the most succinct summary of biblical eschatology anywhere in the Scriptures is in 1 Corinthians 15:24-26. Some consider eschatology to concern only the last things. But it is also a view of Christ's kingdom, and a view of unfolding history. Paul considered eschatology to be of first importance. Paul gives the Corinthian Christians an order of coming events:

> Then comes the end, when He delivers the kingdom to God the Father, when He puts an end to all rule and all authority and power. For He must reign till He has put all enemies under His feet. The last enemy that will be destroyed is death.

Death will be the *last* enemy to be defeated. If death is the last enemy to be defeated, what has to happen before that? All of God's other enemies have to be defeated *before* death, before Jesus returns.

Christ's resurrection begins the expansion of His reign as the new Adam. And as 1 Corinthians 15:25 says, "He must reign till He has put all enemies under His feet." Christ will destroy death when He comes again to earth and raises His people bodily from the grave. The map of the course of human history, beginning with the resurrection of Jesus down to the resurrection at the end of history is very straightforward. This is the shape of things to come: Christ's resurrection begins the expansion of the kingdom, the kingdom will grow through history as Christ is putting all His enemies under His feet, and Christ will return at the end of history to consummate His kingdom, raising His people from the dead and delivering the completed kingdom over to His Father (1 Cor. 15:24).

The resurrection not only gives us hope for our ultimate future after death and the end of history is completed at Christ's return, but it also gives us tangible hope for *this life*. It gives us hope for *this world*. It gives us hope for *unfolding history*. The power of the risen Christ is at work *now*. The risen Christ is reigning *now*. The kingdom is growing *now*. Christ has brought redemption to the world as the last Adam. That redemption means that God's plan for humanity, set up in the beginning of Genesis, has been put back on track. Adam wrecked that plan, but Jesus put it back together. The second Adam will succeed where the first Adam failed. He redeems the creation and He promises to bring the creation to the fulfillment of its original purpose. The long chain of death and decay inaugurated by the first Adam has finally and irrevocably been broken by the last Adam.

In the great chapter on the resurrection, 1 Corinthians 15, Paul supports his argument by alluding to three psalms. He views these passages from the Psalms as prophecies of the kingdom that are coming to fulfillment as the risen Christ presently reigns over the earth.

First, in 1 Corinthians 15:24, Paul is alluding back to Psalm 2:7-8, "You are My Son, today I have begotten You. Ask of Me, and I will give You the nations for Your inheritance, and the ends of the earth for Your possession." The "begotten" language is used by Paul in Acts 13:33 in reference to the resurrection of Jesus. Psalm 2 is about God's Son ruling over the nations. The psalm ends with an ultimatum to the kings of the earth: "Kiss the Son, lest He be angry, and you perish in the way." Paul is saying that this is what is happening in history: Jesus is shaking down the rulers, overcoming the powers and authorities of the earth, inheriting the nations.

Second, in 1 Corinthians 15:27, Paul quotes explicitly from Psalm 8:6, "He has put all things under His feet." Psalm 8 is full of wonder that God not only pays attention to man, but that God has given to man this exalted position within His Creation. Psalm 8 says, "What is man that You are mindful of him...? You have crowned him with glory and honor. You have made him to have dominion over the works of Your hands." Psalm 8 is about Jesus and those who belong to Him. Everything is subdued to Jesus. Everything will be put in its proper place under His reign. The last Adam is crowned with glory and rules over the world.

Last, Paul alludes to Psalm 110. The apostles alluded to Psalm 110 more than any other in the New Testament. They indicate that they were seeing the fulfillment of this psalm beginning in their day. The psalm speaks of God putting His enemies under the feet of His appointed priest-king. In Psalm 110:1, the Father says to the Son, "Sit at My right hand, till I make Your enemies Your footstool." Psalm

110 describes the Messiah on the warpath graciously conquering His foes, with His people participating in the conquest with Him. Now that Christ has been raised from the dead and ascended to the Father's right hand, this is what is happening. How long will He stay seated at the Father's right hand? When will He return to earth in glory? He will not come until *all* His enemies have been made a footstool.

We must get rid of this idea that Jesus is cherry-picking a few individuals here and there for salvation and casting the rest of the world into the flames. That is not why Jesus came. He came to establish His kingdom, to redeem the world, to save the nations, to grow God's kingdom until it fills the whole earth. And He will do it! The empty tomb and the occupied throne go together. Jesus is king right now. Christ is risen; therefore, Christ is king. Because Christ is king, He is claiming the nations as His inheritance. The scope of God's saving work through the last Adam is vast. God is not stingy with His grace and mercy. He is pouring out His grace and mercy on a lost world, and as history continues to unfold, the kingdom will continue to expand.

Resurrection Mission

In John 11, after Lazarus had died, Jesus told Martha that her brother would live again. She said in response, "I know that he will live again in the resurrection at the last day." That was a standard Jewish hope and expectation: at the end of history, God would raise up the righteous dead. But no one seems to have been expecting the resurrection of the Messiah in the middle of history.

We cannot make the same mistake as Martha and place the impact of the resurrection only at the end of history. The New Testament tells us that what God began at Christ's resurrection continues on *now*, and it will not be complete until Jesus comes again in glory and we are raised up bodily ourselves. We already participate in Christ's resurrection life. This new life will be fully revealed at the last day when Jesus returns, but it is manifest in advance in us through the way that we live here and now. The same Spirit that raised Jesus from the dead is at work in us, raising us from death in sins and trespasses to live a new life of righteousness and wisdom. Gospel-believing people are resurrection people. While there is a real danger of an over-realized eschatology in some circles, the problem most Christians have today is underestimating the degree to which the life of the future is already here. Even as we live in the present age (which still has sin, marriage, childbearing, suffering, loss, etc.), we live in the power of the age to come.

Karl Marx said that if you believe in an afterlife, you will not be concerned with making this life better. Marx pointed to poor laborers who were putting up with all kinds of injustices and bad working conditions because they figured that they would die and go to heaven and all their pain would be over. This is why he called religion "the opiate of the masses." In his view, religion makes us passive and indifferent to the pains of this world, because a better life is coming after death. But if our hope is in the resurrection and new creation, the truth is just the opposite of Marx's assertion. If other religions are the opium that drugs us and that lulls us to sleep, the resurrection is like smelling salts that jar us awake.[18] Since this whole world is going to be put to rights and since this whole physical cosmos is going to be perfected when Jesus comes at the last day, our calling in the present is clear. Our mission is to produce signs of that coming new creation in the present.

The Christian faith has been called a fighting religion—in some senses, it is the only fighting religion we've got.[19] Only Christian faith will consistently fight cancer in a hospital, slums in the inner city, abuse in a broken home, tyranny in civil government, and everything else that is wrong with this world. This is because the Christian faith has a vision of a renewed world. We know a new world is coming and we are to be signposts and agents pointing to that world in the present.

The Eastern religions and philosophies say that the physical world is just an illusion, so transforming the world doesn't really matter at all. In Western philosophies like Platonism, the physical is either regarded as evil or greatly inferior to spiritual and immaterial reality, so transforming the world doesn't matter there either. The gospel says "No!" to all of this. The gospel says this is God's good world. God made it, God loves it, God entered into it in the incarnation, God is redeeming it, and God will perfect it and glorify it in the end. When that story becomes our story, it changes the way we live in the present.

Rather than being an opiate to numb us, resurrection hope makes Christians alive, alert, active, energetic, and

---

18. Timothy Keller, *The Prodigal God* (New York: Dutton, 2008), 113.

19. Lewis, *Mere Christianity*, 45.

hopeful for kingdom growth. It makes us want to work to transform the world, to be as the early Christians who were said to "have turned the world upside down" (Acts 17:6). The world is on a road that leads to resurrection glory and the process of that glory breaking into history has already started. God calls His people to be a part of it. The resurrection does not make us less concerned for life in this world; it makes us *more* concerned for life in this world. If we have this resurrection hope, we cannot be cynical or indifferent about the world. We cannot be escapists. We are called to participate in God's triumph over evil and over every last thing that disfigures, stains, and mars God's beautiful creation.

Christ's resurrection gives us a mission. It shows us that the Gospel is not about escaping earth for heaven, but it is about God bringing His reign from heaven to earth, even as we pray, "Thy kingdom come, Thy will be done on earth as it is in heaven." Our task in the here and now is to act as God's resurrection, new creation people living between Easter and the final day. We are called to show people signs that Christ is already risen and that glory is coming. We are to give the world a foretaste and foreshadowing of that coming glory that will appear when Jesus returns. We are called to fight passionately for beauty, justice, goodness, truth, and peace. Easter calls us to live as lights shining amidst the darkness, fighting poverty, hunger, disease, tyranny, and oppression. As God's people in the world, we are here bringing gospel change to renew the culture, so that the world can say of us that we "have turned the world upside down" (Acts 17:6). This is Christ's mission, and we are co-laborers in His kingdom.

It is precisely this resurrection hope that keeps us from chasing false messiahs and false saviors. For example, those who are rooted firmly in a resurrection hope will resist the pull to see the state, or socialism, or any other political program, as the answer to cultural ills. Statism puts hope in a political agenda to correct every injustice and perfect society. The resurrection means Christ is Lord—which means Caesar is not. Thus, civil government's aims and scope must be limited. The state can be a servant of Christ, like other institutions, and we trust that the risen Christ, as the new Adam, will tame the totalitarian leviathans that have often wreaked havoc on humanity. Resurrection hope is not just for the world to come. It shapes the way we live in the present, as we seek to disciple every individual, every family, every nation. The risen Christ is Lord and as Lord He equips and empowers us to live lives of true freedom and wisdom in accord with His design. His resurrection means we are safe and secure, justified and renewed. His resurrection guarantees our future resurrection; his resurrection life at work in us now assures us of growth, maturation, and victory in history.

Chapter 5

Ascended to Reign

The resurrection of Jesus doesn't always get the coverage it deserves, but at least it gets some attention on at least one Sunday per year, Easter. The next major redemptive-historical event, the ascension of Jesus, is an even more neglected episode in the gospel story. It is more likely that a modern evangelical church will celebrate Mother's Day or Memorial Day rather than the ascension. We must repent of this oversight and elevate the ascension to its proper place.

The ascension is a real, historical event in which Jesus was bodily lifted up from the earth into heaven and was seated at the right hand of God the Father Almighty. It is loaded with theological and practical meaning. Between the resurrection and the ascension, Jesus "presented Himself alive after His suffering by many infallible proofs, being seen by them during forty days and speaking of the things pertaining to the kingdom of God" (Acts 1:3). Assembling the disciples together, He commanded them to remain in Jerusalem to receive the promised Holy Spirit for the purpose of being witnesses and spreading the kingdom.

Before Jesus ascended, He said, "But you shall receive power when the Holy Spirit has come upon you; and you shall be witnesses to Me in Jerusalem, and in all Judea and Samaria, and to the end of the earth" (Acts 1:8). The mission of the church began in Jerusalem and continues to move out from there to all the nations of the earth, to enfold the whole world into the kingdom of Christ. Acts 1:9-11 records the historical account of the ascension of Jesus:

> Now when He had spoken these things, while they watched, He was taken up, and a cloud received Him out of their sight. And while they looked steadfastly toward heaven as He went up, behold, two men stood by them in white apparel, who also said, "Men of Galilee, why do you stand gazing up into heaven? This same Jesus, who was taken up from you into heaven, will so come in like manner as you saw Him go into heaven."

Daniel's Prophetic Vision of the Ascension

Daniel 7 gives the Old Testament prophetic vision of the ascension event as seen from heaven. Daniel saw the Son of Man coming *up* to the Ancient of Days. We should not misconstrue this passage to be about Christ coming down at the end of history in final judgment. Son of Man is a title that essentially means Son of Adam, e.g., the new Adam God promised to send to fulfill the dominion mandate. In Daniel 7, the Son of Man tames beastly empires, just as the original Adam ruled the animals. This is an ascension scene, the coronation and enthronement of the Son of Man.

God gave Daniel a preview of coming history from Daniel's own time down to the time of Christ. This vision covered about 600 years of world history, *before it happened*. Daniel saw four great beasts, representing different world empires that would successively come onto the center stage in world history: Babylon (Dan. 7:1-4), Medo-Persia (Dan. 7:5), Greece (Dan. 7:6), and the Roman empire (Dan. 7:7-8). All of these different empires, represented by the beasts, were under God's sovereign control. When one of the beasts rose to power, "dominion was given to it" (Dan. 7:6). Likewise, when the beasts lost power, "they had their dominion taken away" (Dan. 7:12).

The beasts were not autonomous; they only had the power that God had sovereignly chosen to give them for a time. This amazingly accurate and detailed prophecy of Daniel shows that history really is *God's story*. History is under God's control and direction. God causes empires to rise and fall, as He wills.

Daniel also saw something that would happen during the days of the fourth beast. There would be one like the Son of Man coming on the clouds of heaven who would ascend to the Ancient of Days. He would be given dominion, glory, and a kingdom, so that all the nations and peoples would serve Him. Unlike the previous kingdoms of the four beasts, this kingdom would have durability, power, and indestructibility that the other kingdoms did not possess. Daniel 7:13-14 records:

> And behold, One like the Son of Man, coming with the clouds of heaven! He came to the Ancient of Days, and they brought Him near before Him. Then to Him was given dominion and glory and a kingdom, that all peoples, nations, and languages should serve Him. His dominion is an everlasting dominion, which shall not pass away, and His kingdom the one which shall not be destroyed.

This kingdom, inaugurated during the days of the Roman empire, is destined to fill the whole earth.

As the people of God, we can look at civil governments today and realize that they are often beastly and rage against God. They persecute God's people and disregard God's truth, but the ascension means that there is a new Adam who reigns over the beasts. This last Adam will slay them with the sword of the Spirit that comes out of His mouth (Rev. 19:15). He will tame and domesticate these wild beasts. Like Daniel, we may look at the scene around us and be grieved and troubled (Dan. 7:15). But the ascension means that sin, death, and Satan do not reign over us. The beasts do not reign over us. Any time the beasts rear their ugly heads, we have nothing to fear.

We are citizens of the kingdom of God which cannot be destroyed. The Son of Man reigns, and that means that all presidents, prime ministers, kings, legislators, and judges are under His rule whether they acknowledge it or not. We may suffer at their hands, as many Christians do around the world, but it is not suffering unto defeat. It is always suffering unto victory, because we share in a kingdom that cannot fail. Every earthly kingdom will rise and fall, but there is one kingdom that will last forever, the kingdom of the Son of Man. We belong to that kingdom and share in the rule of that kingdom. We are kings in union with Him (Rev. 1:6, Eph. 2:6).

God used Daniel to convert Nebuchadnezzar and transform the Babylonian kingdom (Dan. 4:34-37). He tamed a beast and made it into a man (Dan. 7:4). If we want to see this happen in our time, we must live like Daniel did. He held to God's truth as public truth and not a privatized religion.

The Babylonians of Daniel's day did not mind various expressions of "private piety" in the empire, provided people were willing to bow down to the civic religion in the public square. You may worship who or what you want in private, but you must pledge loyalty to the empire in public, or else be accused of treason. Modern secularists are similar to the ancient Babylonians, placing religion within the confines of "personal values" in which believers are free to exercise their religion within their homes and churches but not in the public square in which supposedly neutral "facts" hold together society. Despite the decree to pray only to the state-sponsored god, Daniel faithfully served King Darius (Dan. 6:4), and prayed to the true God with open windows (Dan. 6:10). He exercised his piety in public; Daniel knew there was no space where God did not belong for He is the lord over all. Because of this stance, he was thrown into the den of lions (Dan. 6:16). He had to suffer patiently and pray faithfully, but he continued to bear witness to the truth. When Daniel was delivered from the lions, Darius proclaimed the true God: "For He is the living God, and steadfast forever; His kingdom is the one which shall not be destroyed, and His dominion shall endure to the end" (Dan. 6:26).

A Human is Reigning in Heaven

The ascension is a comfort to the people of God. A human being is now ruling in heaven; the dust of the earth now sits on the throne of God. It is important for us to remember that Jesus remains a human being. He did not shed His humanity when He returned to the Father at the ascension. In the incarnation of Jesus, God descended from heaven to earth, and in the death of Jesus, God descended even further to rescue us from hell. In the ascension of Jesus, the people of God are raised up to the heavenlies with Him. The church is united with Christ; thus, His ascension is our ascension. This is why Ephesians 2:6 says that God "raised us up together, and made us sit together in the heavenly places in Christ Jesus," for we reign with Him. The gospel includes both a descent and an ascent. Christ descended so that we may ascend; His humiliation leads to our exaltation; his heaven is our ascent.

In His ascension, Jesus became the first human being to arrive at God's goal for humanity. God always intended for humanity to be at the helm of the creation, reigning over all things in wisdom and righteousness under His kingship. In Jesus, God's plan for humanity came to fulfillment. The original trajectory that God put Adam on in the garden came to its final destination in Jesus, as the new Adam. In Ephesians 1:19-23, Paul describes the ramifications of the ascension:

and what is the exceeding greatness of His power toward us who believe, according to the working of His mighty power which He worked in Christ when He raised Him from the dead and seated Him at His right hand in the heavenly places, far above all principality and power and might and dominion, and every name that is named, not only in this age but also in that which is to come. And He put all things under His feet, and gave Him to be head over all things to the church, which is His body, the fullness of Him who fills all in all.

All rule has been given to Jesus, and the church is the fullness of Christ who fills all in all. When Paul talked about the ascension, he spoke of Christ's ruling and filling. This takes us straight back to Genesis 1 and what the first Adam was supposed to do: rule and fill the earth. Jesus, the last Adam, is seated at the right hand of God the Father, exalted above all principalities and powers. With the help of his bride, the church, he completes the dominion project, filling all things (note the way the vocabulary of Ephesians 1 echoes Genesis 1, with words like "dominion" and "filling").

This is the comfort of the ascension: a human being is seated at the Father's right hand ever living to intercede for us "because He…has an unchangeable priesthood…He is also able to save to the uttermost those who come to God through Him, since He always lives to make intercession for them" (Heb. 7:25). The ascended king puts us back in fellowship with God and enables us to fulfill His mission of ruling and subduing the earth, the project that was originally given to humanity.

The Ascension and Mission

The ascension of Jesus, as witnessed by the disciples, is the gospel. It is *good news*. The fundamental truth of the ascension is that Jesus has ascended to reign. He is king. He rules the nations, *right now*. Christ's rule and reign has been established, and He rules from the right hand of the Father in the present age. At the end of Matthew's Gospel, Jesus didn't say, "All authority will be given to me someday at the end of history." Rather, in Matthew 28:18-20, He said:

> All authority has been given to Me in heaven and on earth. Go therefore and make disciples of all the nations, baptizing them in the name of the Father and of the Son and of the Holy Spirit, teaching them to observe all things that I have commanded you; and lo, I am with you always, even to the end of the age.

His kingly power is with us to the end of the age so that His mission can be fulfilled. No matter how things look at any given point in history, we must remember that Jesus is reigning from the Father's right hand and things look quite different from his vantage point. He has everything under control.

Because Christ ascended, He is lord over all of life and all of culture. All of life is to be lived out under His lordship. If we think of our life as slices of pie such as work, family, recreation, church, etc., we must understand that every slice of the pie belongs to Jesus. As Abraham Kuyper said, "There is not a square inch in the whole domain of our human existence over which Christ, who is Sovereign over all, does not cry: 'Mine!'"[20] We must press the crown rights of King Jesus into every facet of life.

The ascension is the sign of Christ's total rule and total kingship. This is *good news* because Christ's reign brings harmony to our life. His kingship gives our life meaning and transcendent purpose. Under Christ's lordship, life becomes whole and integrated. This creation—all of life, all of culture, every kind of human endeavor—is the field in which we are to work out the implications of Christ's lordship, making His reign visible. Christ's lordship covers institutions as well as individuals. He reigns over public affairs as well as private matters. The reign of the incarnate Son covers bodies as well as souls.

The ascension of Christ was an event of great importance to the public proclamation of the gospel. The ascension was the enthronement of the king, and there is no getting around it. This cannot be labeled as a private vision, with implications only for Christians behind the closed doors of their churches. It is a historical fact. It is public truth. It is a universal reality. At the ascension, Jesus entered into His office as king over all things. While He reigns from heaven, His rule bears upon this world. This is why John Calvin said the vocation of the church is to make the invisible reign of Christ visible to the world. This means, among other things, that we need to pray for

---

20. *Abraham Kuyper: A Centennial Reader*, ed. James D. Bratt (Grand Rapids, MI: Eerdmans, 1998), 488.

and encourage earthly political powers to be submissive to Christ, to heed His Word in their official capacity, to be attentive to His church, and to make space in the world for the mission of the church to move forward.

The state, as well as every other institution, has a duty to acknowledge God's revelation of Himself in history in Christ, as lord and king. As Psalm 2:10-11 says: "Now therefore, be wise, O kings; be instructed, you judges of the earth. Serve the Lord with fear, and rejoice with trembling. Kiss the Son, lest He be angry and you perish in the way." Sadly, in America this has been cheapened and twisted in all sorts of ways. Progressives obviously deny these realities. But the "religious right" has also given us all sorts of misguided notions about Christ's reign, privatizing the faith and failing to grasp the centrality of the church. But however wrongly some people may act, that doesn't change this fundamental truth: all authorities are called to submit to King Jesus as He reigns over every nation from heaven. As T.S. Eliot said, "The Christian can be satisfied with nothing less than a Christian organization of society."[21] Eliot explained that he wasn't imagining a society in which every individual is a Christian or is forced to make a Christian confession, but rather a society organized upon biblical principles, seeing the story of the Bible as the over-arching story in which every nation must take its place.

---

21. T.S. Eliot, "The Idea of a Christian Society" in *Christianity and Culture* (New York: Harcourt, Brace and World, 1949), 27.

As He Left, so Shall He Return

In Acts 1:11, the two angelic messengers made a promise of the final coming of Jesus that will occur after the church has completed her mission: "This same Jesus, who was taken up from you into heaven, will so come in like manner as you saw Him go into heaven." Jesus will come back in the same visible, glorious way that He left. Christ's leaving is a good thing for now, because it means the sending of the Spirit. But His leaving is not the end of the story.

History is a story with a beginning, middle, and end. It finds its beginning in creation, when God spoke the world into being in Genesis 1. It finds its center in the death, resurrection, and ascension of Jesus. History will find its ending in His glorious return, when Jesus will join heaven and earth together and glorify all things.

The kingdom that was inaugurated in His death and resurrection continues to be built by His Spirit. But the conclusion of it all is His Second Coming in glory to consummate all things: to join heaven and earth together, to join God and His people together, to resurrect the saints, and to bring the final judgment. Alluding to the ascension and final coming, Philippians 2:9-11 reminds us:

> Therefore God also has highly exalted Him and given Him the name which is above every name, that at the name of Jesus every knee should bow, of those in heaven, and of those on earth, and of those under the earth, and that every tongue should confess that Jesus Christ is Lord, to the glory of God the Father.

Everything that happens in history is moving toward this final goal, when Christ will come and restore all things. Jesus will reign from heaven for however long it takes for the church to complete her mission. After the mission is accomplished, Christ will return in glory and hand the completed, fulfilled kingdom over to His Father (1 Cor. 15:24). But in the meantime, He reigns over every nation, until every nation has bowed the knee to Him, no matter how long that takes. Christ will continue to sit at the Father's right hand, ruling over all things, until the church finishes her task of bringing all peoples under the loving lordship of Christ and the gracious government of God.

After Jesus ascended into heaven, the two angelic messengers said in Acts 1:11, "Men of Galilee, why do you stand gazing up into heaven?" In other words, "Don't you realize, you've got work to do? You can't just stand here staring up into heaven. You've got a mission and you had better be preparing for it." Christian living is not just gazing into heaven, but working to extend the kingdom on earth by living as witnesses to King Jesus in word and deed.

Chapter 6

The Pentecostal Church

Because Jesus ascended, He rules over all for the good of His church. Consider again Ephesians 1:20-23:

> He worked in Christ when He raised Him from the dead and seated Him at His right hand in the heavenly places, far above all principality and power and might and dominion, and every name that is named, not only in this age but also in that which is to come. And He put all things under His feet, and gave Him to be head over all things to the church, which is His body, the fullness of Him who fills all in all.

The church is the apple of His eye and the center of His plan. Jesus rules all for her sake and for her good. In Christ, we are seated on the throne at God's right hand as well (Eph. 2:4-7). God's plans in the world revolve around the church. As the ascended one, Christ rules the world for the sake of His church and He rules over the church for the sake of the world. This is why the church is the institution that most shapes history—not the state, not the family, not the corporation.

The Ascension opens up space for the church's mission. When Jesus went away, He left His church with a mission in the world. Even as the Father so loved the world that He sent His only begotten Son, so the Son so loved the world that He sent His Spirit to His church. Because Jesus has ascended, the Spirit has descended. The Son went up so the Spirit could come down.

Jesus has physically left us, but He has not left us alone. Pentecost, like the death and resurrection of Christ, is a once-and-for-all event. But this event continues to shape the world today. The sending of the Spirit at Pentecost shows the church's union with the glorified and risen Christ. Jesus was baptized with the Spirit before He launched His public ministry to Israel. At Pentecost, the church was baptized with the Spirit to launch her mission to the nations. In the Old Testament prophets, God had promised to baptize many nations, to pour out His Spirit on all flesh. This came to pass at Pentecost.

In Acts 1, Jesus gave the promise of the Holy Spirit, then ascended into heaven. Ten days after His ascent into heaven, Jesus poured out His Holy Spirit on His disciples. After the Spirit was poured out in Acts 2, Peter explained how the Ascension led to Pentecost: "Therefore being exalted to the right hand of God, and having received from the Father the promise of the Holy Spirit, He poured out this which you now see and hear." This is why Jesus said in John 16:7, "It is to your advantage that I go away; for if I do not go away, the Helper will not come to you; but if I depart, I will send Him to you." By sending His Spirit, Jesus is now present in a much more comprehensive way in the world than He was during His earthly ministry. Heaven now has the holy body, and the earth has the Holy Spirit. Now, through His Spirit, Jesus is with us to the end of the age.

Because Jesus has ascended, He has given gifts to His church. In ancient times, the greatness of a king was shown in the greatness of the gifts that he bestowed upon his people. Jesus, as the ascended king, has opened up His treasury and given us the greatest gift of all: the person of the Holy Spirit. Through that gift of the Spirit to the whole church, He gives each of us particular gifts to equip us for service in His body. Ephesians 4:7-8 says, "But to each one of us grace was given according to the measure of Christ's gift. Therefore He says: 'When He ascended on high, He led captivity captive, and gave gifts to men.'" When the Spirit enters our lives, He gives us customized gifts suited to who God has made us to be. In God's grace, it is our privilege to be able to serve so great a king and point others to His kingdom, equipped and empowered by the Holy Spirit.

The Old Testament Roots of Pentecost

In the Old Testament, Pentecost was a feast day ordained for Israel in the law of Moses. It was the feast when Israel commemorated the receiving of the law. The word Pentecost means "fifty." In Exodus, it was fifty days after the Passover in Egypt when Moses went up on Mount Sinai and came back down with the Ten Commandments. On that day, three thousand people died because of their idolatry (Exod. 32:28). At the new covenant Pentecost, the Spirit gave new life to three thousand people (Acts 2:41). The law brought death, but the Spirit brings life. Moses went up the mountain and the law came down written on stone. Jesus ascended to heaven to sit at the Father's right hand, and the Spirit came down to write the law on our hearts.

Pentecost, also known as the "Feast of Weeks" or the "Feast of Harvests," is described in the Old Testament law mainly in Leviticus 23:15-22 and Deuteronomy 16:9-12. It celebrated the beginning of the land's fruitfulness. There were three main festivals in the Jewish calendar: a firstfruits festival at the end of Passover, the Pentecost festival which celebrated the ongoing harvest, and the Feast of Tabernacles, which celebrated the ingathering of the harvest. In Acts 2:1, Luke said that "the Day of Pentecost had fully come." When Luke said this, he did not just mean that Pentecost happened that year in the Jewish calendar. Rather, he meant that everything the Old Testament festival pointed to had come to its fulfillment.

At Pentecost, the Feast of Harvests, the Spirit had been poured out as a sign that God was beginning to harvest the nations. These were the firstfruits of the new age. The sacrificial lamb of Passover that was slain at Calvary was now beginning to bear fruit in the world as people were drawn into the kingdom of God in its new form. Jesus died and rose again to form a Spirit-indwelt community that would bear His name, worship the Father through Him, and carry on His mission in the world. From Pentecost on, the public work of Jesus in the world would be concentrated in His church, through the Holy Spirit.

The New Israel and New Temple

Acts 2:2 says the Spirit came like a "rushing mighty wind." In both Hebrew and in Greek, the words for "wind" and "spirit" are the same words. This is reminiscent of Genesis 1, where the Spirit hovered over the waters of the earth at the beginning of the creation week. In Genesis 2, God breathed life into Adam, filling him with a rushing wind so that he became a living being. The rushing mighty wind also resembles Ezekiel 37, in which the prophet had a vision of Israel in exile: dry bones down in a valley. The wind of God rushed upon the bones and brought them to life, forming them into a great army. Israel was restored through the wind of God.

Pentecost fulfilled all these things, marking a new creation and signaling the last days of the old world order. Pentecost showed that a seismic shift had taken place in redemptive history. No longer would God's work be primarily with the single nation of Israel, sending prophets to them who spoke their native language of Hebrew. Rather, the kingdom was now open to all peoples. Through the Spirit, God spoke in the languages of the nations. The new humanity would not have racial or ethnic barriers. Rather, the church would be one new family formed by the Spirit, composed of people from every nation, tribe, and language.

The rushing wind of the Spirit "filled the whole house where they were sitting." This language of "filling" the house was used in several places in the Old Testament. Moses had the people build the tabernacle according to God's instructions, and Exodus 40:34 states that "the glory of the LORD filled the tabernacle." Later, Solomon built the temple and 1 Kings 8:11 reports "the glory of the LORD filled the house of the LORD." The filling of the house at Pentecost points to the church as the new and true temple. The old temple in Jerusalem was now obsolete and would eventually be destroyed, as Jesus prophesied in Matthew 24:1-35. In Exodus 40 and in 1 Kings 8, no one could enter because the house was filled with the glory of God. On the day of Pentecost, when God filled His house, three thousand enter (Acts 2:41). The new covenant brings a welcome that was not there in the old covenant. God now invites all nations to come and be a part of His Temple, the church. The church is a house filled with the promised Spirit of God.

Acts 2:3 says, "Then there appeared to them divided tongues, as of fire, and one sat upon each of them." This fire falling from heaven also takes us back to the inauguration of Solomon's temple in 1 Kings 8. In that passage, when God moved into the temple, sacrifices were prepared, and fire fell from heaven to consume them. In Pentecost, God the Holy Spirit came to dwell in His new and true temple, the church. Just as fire consumed those old covenant sacrifices, we are the new covenant sacrifices, offering ourselves as a living sacrifice in union with the Lord Jesus Christ (Rom. 12:1). John the Baptist said that Jesus would baptize with the Spirit and with fire (Matt. 3:11). Just as Jesus' baptism launched His ministry to Israel, the church's baptism by fire launched her ministry to the nations.

Reversal of Babel: Speaking in Tongues

On Pentecost, the apostles spoke the gospel in foreign languages: "And there were dwelling in Jerusalem Jews, devout men, from every nation under heaven. And when this sound occurred, the multitude came together, and were confused, because everyone heard them speak in his own language" (Acts 2:5-6). Clearly from the text, the act of speaking in tongues is not some other-worldly language. Rather, it is the Spirit-enabled ability to speak in human languages that the apostles would not have ordinarily known. Everyone who gathered in Jerusalem for the Jewish Pentecost feast, including distant travelers, heard the gospel in his own native language.

This is a reversal of the tower of Babel. At Babel, God separated the peoples according to language. The effect of Babel is summarized in Genesis 11:9, "Therefore its name is called Babel, because there the LORD confused the language of all the earth; and from there the LORD scattered them abroad over the face of all the earth." Just as the broader context of Genesis 10 and 11 gave us a table of nations, Luke wrote a table of nations in Acts 2:3-12. Genesis lists seventy (seven times ten) nations; Luke lists seventeen (seven plus ten) nations. At Babel, the different tongues brought division into the many nations. At Pentecost, God is reuniting humanity into one new family by His Spirit. Babel was a curse; Pentecost is a blessing. Babel scattered; Pentecost gathered. At Babel, man had tried to build a tower into heaven. At Pentecost, through the gift of the Spirit, heaven came down to earth as God's gracious gift to His people.

A reversed Babel does not mean nations will no longer exist. Perhaps it would be more accurate to call Pentecost the sanctification of Babel rather than its reversal. Nations, as identifiable groups of people with a common culture (and usually a common civil government) living in a defined geographic area still exist, obviously, and there is nothing wrong with that. But Pentecost does make it possible for the nations to be united in love. This becomes a major theme in the rest of the New Testament: Jews and Gentiles are brought together in Christ and made one in his church. This does not mean they have to give up all their cultural distinctives. The nations can remain distinct people groups. But as the Pentecostal Spirit permeates each group, as the leaven of the gospel gets worked into each culture, these cultures will be transformed and matured. The nations do not meld together into a Babelic blob; rather the nations in their distinctiveness can become Christian nations, sharing a common faith, while remaining diverse. The unity and diversity of the nations is pictured in passages like Isaiah 60:1-7, where the multitude of nations bring their many different gifts into the one kingdom of Christ.

Speaking in tongues in Acts 2 was a sign of blessing to the nations, but there was also a sense in which tongues served as a sign of judgment upon Israel. In several places in the Old Testament, God said He would speak to Israel in foreign tongues as a judgment upon them; if they would not listen to Him when He spoke to them in Hebrew (through the prophets), He would confuse them with the tongues of Gentiles. In Deuteronomy 28:49-50, this was one of the curses of the covenant. In Isaiah 28, the foreign languages were a sign that God was bringing a curse upon His people. It was as if God was saying, "You won't listen to me when I speak Hebrew. Maybe you'll listen to me when I send these Assyrian invaders, speaking a strange tongue, to defeat you and carry you off into exile." In 1 Corinthians 14:21, Paul quoted from Isaiah 28:11-12, "With men of other tongues and other lips I will speak to this people; and yet, for all that, they will not hear Me." Paul is indicating the apostolic era's gift of tongues was a sign Gentiles are being grafted into the kingdom, but also a sign to Jews of impending judgment (which was fulfilled in A.D. 70 when the temple was destroyed and the old covenant ended).

In the Old Testament, when Israel did not listen to God and the prophets, they were sent into captivity. In the New Testament, when Israel did not listen to Christ and His apostles, God judged them and gave the covenant blessings to other nations. As the apostle Paul said in 1 Corinthians 14:22, "tongues are for a sign, not to those who believe but to unbelievers," particularly the unbelieving Jews of that generation. The church is the new temple of God, which the destruction of the temple in Jerusalem in A.D. 70 would make unmistakably clear.

The Holy Spirit:
The Spiritual Gift Given at Pentecost

The principal spiritual gift that Jesus gives to the church is the Holy Spirit. The Holy Spirit is not just a person, He is a divine person. The Spirit does works only God can do. He was active in the creation, and continues to act in the sustaining and redeeming of this world.

In Genesis 1, the Spirit hovered over the waters of the earth. Throughout the creation week, He carried out the Word the Father spoke. The Spirit was the architect and builder of the world. In Genesis 2, the Holy Spirit breathed life into man, so that man became a living being. This is why the church has confessed that the Spirit is "the Lord and giver of life."

The Spirit is also active in God's works of redemption. In Isaiah 63, the exodus is a work attributed to the Holy Spirit. Jesus was conceived by the Holy Spirit in the womb of the virgin Mary. Jesus said that we must be born of the Spirit to enter His kingdom. The Spirit gives life to us in re-creating us. And the Holy Spirit raised Jesus from the dead (Rom. 8:11). The Spirit bears fruit in our lives, working in us faith and repentance. The way of salvation is described as "walking in the Spirit" (Gal. 5:16).

One of the major acts that the Holy Spirit performed on behalf of the church is His inspiration of the Scriptures. The Bible is authored by the Spirit. In John 14:26, Jesus said, "the Helper, the Holy Spirit, whom the Father will send in My name, He will teach you all things, and bring to your remembrance all things that I said to you." Jesus said a similar thing in John 16:13, "when He, the Spirit of truth, has come, He will guide you into all truth; for He will not speak on His own authority, but whatever He hears He will speak; and He will tell you things to come." The gospels are trustworthy accounts of Jesus' life, not just because they rely on eyewitness testimony, but also because the Spirit directed and guided their writing. The entirety of the Scriptures is attributed to the inspiration of the Holy Spirit (2 Tim. 3:16).

There is a lot of talk about the miraculous gifts of the Spirit in the church today, but the most miraculous work of all that the Spirit does is to raise sinners from death to life, uniting them to Christ Jesus. It is not as though salvation is a joint project between us and God, where Jesus did His part by dying on the cross and now we do our part by believing in Him and obeying Him. No, even our faith comes as a gift that the Spirit works in us (Eph. 2:8-9), and our obedience is God's workmanship (Eph. 2:10).

Left to our own devices, we are dead in our sins and trespasses, and we despise God and His Word. But when the Spirit goes to work in us, He turns our hearts and causes us to cry out to Jesus for salvation. The Spirit comes to ensure that all of Christ's benefits won for us in His life, death, and resurrection, actually reach us. The Spirit opens up our hearts, that Christ may enter in.

However, the Holy Spirit does more than apply redemption to us. The Holy Spirit has not come into our lives for our sole, private benefit. The Spirit is the life and power of God in us for the sake of others. The Spirit transforms us, so that through the church the world may be transformed. God has given us His Spirit because He wants to bring the kingdom of heaven to earth. He wants to renew the whole world. This is the ultimate purpose of the Spirit's ministry in us.

The Holy Spirit continues and expands the mission of Jesus. Jesus went away at His Ascension, but the reigning king sent the gift of the Holy Spirit. The Spirit does not have His own mission; His mission is to make us partakers in the mission of Christ.

In John 14:12, Jesus made this astounding claim: "Most assuredly, I say to you, he who believes in Me, the works that I do he will do also; and greater works than these he will do, because I go to My Father." Jesus did not convert that many people during His earthly ministry. Yet, as a result of Peter's first sermon after the sending of the Spirit at Pentecost, three thousand people became believers (Acts 2:41). The greater works that we do now since the time the Spirit has come are not miracles, but mission. This is why the Spirit has come: to lead the church in converting and discipling the world.

Conclusion

Pentecost was not just a private event in the experience of those first disciples. It was a public event in the history of the world. The first Christian Pentecost is not just a part of church history, but one of the most important events in world history. The church was given the Spirit on behalf of the world so that through the church the world may come to know God through the same Spirit. Pentecost was another chapter in the divine invasion, as part of God's rescue mission.

God's mission is not just to save a tiny handful out of the nations. God is determined to renew the whole world by His Spirit. This is why when the Spirit was poured out, immediately the church began to speak in tongues. The gift of tongues may have expired but the global mission of the Spirit-filled continues. The gospel must go forth and the whole world must come to know Jesus and bow before Him. When the Holy Spirit was poured out on the people of God, a new age began in human history. From that point on, the Holy Spirit guides the church, in accordance with the Spirit-inspired Scriptures, shaping the course of human history.

When the new wine of the Spirit was poured out, the old wineskin of Israel could not contain it. This wine is poured into the new wineskin of the church, which is destined to fill the whole world by discipling every nation. The Spirit not only changes individual lives, He changes nations. He changes the whole structure and order of the world. The Spirit fills and transforms the church precisely so the church can fill and transform the world.

Chapter 7

Jesus Christ and the Temple of Doom

In his Pentecost sermon in Acts 2, Peter spoke in this way:

> Men of Judea and all who dwell in Jerusalem, let this be known to you, and heed my words. . . But this is what was spoken by the prophet Joel: "And it shall come to pass in the last days, says God, that I will pour out of My Spirit on all flesh; your sons and your daughters shall prophesy, your young men shall see visions, your old men shall dream dreams."

Joel made a prophecy about "the last days," and it was coming to fulfillment in Peter's day. Peter realized that by "last days," Joel was not referring to the end of human history, but the end of the old covenant.

The coming of the Spirit meant the coming of a new age. In the last days of the old covenant, God was going to begin something new by pouring out His Spirit. In his sermon in Acts 2:40, Peter also said, "Be saved from this perverse generation." That generation then living was in the last days of the old covenant, and they would face judgment.

The outpouring of the Spirit at Pentecost around A.D. 30 was a prelude to the destruction of the Temple in A.D. 70. During the time between A.D. 30 and A.D. 70, there was *covenantal overlap* between the old covenant and the new covenant. The old covenant was winding down and the new covenant was being inaugurated. The real questions during this time period included, Where is the presence of God to be found? Where is the true priesthood to be found? Where is true sacrifice offered? Are these to be found in the temple building in Jerusalem or in the church, in Christ?

Much of the New Testament was written to answer these questions. The New Testament declares that God's presence was no longer to be found in the desolate temple building, but in the people of Christ. The true priesthood was not to be found in Jerusalem, but in the church (1 Pet. 2:9-10). True sacrifice was no longer to be found in the animal sacrificial system, but in the sacrifice of praise in Christian worship (Heb. 13:15). The Jewish people were being "replaced" as the covenant people of God by the new covenant people, Christians. The Jewish temple building was becoming obsolete and replaced with the greater new covenant temple, the church (1 Cor. 3:16-17). Some Jews made the transition by believing in Jesus; the rest were like fruitless branches broken out of the olive tree of the covenant (Rom. 11).

From A.D. 30 to 70, there were two temples vying to be the true temple of God. There was the temple building in Jerusalem, and there was the people-temple of the church (Eph. 2:11ff; 1 Pet. 2:4ff). The destruction of the temple in A.D. 70 was the definitive answer to this debate. It was the vindication of Jesus and His people. The old covenant was winding down and the new covenant was beginning from the time of Christ until the destruction of the temple in A.D. 70. These are the "last days" so often mentioned by the apostles and "the end of the age" that Christ prophesied in Matthew 24:1-35.

Perhaps no text in the gospels has been as misinterpreted as Jesus's prophecy in Matthew 24:1-35.[22] Despite Jesus's own words that "this generation will by no means pass away till all these things take place," some biblical interpreters still insist on placing these events at the end of history. The entirety of this portion of the Olivet discourse is a prophecy by Jesus of the destruction of the temple in Jerusalem. Moreover, the destruction of the Jewish temple is a *fulfilled* prophecy which came to pass in A.D. 70 when the Roman army crushed the city. The destruction of Jerusalem and the temple connects together Jesus's life, death, resurrection, ascension, Pentecost, and the establishment of the church as God's new temple that will fill the earth.

---

22. The parallels to Matthew's Gospel account of the Olivet discourse are found in Mark 13 and Luke 21. John's version of these now fulfilled prophetic events is found in Revelation.

The Historical Significance of A.D. 70

Modern theology does not give much significance to the events of A.D. 70, and many of us are not fully aware of the importance of these events in the first century. However, what happened to the city of Jerusalem and the temple is of tremendous importance as a redemptive-historical event. The temple was the center of religion, politics, and culture for Israel, the centerpiece of their life. It was the heart of the sacrificial system and old covenant priesthood. The destruction of the temple was the definitive end of the old covenant and its system.

The Jewish war with Rome lasted three and a half years, from A.D. 66 to 70. Tensions had been boiling between Jews and Rome for at least a century. There had been previous attempts at revolt but they had been put down. In the New Testament itself, there is reference to the zealot party, those who were most keen on going to war with Rome. There was a very strong nationalistic fervor amongst the Jews at this time, which led them into conflict with Rome. However, the war with Rome was suicidal for Israel. An abundance of troops and supplies made the Romans virtually unbeatable. Many Jews fought to the end, expecting a Messiah to deliver them, not realizing their Messiah had already come, been rejected by them, and had sovereignly dispatched the Roman army to carry out His will. The Romans besieged Jerusalem, and of the Jewish people who were not killed by Roman attacks, many starved to death.

According to the historian Eusebius, the only survivors of Jerusalem were Jewish Christians who had heard Jesus's prophecy. They knew that when the Roman army came, it was time to head for the hills. In Luke 21:20, Jesus had warned the disciples, "But when you see Jerusalem surrounded by armies, then know that its desolation is near." It would seem that at that point it would have been too late to flee, but the historical record is that the Roman army surrounded the city, then pulled back. At this time, the Christians left the city. Not a single Christian perished for this reason. This confirms that the early Christians believed that Christ's prophecy in Matthew 24 was about a coming conflict with Rome within that generation, and not the end of the world.

There were a few Jews who were spared and were made part of Titus's triumphal procession in Rome as he celebrated his victory.[23] All told, about one million Jews were killed in the conflict and another four hundred thousand enslaved. Josephus the historian gave an eyewitness account of the tragedy that happened to the Jewish people in this war. He recorded massacres that were so great the Sea of Galilee turned to blood. He detailed the infighting among the Jews in Jerusalem and the desecration of the temple. He reported famine and cannibalism with mothers eating their own babies, the ultimate covenant curse (Lev. 26:29; Deut. 28:53-57). Josephus recorded that Jews were crucified at a rate of five hundred a day at the hands of the Romans. The temple was burned to the ground. Virtually the entire city and temple were leveled. Jesus said that not one stone would be left upon another, and it came to pass. The once great city became a barren wasteland and a pile of rubble.

---

23. The Arch of Titus in Rome stands to this day, depicting a portion of this triumphal procession.

The most important thing to understand about the Jewish wars that culminated with the destruction of the temple in A.D. 70 is that Jesus is the one who brought the great tribulation to pass. He used the Roman army to do it, just as God has used Babylonians and Assyrians in the past to bring judgment against Israel. The judgment that fell on unbelieving Israel was the "coming" of Jesus that He prophesied in Matthew 24:1-35.[24]

Impending Judgment upon First Century Israel

The climactic moment in Israel's history came in the person of Jesus of Nazareth. God had sent to Israel her promised Messiah; Israel needed to bow before the Messiah in order to receive all the promises. But if Israel rejected her Messiah, the curses of the covenant would fall upon her. This theme of impending judgment on Israel for her unbelief and covenant unfaithfulness is highlighted throughout the gospels. Consider a few of the passages which indicate that judgment on Israel was coming soon.[25]

Jesus prophesied impending judgment, and the destruction of Jerusalem brought tears to His eyes. In Luke 13:34-35, Jesus lamented:

> O Jerusalem, Jerusalem, the one who kills the prophets and stones those who are sent to her! How often I wanted to gather your children together, as

---

24. This is not to be confused with Jesus's final coming on the last Day of Judgment.

25. See also Matthew 3:7-12, 21:18-20, 21:33-46; Luke 13:1-9, 13:22-30, 23:28-31.

a hen gathers her brood under her wings, but you were not willing! See! Your house is left to you desolate; and assuredly, I say to you, you shall not see Me until the time comes when you say, "Blessed is He who comes in the name of the LORD!"

Christ was lamenting over Jerusalem, for He knew the looming destruction that was to come upon her for lack of faith and repentance. Jesus said, "Your house is left to you desolate," referring to the temple. After the triumphal entry, in Luke 19:41-44, Jesus again wept over Jerusalem, saying:

If you had known, even you, especially in this your day, the things that make for your peace! But now they are hidden from your eyes. For days will come upon you when your enemies will build an embankment around you, surround you and close you in on every side, and level you, and your children within you, to the ground; and they will not leave in you one stone upon another, because you did not know the time of your visitation.

Jesus was talking explicitly about a coming judgment upon Israel from the hand of God through the Roman army.

Christ's parable of the wedding feast is recorded in Matthew 22:1-14. In this parable, there was a "king who arranged a marriage for his son." The king sent out servants to summon those invited to the wedding, but none come. Eventually, some "seized his servants, treated them spitefully, and killed them." Matthew 22:7 gives the king's response: "when the king heard about it he was furious. And he sent out his armies, destroyed those murderers, and burned up their city." This description fits the history of what happened to Jerusalem in A.D. 70 at the hands of the Roman army, dispatched by the King of Kings.

The words and actions of Jesus, such as the temple cleansing and the withering of the fig tree (Matt. 21:12-22), are prophetic actions which foretell the destruction of the temple itself. These enacted parables show that Jesus came not as a temple reformer, but a temple destroyer. The temple was doomed.

Selective Exposition of Matthew 24:1-35

Referring to all he prophesied in Matthew 24:1-33, Jesus said in Matthew 24:34, "Assuredly, I say to you, *this generation* will by no means pass away till all these things take place." Despite Jesus's clear teaching in the Olivet discourse, many modern interpreters cannot accept these events as having happened within that generation but instead project these events into the future. This is mainly due to misunderstanding the language Jesus used in Matthew 24, leading up to verse 34. Jesus talked about the end of the age, the great tribulation, the coming of the Son of Man, the sun and moon darkening, and the angels calling the elect from the four corners of the world. Surely this is about the end of the world, right? Modern readers, unversed in the Old Testament, and without skill in reading Scripture typologically, frequently misinterpret these comments of Jesus. This kind of reading makes Jesus's prophetic statement that "this generation will by no means pass away till all these things take place" into an erroneous assertion.[26]

The Beginnings of Birth Pains (Matt. 24:4-8)

In the Olivet discourse, Jesus describes a series of signs that will presage the end of the old covenant order. In Matthew 24:6-7, Jesus said they "will hear of wars and rumors of wars…. For nation will rise against nation, and kingdom against kingdom." The era into which Jesus was born was marked by the Pax Romana, the Roman peace. Rome had conquered the Mediterranean world and because of their military might, they were able to keep the peace. Jesus was saying that the Pax Romana would be interrupted. According to the historian Josephus, in the period after Christ's ascension and before A.D. 70, one violent war after another broke out, as Jesus predicted. In Matthew 24:7, Jesus prophesies natural disasters: "And there will be famines, pestilences, and earthquakes in various places." Famine was clearly a big problem in this period of history, such as in Acts 11:27-28, where we read:

---

26. The atheist Bertrand Russell wrote in *Why I Am Not a Christian* that Christ believed He would return within a generation but was wrong. This misinterpretation of Matthew 24 is part of the reason Russell rejected Christ. Ironically, the proper interpretation of the passage is a great defense of Christ as prophet, king, and God in the flesh. If we properly understand the biblical text, that His coming is not His final coming at the end of history, but a coming judgment on Israel and Jerusalem in A.D. 70, then Matthew 24 becomes an amazingly accurate foretelling of events that can only be accounted for if Jesus was indeed a prophet of God.

And in these days prophets came from Jerusalem to Antioch. Then one of them, named Agabus, stood up and showed by the Spirit that there was going to be a great famine throughout all the world, which also happened in the days of Claudius Caesar.

Jesus also mentioned earthquakes. There are two accounts of earthquakes in Matthew 27:50-52 and 28:1-2, associated with Christ's death and resurrection. Acts 16:26 also records an earthquake while Paul and Silas were imprisoned. All these signs, the false messiahs, wars, and natural disasters, are not signs of the end, as verse 6 indicates: "See that you are not troubled; for all these things must come to pass, but the end is not yet." In other words, these were *not* signs of the end. As verse 8 says, "these are the beginning of birth pains," convulsions that are rocking the old world before its final collapse.

The Spread of the Gospel of the Kingdom (Matt. 24:9-14)

Matthew 24:14 says, "And this gospel of the kingdom will be preached in all the world as a witness to all the nations, and then the end will come." At first glance one might believe this is obviously not about events in the first century, but about the end of history. Surely by A.D. 70., the gospel had not advanced to all the nations? The key to understanding this statement is noting that when Jesus said "all the world" in Matthew 24, the word for "world" in the Greek language is not *cosmos* but *oikumene*, which *oikumene* is a reference to the Roman empire. The root word for *cosmos* is used by Jesus in the familiar John 3:16 passage:

"For God so loved the world [*kosmon*] that He gave His only begotten Son, that whoever believes in Him should not perish but have everlasting life." Passages like John 3 speak of the "cosmos," the entire world or universe. But here in Matthew 24, Jesus's word *oikumene* ("world") is specific to the Roman empire.

This usage of the word *oikumene* for the inhabited world is supported by other texts in the New Testament. In Colossians 1:5-6, Paul speaks of "the gospel, which has come to you, as it has also in all the world, and is bringing forth fruit, as it is also among you since the day you heard and knew the grace of God in truth." In Romans 1:8, Paul writes, "I thank my God through Jesus Christ for you all, that your faith is spoken of throughout the whole world." Paul ends the Romans letter with the benediction of the gospel that is "now made manifest, and by the prophetic Scriptures made known to all nations, according to the commandment of the everlasting God, for obedience to the faith." And back in Luke 2:1, before Christ's birth, "it came to pass in those days that a decree went out from Caesar Augustus that all the world should be registered." In each of these passages, the usage of "all the world" or "the whole world" or "all nations" refers to the territory of the Roman Empire, the *oikumene*.

Jesus was saying that before A.D. 70, the gospel would spread to all the boundaries of the Roman empire. The foundation for the new world would be laid in the old world. Beginning in Acts 2 and Pentecost, the gospel spread through the Roman empire very quickly. The persecution of Christians led to the scattering of believers, who took the gospel with them. Paul's letter to the Romans was really a missionary fundraising letter. He wanted to go to Spain because he did not want to build on another apostle's foundation. Paul said in Romans 15:20, "I have made it my aim to preach the gospel, not where Christ was named, lest I should build on another man's foundation." This means that at the time he wrote Romans, there must have been gospel foundations and churches planted throughout most of the Roman empire. There was a gospel witness in all the Roman world by A.D. 70.

The Abomination of Desolation (Matt. 24:15-28)

Continuing in Matthew 24:15-16, Jesus said, "Therefore when you see the 'abomination of desolation,' spoken of by Daniel the prophet, standing in the holy place...then let those who are in Judea flee to the mountains." When the abomination of desolation happened, that marked the point when the disciples knew it was time to flee the city of Jerusalem. In Matthew 23:38, Jesus had said that their house would be left desolate, as He left the temple area. There would be some kind of sacrilege in the temple. In Old Testament language, this was an abomination committed by the Jews that is specifically connected with the Jewish high priest. Paul speaks this way in 2 Thessalonians 2:3-4:

> Let no one deceive you by any means; for that Day will not come unless the falling away comes first, and the man of sin is revealed, the son of perdition, who opposes and exalts himself above all that is called God or that is worshiped, so that he sits as

God in the temple of God, showing himself that
he is God.

This man has done what ought not to be done in a
holy place, therefore defiling the temple, causing it to be
left desolate. In Matthew 24:15-20, Jesus told His followers to flee the city after the abomination occurred, for the
time of destruction by the surrounding Roman army was
near. This cannot be a reference to the end of the world, for
who could flee from God's wrath?

The Darkening of the Sun,
Moon, and Stars (Matt. 24:29)

In Matthew 24:29, Jesus said, "Immediately after the tribulation of those days the sun will be darkened, and the
moon will not give its light; the stars will fall from heaven,
and the powers of the heavens will be shaken." Jesus was
using the language of the Old Testament prophets that describe the end of a nation. Imagine that a prophet came
today and said, "I had a vision that fifty stars fell from the
sky." We would associate that with the fifty stars of the flag
of the United States. In a similar way, Jesus was using the
symbolic language and imagery of the Old Testament. This
symbolism was built into the fabric of creation. God designed the sun, moon, and stars to be heavenly symbols of
earthly rulers. In Genesis 37, Joseph had a dream in which
the sun, moon, and eleven stars bowed down before him.
When he relayed this dream to his family members, they
did not interpret it to mean the end of the world, but rather
that their authority would be subservient to his authority.
Throughout the Bible, this symbolic language of the sun,

moon, and stars continues to be used. Concerning the end of the Babylonian empire, the prophet says in Isaiah 13:

> Behold, the day of the LORD comes, cruel, with both wrath and fierce anger, to lay the land desolate; and He will destroy its sinners from it. For the stars of heaven and their constellations will not give their light; the sun will be darkened in its going forth, and the moon will not cause its light to shine.

The sun, moon, and stars that are the Babylonian empire were going to come crashing down. In Matthew 24:29, Jesus was using symbolic language to describe the destruction of the Jewish nation and the city of Jerusalem.

The Sign of the Son of Man (Matt. 24:30)

In Matthew 24:30, Jesus said, "Then the sign of the Son of Man will appear in heaven." The sign that Jesus is the Son of Man and that He is reigning from heaven was that this whole series of events was coming to pass, culminating with the destruction of the temple. The destruction of the temple proved that Jesus had been enthroned at the Father's right hand at the Ascension. It proved that all authority on heaven and on earth had been given to Him. Indeed, the destruction of the temple can be understood as the vindication of Jesus. Just as God Himself was behind the Babylonians when He had them destroy the temple (Dan. 1:1-2), so Jesus is behind the Roman army's decimation of the temple in A.D. 70.

Jesus said, "they will see the Son of Man coming on the clouds of heaven with power and great glory." In the Old Testament, the clouds were associated with the presence of God. The Israelites were led in the wilderness by a cloud and a pillar of fire. On Mount Sinai, as Moses received the Ten Commandments, a cloud enveloped the mountain. When the tabernacle was completed and God moved into it to make it His home, His presence was manifested as a cloud. Nehemiah 9 links the cloud with the Spirit of God. Jesus described Himself as the Son of Man coming on the clouds of heaven. The cloud rider is God Himself; the Lord is the one who rides swiftly on the clouds. Jesus is the truly human one who is also God. This is why in Matthew 26:64, when Jesus says that He will ride on the clouds of heaven, the Jewish high priest believed this was blasphemy. When we see that Jesus was speaking here in light of the Old Testament, we can make sense of statements that at first appear difficult to understand.

The Sound of the Trumpet (Matt. 24:31)

When Jesus talked about His angels gathering the elect at the sound of the trumpet (Matt. 24:31), He was not referring to a physical gathering, but a spiritual gathering. Christ was gathering His elect into the kingdom of God, into the new covenant family, the church. We tend to view the word "angel" as being exclusively about heavenly beings, but the Greek word *angelos* means "messenger," "ambassador," "envoy," or "one who is sent." The New Testament uses the word *angelos* one hundred and seventy five times. In the majority of occurrences, *angelos* is used for a heavenly messenger, but in some occurrences, it can be a human messenger. In Matthew 11:10, John the Baptist is called an "angel," a messenger. Christ's usage of the term "angels" in Matthew 24:31 refers to human messengers being sent out to proclaim the gospel to gather together God's elect. The "sounding of a trumpet" refers to preaching, the heralding of good news. This metaphor of sounding the trumpet is used in many places in the Scriptures, such as Isaiah 58:1, Ezekiel 33:2-7, Jeremiah 6:17, Isaiah 27:13, and 1 Corinthians 14:8, to refer to a message from God being openly declared.

This Generation (Matt. 24:32-35)

In Matthew 24:1-2, after the disciples pointed to the grand temple, Jesus prophesied its destruction by saying, "not one stone shall be left here upon another." The disciples asked questions: "Tell us, when will these things be? And what will be the sign of Your coming, and of the end of the age?" They wanted to know *when* the destruction of the temple was going to occur.

As we have seen, Jesus gave a full description of events that would occur. If an Old Testament prophet had predicted the destruction of Jerusalem in A.D. 70, the language used would have sounded like the symbolic language that Jesus used in Matthew 24 with the "darkening of the sun, moon, and stars," and "the abomination of desolation." Jesus concluded the section in verse 34: "Assuredly, I say to you, this generation will by no means pass away till all these things take place."

To answer His disciples' question about *when* the destruction of the temple would occur, Jesus said it would occur within *this generation*. Verse 34 is the key which unlocks the prophecy as a whole: the wrath of God was coming upon *this generation* of Jews. A "generation" in Scripture typically corresponds to forty years, and this wrath in A.D. 70 would happen within forty years of Christ's death, resurrection, and ascension, which occurred around A.D. 30-33.

There are some who attempt to interpret Matthew 24:1-35 as unfulfilled prophecy, with events yet in the future. These "futurists" are forced to take "this generation" from Matthew 24:34 and make it mean something other than what the text says. The word "generation" in Greek is *genea*. Futurists attempt to translate the word *genea* as "race." As an interpretation of the passage, reading *genea* as "race" does not work for three reasons. First, translating the word "race" instead of "generation" makes the entire passage meaningless. Jesus has foretold a series of judgments that would fall on Israel. It would be nonsense for Him to get to the end of the prophecy and say, "This race won't pass away until all these things happen to this race." Of course the Jewish race has to continue to exist for these things to happen to them! Second, it would be an unintelligible answer to the disciples' question. They asked "*When* will these things take place?" not "Who will these things happen to?" The *who* was obvious: Israel and her temple. Last, from the clear teaching in Scripture, every time this word *genea* is used, it is of a generation living approximately forty years. In Luke 1:50, as part of the Magnificat, Mary says, "His mercy is from *genea* to *genea*." In Matthew 1:17, the ancestry of Jesus is summarized by three sets of fourteen generations, or *geneas*. In Hebrews 3:10, the Holy Spirit says He was angry with "that generation," that *genea*. In all these passages, the word *genea* simply means "generation," indicating a forty-year period.

In Matthew 11:16, Jesus said, "to what shall I liken *this generation*?" They rejected John the Baptist for being an ascetic and they rejected Christ as "a glutton and a winebibber, a friend of tax collectors and sinners!" In Matthew 11:20-24, He pronounced woes upon "this generation's" cities of Israel, concluding that "if the mighty works which were done in you had been done in Sodom, it would have remained until this day. But I say to you that it shall be more tolerable for the land of Sodom in the day of judgment than for you."[27]

In Matthew 23, Jesus pronounced eight woes upon the leaders of Israel, the scribes and the Pharisees, because of their hypocrisy, unbelief, and disobedience. Jesus summarized the woes in verses 34-36:

> Therefore, indeed, I send you prophets, wise men, and scribes: some of them you will kill and crucify, and some of them you will scourge in your synagogues and persecute from city to city, that on you may come all the righteous blood shed on the earth, from the blood of righteous Abel to the blood of Zechariah, son of Berechiah, whom you murdered between the temple and the altar. Assur-

---

27. See also Matthew 12:38-45, in which Jesus said that "*an evil and adulterous generation* seeks after a sign" and only the sign of Jonah will be given. "The men of Nineveh will rise up in the judgment with *this generation* and condemn it." And one unclean spirit was replaced with seven more wicked: "So shall it also be with this *wicked generation*."

edly, I say to you, all these things will come upon this generation.

In the Old Testament, Abel was the first martyr in the book of Genesis and Zechariah son of Berechiah was murdered in 2 Chronicles, which was the last book in the Old Testament canon, according to the Jewish arrangement of the books. Jesus was saying that for all the righteous saints and martyrs who were killed in the Old Covenant era, their blood would come upon "this generation." This generation was going to commit the greatest act of murder: killing Christ, the righteous servant that God had sent. *This generation* would be held accountable for all the righteous blood that had been shed.

What Jesus meant by "the end of the age" was the decisive end of the old covenant era, not the end of world history at His final coming. The end of the temple was the end of the sacrificial system and the end of the distinction between Jew and Gentile. The new distinction that matters is Christian and non-Christian, not Jew and Gentile. The whole book of Hebrews is about the winding down of the Old Covenant and the arrival of the New Covenant. Hebrews 8:13 says, "In that He says, 'A new covenant,' He has made the first obsolete. Now what is becoming obsolete and growing old is ready to vanish away."

The book of Hebrews was written in the mid-60s, just before the Jewish war with Rome, to discourage Jewish Christians from taking up arms with their countrymen to defend an obsolete covenant structure. Many were being pressured to fight for their nation, but they should not turn away from the new covenant in Christ to something that was obsolete and ready to vanish away. Hebrews 9:26 says, "He then would have had to suffer often since the foundation of the world; but now, once at the end of the ages, He has appeared to put away sin by the sacrifice of Himself." All the ages that were in the old covenant were the ages being put to an end by Christ. His death brought the previous covenantal ages to a climax and conclusion because He founded a new age. The Jewish kingdom was being shaken and passing away, but the kingdom of God cannot be shaken (Heb. 12:27-28).

Conclusion

In Matthew 24:34, Jesus concluded that the events prophesied would occur within the next generation: "Assuredly, I say to you, this generation will by no means pass away till all these things take place." Jesus added to this certainty, "Heaven and earth will pass away, but My words will by no means pass away." This is not so much physical language as it is covenantal language. He was not saying, "My words are more sure than the physical creation itself," but "My words are more sure than the temple itself." The temple was the shadow; Jesus's words are the reality. The temple would become a pile of rubble, but the word of Jesus will last forever.

As Jesus was on trial to be crucified, the Jews cried out in Matthew 27:25, "His blood be on us and on our children." Sovereignly, the ascended Christ dispatched the Roman army in A.D. 70, to fulfill His prophecy that "this generation will by no means pass away till all these things take place." The obsolete and desolate temple was destroyed, and the old covenant passed away. The new covenant had dawned, with a new temple, a royal priesthood, and the sacrifice of praise. The church of the Lord Jesus Christ had been established as the covenant people of God, the new Israel.

Section 2

Kingdom Central:
The Church

Chapter 8

Welcome to The Church

The destruction of Jerusalem in A.D. 70 was the judgment of God on unbelieving Israel and the sign that Jesus was forming a new Israel in the church, which is no longer divided between Jew and Gentile. As Paul explained in Romans 11, the unbelieving, unfruitful branches (much of national Israel) were broken off, and the wild olive shoots (believing Gentiles) have been grafted into God's covenant people. The people of God would no longer be confined primarily to the nation of Israel, its temple, and the sacrificial system.

In the new covenant, the church of the Lord Jesus Christ is now the holy people of God, whether Jew or Gentile (Rom. 10:12-13). Although redemptive history is filled with various developments and covenant administrations, there has always and only ever been one covenant of grace by which God relates to His people. Israel's mission as a priestly nation was to mediate God's blessings to the Gentiles, but they failed in that task to a great extent because of their unbelief and rebellion. Jesus came as the promised Messiah of Israel who fulfilled Israel's mission and in whom God's promises to Israel are fulfilled. He is the one faithful Israelite who brings God's blessings to the Gentiles and pronounces judgment on unbelieving Israel. Rather than the Levitical priesthood of the old covenant, now every believer in union with the crucified and risen Jesus Christ is a priest:

> But you are a chosen generation, a royal priesthood, a holy nation, His own special people, that you may proclaim the praises of Him who called you out of darkness into His marvelous light; who once were not a people but are now the people of God, who had not obtained mercy but now have obtained mercy (1 Pet. 2:9-10).

Rather than the temple mount in Jerusalem being the center of God's activity in the world, the church is now the true temple where God's special presence was located.

> Now, therefore, you are no longer strangers and foreigners, but fellow citizens with the saints and members of the household of God, having been built on the foundation of the apostles and prophets, Jesus Christ Himself being the chief cornerstone, in whom the whole building, being fitted together, grows into a holy temple in the Lord, in

whom you also are being built together for a dwelling place of God in the Spirit (Eph. 2:19-21).

Church-Centered

God has placed His church, the new humanity, at the center and summit of the world. The church is the bride of Christ, created from the wound in His side. To be Christ-centered leads us to be church-centered, for Christ's gaze is continually upon His bride.

> Christ...loved the church and gave Himself for her, that He might sanctify and cleanse her with the washing of water by the word, that He might present her to Himself a glorious church, not having spot or wrinkle or any such thing, but that she should be holy and without blemish (Eph. 5:25-27).

You cannot claim to know the head of the church without being a living member of the body of Christ—the church. First John 2:9 says, "He who says he is in the light, and hates his brother, is in darkness until now," and 1 John 4:20 says, "If someone says, 'I love God,' and hates his brother, he is a liar; for he who does not love his brother whom he has seen, how can he love God whom he has not seen?"

The church is central, not peripheral, to God's plan for creation. God created the world that He might have a redeemed people to the praise of His glory. Martin Luther said, "The Holy Christian Church is the principal work of

God, *for the sake of which all things were made*."[28] God did not create us because He *needed* our fellowship. Rather, because the triune God was bursting with love and joy, a love and a joy He desired to share with creatures made in His image, God called forth the world, and within the world, the church. Jonathan Edwards argued that God created so He might form a spouse for His Son. If that is true, then, again, the church is central to the divine purpose for history and creation.

The church is not merely God's rationale for creation, but also the goal toward which He is directing history. God not only created the world that He might have a church; He also rules all things for the sake of the church, especially for the sake of her future glorification and exaltation: "And [God] put all things under [Christ's] feet and gave him to be head over all things *to the church*, which is his body, the fullness of Him who fills all in all" (Eph. 1:20-22). Thus, we see the church's centrality in God's providence and in Christ's kingdom.

If we conceive of history as a river, the church's own history is the central current. Church history is the core of world history. The church is the central place of God's action in the world. In other words, if you want to know what God is up to, look at His gathered people. This view is sometimes referred to as "ecclesiocentrism," and it is the view of society and history that most Christians have held over the years. It was represented in architecture (churches were the greatest of all buildings), geography (churches

---

28. Philip J. Lee, *Against the Protestant Gnostics* (New York: Oxford University Press, 1987), 59.

were often places physically in the center of the city square to represent the church's spiritual position), aesthetically (as much of the best and most beautiful art was produced in and for the church's use in worship), and so on. There are times in history when it has been obvious that the church is the most powerful institution on earth (e.g., the way the church changed history during the Reformation), but even when the church's power is hidden (such as in the early pre-Constantinian days of church history), the church exerts incredible power in the world. The church has been entrusted with the Word of God and the sacraments, which God uses to bring about salvation. The church holds the keys to the kingdom of heaven, to open and close, bind and loose (granted, in ministerial and declarative ways, according to God's Word, not autonomously). The church's weekly liturgy is the most important thing that happens on earth (in part because it actually happens in heaven!).

Historically, the church has held to the Scriptural truth that she is the center of Christ's kingdom and of human civilization. Without taking on airs, and without a hint of pretense, the church has viewed herself as the most important social institution on earth. The church—not the state or the family—is the institution that can provide social cohesion, cultural unity, and hope to an otherwise fragmented, chaotic, and despairing world. The church can unite divided families, cultures, nations, and empires.

While acknowledging that the kingdom is ultimately broader than the church, embracing and transforming *all* social institutions and bringing them under Christ's lordship, Christians over the ages understood the church is *central* to the kingdom. Indeed, they viewed the church as the nursery of the kingdom, the wellspring of Christian culture, the engine that powered the Christianization of every area of life.

Holding to a High View of the Church

The centrality of the church entails a high view of the church's ministries, unity, authority, and discipline. It has been well said that a low churchman is a man with a low view of the church and a high view of himself, whereas a high churchman holds himself in low esteem and the church in high esteem. Historically, the one holy catholic and apostolic church that Christians confess in the Nicene Creed has been "high church."

Most American evangelicals today, by contrast, are low church, viewing the church as an optional add-on to a "personal relationship with Jesus." Modern Christians were saved, in their view, apart from the church and can stay saved apart from it. This individualized, privatized connection with Jesus is considered the essence of true religion. But historically, the Christian faith has been defined by participation in the new life and community found in the body of Christ. Whereas many modern evangelicals see the church as merely a voluntary organization, a club of sorts, the church fathers and Reformers saw the church as the mother of all the faithful.

Since formal church membership, when practiced in modern evangelicalism, is a "take it or leave it" proposition, it is not surprising that church authority, particularly the church's right to make binding pronouncements on matters of doctrine and discipline, is scorned. The church's preaching ministry is treated as less important than one's private Bible reading. The church offers, at best, vitamins to supplement a staple spiritual diet of personal quiet times, podcasts, and fictional books thinly disguised as theology. Sermons are not authoritative proclamations of the whole counsel of God, but after-dinner speeches, pep talks, and group therapy sessions.

Similarly, the sacraments have been turned into needless appendages to the individual's private relationship with Jesus. At most, they are means of personal devotion and acts of piety, rather than means of grace in which God acts through creaturely instruments. In short, we could say the malady afflicting modern evangelicalism is its low view of the church. Sure, we can find a use for the church every now and then, but for the most part, we look for the real action elsewhere—in the family, in politics, or our own individualized, churchless form of spirituality. Our church consciousness has sharply declined. Amazingly, the church has been shoved out to the margins of culture, not only by our secularized neighbors, but also by professed Christians.

Most modern evangelical Christians do not think in terms of a high view of the church because we have a bankrupt ecclesiology. This modernized understanding of Christianity would have been incomprehensible to most Christians throughout history, and especially the Reformers like Martin Luther and John Calvin. For them, religion was centered in (though not confined to) the church because in the church God is present to offer Christ in the means of grace, the public administration of Word and sacrament. For these theological giants, religion was a matter of fact, not subjectivity. The Christian religion was a public, communal, holistic way of life centered in the ministry of the church, rather than a private compartment tucked away within an individual's mind or heart.

The Necessity of the Church

Calvin was one of the great ecclesiologists in the history of the church. In large part, this is because he was not afraid to build on the work of those who had gone before, especially Augustine. The four-book plan of Calvin's *Institutes of the Christian Religion* basically tracks with the Apostle's Creed, moving from God the Father, to the Son, to the Holy Spirit, and finally concluding with the church. But the last book, on the church, is the longest, and in some ways the most mature.

The title of Book IV is telling: "The External Means or Aids by Which God Invites Us Into the Society of Christ and Holds Us Therein." In particular, the title reveals Calvin's tight link between soteriology and ecclesiology. He has what may be called an *ecclesial soteriology*. Whereas modern Protestants tend to conceive of salvation as a personal relationship with Christ apart from the church, prying apart the *ekklesia* and salvation, for Calvin, the church and salvation are much more closely aligned. Christ is found in and through the means of grace entrusted to the church. Through these means, we enter the "society of Christ," and through these means, we remain in that society. For Calvin, an unmediated salvation enjoyed apart from the church is (ordinarily) unthinkable. In harmony with virtually the whole Christian tradition before him, Calvin conceived of salvation as coming from God's means of grace to the sinner rather than from the sinner's heart toward God. A high view of the means of grace was regarded as a necessary safeguard against Pelagianism, the ancient heresy that placed man's efforts in front of God's grace as the cause of salvation.

The Westminster Confession of Faith echoes Calvin in Chapter 25.2: "The visible Church, which is also catholic or universal under the Gospel (not confined to one nation, as before under the law), consists of all those throughout the world that profess the true religion; and of their children: and is the kingdom of the Lord Jesus Christ, the house and family of God, out of which there is no ordinary possibility of salvation." Modern Protestants have tended toward making the exception the rule, that inside the church, through the means of grace, there is no expectation of God to save sinners. We have severed salvation from the church, and in doing so we have ripped apart what God intended to come as a package. We have individualized the communal and privatized the public.

Even though Calvin proclaimed a church-centered salvation, a shift happening centuries later within Protestantism came to view the church's role in salvation with suspicion. Charles Hodge depicts this change as he argued that the distinction between Roman Catholicism and Protestantism hung on this very issue. Hodge wrote:

> So long as [the fact that all men have access to Christ by faith] is asserted, do we protest against the great error of Rome, that men can only come to God through the church, or through the mediation of other men as priests, by whose ministrations alone the benefits of redemption can be applied to the soul. The reverse of this is true, and the reverse

of this is Protestantism. We are in the church because we are in Christ, and not in Christ because
we are in the Church.[29]

B. B. Warfield followed Hodge in this theological shift
when he argued for "the immediacy of the operations of
the divine grace" apart from any "instrumentalities [that]
are committed to human hands for their administration."
Warfield labeled the "means of grace" view as sacerdotal-
ism.[30] When taken to their logical conclusion, Hodge and
Warfield's conception not only marginalizes God working
through the sacraments but also preaching, for both of
these means of grace are God's action through fallible human instruments. In the work of great theologians such as
Augustine and Calvin, the sovereignty of God's grace is not
at odds with the means of grace. Obviously not everyone
who receives the means of grace is saved; these means must
be received by a persevering faith.

But for Calvin, the church's necessity was a non-nego-
tiable starting point. Calvin's opening sentences shows us
where he's going:

As explained in the previous book, it is by faith
in the gospel that Christ becomes ours and we are

---

29. Charles Hodge, "Schaff's Protestantism: A Review," *The Biblical
Repertory and Princeton Review* 17 (1845), 627-628, quoted in W.
Bradford Littlejohn, *The Mercersburg Theology and the Quest for Re-
formed Catholicity* (Eugene, OR: Wipf and Stock, 2009), 36-37.

30. B. B. Warfield, *The Plan of Salvation* (1915, repr., Eugene, OR:
Wipf and Stock, 2000), 49, 86.

made partakers of the salvation and eternal blessedness brought by him. Since, however, in our ignorance and sloth (to which I add fickleness of disposition) we need outward helps to beget and increase faith within us, and advance it to its goal, God has also added these aids that he may provide for our weakness.[31]

He then goes on to explain what these means are: Pastors and teachers, through whom God instructs His own, and the Sacraments, through which He fosters and strengthens faith. Calvin has already argued that faith receives salvation. But how does the Spirit work faith in the heart? Where does faith find and lay hold of this gracious God and his gifts? Calvin's answer is clear: through these outward means, the Spirit cultivates and matures the heart of faith.

Jesus formed a community around Himself—a community that shares in His very life and mission (John 20:21). The church is the restoration and reconstruction of our shattered humanity in and through Christ. God's redemptive target is not isolated, fallen individuals; it is the entirety of creation, represented by a new human race formed by virtue of the church's union with Christ.

The church "is the kingdom of the Lord Jesus Christ" according to Westminster Confession (Chapter 25), and thus exists to display the kingdom of God to the world. The church does not contain the kingdom, but it is cen-

---

31. John Calvin, *The Institutes of the Christian Religion*, ed. John T. McNeill, trans. Ford Lewis Battles, 2 vols. (Philadelphia: Westminster Press, 1960), IV.1.1, 1303.

tral to the kingdom. The primary ways through which the church portrays the kingdom of God to the kingdoms of this world are mission, community, discipleship, and worship.

Chapter 9

The Church is Mission

In John's Gospel, after the risen Jesus showed the disciples His hands and side, He said, "As the Father has sent Me, I also send you." The mission that the Father gave to Jesus is to be entrusted, continued, and fulfilled *by the church*. Christ completed His phase of the mission, accomplishing redemption through His death and Resurrection; now the Holy Spirit applies redemption though the mission of the church. We have been given a "Great Co-Mission," shared between Christ and His bride, the church. After Jesus spoke these words in John 20, He breathed on the disciples and said, "Receive the Holy Spirit." Christ gave His disciples the Holy Spirit to be with them and equip them, so that the mission would be fulfilled. The church is to carry on the mission of Jesus in the power of the Holy Spirit, declaring the kingdom in preaching and enacting the kingdom in the sacraments of baptism and the Eucharist. It is through these means of grace that the world is to be saved; it is through these that Christ applies His accomplished redemption to the nations.

Every Sunday for almost two thousand years, Christians all around the world have confessed that there is "one holy catholic and apostolic church." To describe the church as "apostolic" certainly means maintaining and passing along the doctrine of the apostles that was encapsulated by the Holy Spirit in the Scriptures. Yet, to be apostolic means more than this. To be an apostle is to be a "sent one." An apostolic church is a sent church.

Jesus is the preeminent apostle, sent by His Father to achieve the redemption of His people. But the church also is apostolic. As Jesus was sent by the Father, so the church has been sent forth into the world to announce and enact the good news of God's kingdom. Just as the Father sent the Son to show His love and service, so the church is sent to reveal the love and service of Christ.

The incarnation and the cross become our models for ministry and mission. We are sent as messengers of hope. We are sent as agents and ambassadors of grace. We are sent to make the transforming and healing love of Jesus known in the world around us through word and deed. The church is apostolic in the sense that she not only has a mission, she *is* mission. Through her, God's purposes for the creation will be fulfilled.

The Scope of the Great Commission

In the context of the gospel story, the Great Commission was given by Christ between His Resurrection and Ascension:

All authority has been given to Me in heaven and on earth. Go therefore and make disciples of all the nations, baptizing them in the name of the Father and of the Son and of the Holy Spirit, teaching them to observe all things that I have commanded you; and lo, I am with you always, even to the end of the age.

The comprehensive aspect of mission is seen in the "alls" of the Great Commission: *all* authority, *all* nations, and *all* His commandments.

Jesus began the Great Commission by giving its basis. He said to His disciples, "*All authority* has been given to Me in heaven and on earth." Jesus has been enthroned by His Father as king. He is now King of Kings and Lord of Lords. When people hear this claim of Jesus concerning "all authority," they might be puzzled. Obviously, there are so many things in the world where the reign of Jesus is not apparent. What Jesus means here is that He has the power to transform the world. The world belongs to Him, so He can do with it what He will.

The world is no longer under the reign of death, sin, and Satan (John 12:31, Col. 2:15). It is under the reign of Christ in principle, and His lordship will become progressively more and more manifest as all things are put under His feet (1 Cor. 15:25). Jesus is the world's rightful lord, and He promises to bring the nations under His gracious dominion. This declaration is the starting point of that world transformation. We can connect this with the Lord's Prayer, where we are taught to pray, "Thy Kingdom come, Thy will be done on earth as it is in heaven." We do not go forward in mission in order to make Jesus king; we go forth because He is *already* king of the nations.

The church is to go and make *all nations* Christ's disciples by baptizing them and teaching them *all things that He has commanded.* The object of the Great Commission is not merely individuals; it is nations. The Great Commission actually requires the nations to be converted, baptized, and discipled. So long as all the *nations* are not converted, baptized, and discipled, the Great Commission has not been fulfilled.

The mission is not just making disciples *from* the nations, but making the *nations* Christ's disciples. Jesus does not just want some Americans; he wants America. He does not just want some Chinese people; He wants China. Successfully discipling the nations in the ways and truth of Christ is mandated by the Great Commission. Of course, the results of our ministry are always up to God. He is sovereign and will have mercy on whom He will have mercy, in His own time according to His eternal plan and purpose. We cannot make the mission successful in our own strength; God has to give the increase and fruit. Yet, we can never use the sovereignty of God as an excuse for failing to do what is commanded: to make the nations Christ's disciples. The church is sent forth to bring to Christ what is already His: all peoples, languages, and nations are His inheritance (Ps. 2:8).

Jesus, as the Last Adam, will bring the creation to its original fulfillment. God's purpose in creation, as given in Genesis 1:26-27, was to fill the earth with His image bearers who served and worshiped Him. The church will be the bearer of God's purposes in history. Jesus will work with and through His bride as the Last Adam to bring it about. There will be a worldwide civilization that reflects the culture of heaven on earth.

In many ways, the modern church has reduced the vastness of the Great Commission. We tend to think of missions as a line item on a church budget or one among many programs of the church.

We truncate the Great Commission by thinking solely in terms of individual conversions, believing that the whole point of preaching the gospel is to save a soul here or there. We have left off the dimension of ever-deepening discipleship, teaching all that Christ has commanded, transforming families and institutions, and bringing *entire nations* to Christ. The modern church has truncated the Great Commission in two primary ways: (1) through accepting secular privatization of the church and (2) by adopting a pessimistic outlook concerning the growth of the kingdom of God. Through recapturing the public proclamation of the gospel and returning to a Scriptural hope for the expansion of the kingdom of God, we can be obedient to Christ's command to disciple the nations.

The Kingdom in a Closet: Privatized Religion

Privatization is the primary way the church in the West has been subverted. Privatization happens when the church accepts the world's way of carving up culture into secular (public) and sacred (private) categories, with all the important earthly and historical aspects of life (such as politics, economics, education, and so forth) on the secular side of the line. Yet historically, the church has thought in terms of Christian civilization, in which Christ's preeminence extended beyond the human mind and heart to every nook and cranny of public life.

Christ is lord of body as well as soul, of the public realm as well as the domestic. The notion that "Christ" and "culture" should be—or even could be—separated was unthinkable. Gospel faith was not something "tacked on" to generic human existence but constituted a new way of living life in its entirety. Nothing is secular, for everything belonged to Christ and came within the scope of His lordship and redeeming grace. In pre-modern expressions of biblical religion, Christ was hailed as lord in the public square every bit as much as in the private sector. Christ's lordship could not be put in a closet.

With modern times, however, came a new version of "Christianity." This truncated version of "Christianity" was an individualistic and introspective version of the faith. The corporate, communal faith seen in the church in Acts was shrunk down to an ideology or to a private experience. "Christianity" in the modernized, truncated form became ideology (propositions to which are paid mental assent) and/or a private experience (which takes place solely in the interior psychology of the individual). Neither of these are based on the public facts of Christ in the gospel accounts, nor are they church-centered. Peter Leithart has captured this drastic change of religion quite well. In Leithart's book *Against Christianity*, "Christianity" becomes a code word for privatized faith. The problem with privatized "Christianity" is that it is all too easy to think of it as a "religious" layer of life added to a religiously neutral human core.

R. J. Rushdoony critiques the anthropological views of Jonathan Edwards and the Great Awakening:

The essence of Christianity was now the religious experience. Man was religious man only when possessed by the religious sentiment or affections. Edwards did not see, as Calvin did, man as always religious man, whether covenant keeper or covenant breaker. Edwards' man was Enlightenment man, basically secular except when possessed by religious experience. Religious experience thus became frenzy, and an addition to nature.[32]

This conception of "Christianity" is just another "ism" or ideology in the consumerist marketplace of ideas. In modernity, biblical faith has been internalized and privatized into an individual belief system. It is a set of doctrines tucked away between one's ears and behind one's eyes. And when this happens, Christ is driven out of the public square.

Thomas Jefferson is emblematic of this view of privatized religion which has gripped the United States of America and the rest of the Western world:

> Believing with you that religion is a matter which lies solely between Man & his God, that he owes account to none other for his faith or his worship, that the legitimate powers of government reach actions only, & not opinions, I contemplate with sovereign reverence that act of the whole American people which declared that their legislature should

---

32. Rousas John Rushdoony, *This Independent Republic* (Fairfax, Virginia: Thoburn Press, 1978), 106.

"make no law respecting an establishment of religion, or prohibiting the free exercise thereof," thus building a wall of separation between Church and State.[33]

When religion is defined as "a matter which lies solely between Man & his God," it has no place in the public sphere. In Jefferson's view, operations of the mind are not subject to legal coercion, but acts of the body are: "The legitimate powers of government extend to such acts only as are [bodily] injurious to others. But it does me no injury for my neighbour to say there are twenty gods, or no god. It neither picks my pocket nor breaks my leg."[34] For Jefferson, religion is in its essence disembodied and individualistic. It is "mere belief," rather than a way of life with communal practices. Religious freedom amounts to the fact that the state cannot tell you what propositions and ideas can flit about in your skull. For Jefferson, and many Americans after him, there is no deep connection between theology (the kind of god one serves) and praxis (the kind of character one embodies).

In our secularized society, individuals are free to exercise their religion, but only in their private lives, according to their conscience. Since the location of religious liberty

33. "V. To the Danbury Baptist Association, 1 January 1802," *Founders Online,* National Archives, https://founders.archives.gov/documents/Jefferson/01-36-02-0152-0006.

34. "Extract from Thomas Jefferson's *Notes on the State of Virginia*," *Jefferson Quotes & Family Letters,* The Jefferson Monticello, https://tjrs.monticello.org/letter/2260

is the individual's conscience, rather than the institutional church, "religion" has already been defined in secular terms rather than biblical terms. It is free from the state's control because it is a matter of disembodied ideas and emotional experiences. It is not "incarnated" in the public square (where, no doubt, it might very well impinge upon the state's agenda). Only religions that are pre-defined according to modernity's model are truly "free." Religions that have "absolutizing" visions—that would desire to reshape and remold all of social life—are not free. *This means that modern nations have essentially outlawed the Great Commission*. The church is still free to disciple individuals, but not nations. This is why Oliver O'Donovan suggested the First Amendment to the U.S. Constitution is the symbolic death of Christendom.[35] Of course, the First Amendment does not have to be understood this way. At the time of its adoption, several of the states actually had established churches. But under pressure from the Enlightenment, the First Amendment has been hijacked to press the privatization agenda.

The net result of the shift to privatization is easy to see. The keys to social and political life as a whole have been turned over to secularists. The church deals with the soul; the state deals with matters of the body. The result of this kind of dualism is witnessed on prime time television every night: America is largely a nation of private evangelicals run by public secularists. Christians are regarded as "free" because, after all, no one tells them what beliefs they can

---

35. Oliver O'Donovan, *The Desire of the Nations* (Cambridge University Press, 1989), 193-195.

and cannot have in their hearts or in their heads. However, the present social structure does not allow Christians to embody those beliefs in public life, at least not without great risk and social ostracism. Privatized "Christianity" is acceptable because it does not interfere with the secular agenda, but public proclamation and application of the Word of God by the church is not tolerated.

The clear teaching of Jesus shows us that this privatization doctrine should be resisted. Christ's parable of the leaven deals with the *intensive* growth of the kingdom of God in cultures. In Matthew 13:33, Jesus said, "The kingdom of heaven is like leaven, which a woman took and hid in three measures of meal till it was all leavened." The kingdom transforms human culture as it penetrates every facet of human life. The leaven will go through all the dough. Earlier in Matthew, Christ told His disciples to be "salt and light" and a "city on a hill" so that God's light shines out into the darkness. This is why we cannot compartmentalize the Great Commission, keeping Christ in our private lives and living as secularists for the rest. The gospel cannot just be a *part* of Christian life. The gospel ought to flavor all that we do, in every aspect of our lives. Like the apostle Paul, we should be able to confess in public as well as private, "I am not ashamed of the gospel of Christ" (Rom. 1:16).

Capitulating to secularists' understanding of the gospel as private opinion is tantamount to being ashamed of the gospel. On the importance of declaring the gospel, Lesslie Newbigin wrote:

> We have a gospel to proclaim. We have to proclaim
> it not merely to individuals in their personal and

domestic lives. We do certainly have to do that. But we have to proclaim it as part of the continuing conversation which shapes public doctrine. It must be heard in the conversation of economists, psychiatrists, educators, scientists, and politicians. We have to proclaim it not as a package of estimable values, but as the truth about what is the case, about what every human being and every human society will have to reckon with. When we are faithful in this commission we are bound to appear subversive to those who believe that the cosmos is a closed system. We may appear to threaten the achievements of these centuries in which this has been the reigning belief. In truth we shall be offering the only hope of conserving and carrying forward the good fruits of these centuries into a future which might otherwise belong to the barbarians.[36]

Another way to resist the pressure to privatization is to keep the Great Commission of Matthew 28 connected to the dominion mandate of Genesis 1. The Great Commission is actually nested inside the dominion mandate of Genesis 1:26-28, to be fruitful and multiply and subdue the earth. In a fallen world, the Great Commission is necessary in order for the dominion mandate to be fulfilled. If the dominion mandate set humanity's agenda—to build a God-glorifying civilization in all the earth—the Great Commission shows how God gets humanity back on track

---

36. Lesslie Newbigin, *Truth to Tell: The Gospel as Public Truth* (Grand Rapids, MI: William B. Eerdmans Publishing Co., 1992), 64.

to fulfill that original vision. Grace restores nature, and thus the Great Commission restores our ability to rule the earth for God's glory.

The reality is that theocracy is inescapable. Every society has a god. Every society has blasphemy laws, though in a humanistic society that makes man into a god, blasphemy gets redefined as hate speech. It is not a question of whether a society will have a god, but which god it will have. The call of the Great Commission is to ensure that every nation has Jesus as its God. The Great Commission requires the transformation and Christianization of every nation on earth. It requires Christian nations, Christian cultures, Christian civilizations—what has traditionally been called Christendom. We should want to form Christian societies through the preaching of the gospel and through discipleship not only because this will save our neighbors from hell as they come to trust in Christ but also because it is best for everyone (including those who do not convert) to live under the acknowledged reign of Christ. When a nation's social life and political life are shaped by the principles and wisdom of Scripture, everyone has a greater opportunity for flourishing. When a nation's customs and culture are informed by the gospel and its implications, everyone benefits. We carry out the Great Commission not only because we love God and want to serve him but also because we love our neighbors and want what is best for them.

If we do not Christianize nations, they will remain in the grip of idols, and ultimately Satan. If we will not have Christian nations, organized under Christ's lordship, we will have tyrannical and anarchic nations under the reign of a false god. The spread of the gospel has brought untold good everywhere it has gone: the rise of science, the establishing of human rights and dignity (especially for women, children, and minorities), the rise of the university and common schooling, the establishment of hospitals and widespread healthcare, the cultivation of publishing and the promotion of literacy, representative and republican forms of government that spread power, free markets and the division of labor, the rule of law and the right to due process, and on and one we could go—all of these are tangible civilizational blessings of living in a highly Christianized society. Today, secular humanism tries to take credit for many of the benefits the Christian faith has bequeathed to the Western world. But we should give credit to where credit is due for the amazing success of the West: Jesus and the Bible. The greatest blessings the world has ever known grow only on one tree, and that is the tree of God's kingdom.

Hope for the Task of Discipling the Nations

Discipling the nations in this extensive manner is a daunting task. This sounds like the original *Mission: Impossible*. Before we throw up our arms in despair, we should consider that what Jesus commands the church to do in the Great Commission dovetails with the promises and prophecies of the Old Testament. In other words, the fulfillment of our mission and God's fulfillment of His promises will coincide. In Matthew 28, we find the number of disciples is small and the task is big. It is almost laughable: a few guys from Galilee are told to go and conquer the world. But when we understand that the Great Commission is really the capstone of God's purpose in creation and the covenant promises that He made with His people, then we can conclude that it is not hopeless. The risen and ascended Christ has all authority in heaven and on earth and He is with us. He sent His Spirit to the church at Pentecost. Therefore, the mission of discipling the nations can and will happen. God is with us; who can stand against us?

The Promise to Abraham

Genesis 12 is a significant passage because virtually everything that the Prophets and the New Testament have to say about salvation and the kingdom refers back to it. The promise that God made to Abraham shows us God's plan for the shape of history:

> Now the Lord had said to Abram: "Get out of your country, from your family and from your father's house, to a land that I will show you. I will make you a great nation; I will bless you and make your name great; and you shall be a blessing. I will bless those who bless you, and I will curse him who curses you; and in you all the families of the earth shall be blessed."

Abraham was blessed so that through him the blessing of salvation would flow out to all the nations and families of the world. The objective of the Abrahamic covenant was nothing less than a saved world. Another way of articulating what Jesus said in the Great Commission is "go and take the Abrahamic blessing to all the nations of the earth." The theme of God blessing all the families of the earth through Abraham's seed is further developed throughout the Old Testament. The first section of Psalm 22, beginning with "My God, my God, why have you forsaken me?" prophesies the crucifixion of Jesus Christ. Psalm 22:27-28 shows the result of His finished work on the cross: "All the ends of the world shall remember and turn to the Lord, and all the families of the nations shall worship before You. For the kingdom is the Lord's, and He rules over the nations." The "turning" language is the language of conversion, coming to faith and repentance. The language of "all the families" points back to Genesis 12 in which all the families will be blessed. This cannot be a description of the consummated new creation, because at that point, it will be too late for conversion.

Psalm 22 is describing a world in which there is still death (verse 29) and procreation (verse 30), so the fulfillment of this cannot be pushed out of history to the Second Coming. This promise in Psalm 22:27-28 is within history, *before* Christ's return. Therefore, it gives hope for the growth of the kingdom within history. The pattern of Psalm 22 is one of suffering followed by glory. Christ's glory includes taking possession of the kingdoms of the earth.

In line with the Abrahamic promise to bless all the families of the earth, Psalm 72:8-11 describes the extent of Christ's kingdom:

> He shall have dominion also from sea to sea, and from the River to the ends of the earth. Those who dwell in the wilderness will bow before Him, and His enemies will lick the dust. The kings of Tarshish and of the isles will bring presents; the kings of

Sheba and Seba will offer gifts. Yes, all kings shall
fall down before Him; all nations shall serve Him.

As the Davidic King, Christ's dominion will be "from
sea to sea, and from the River to the ends of the earth."
The conclusion of this section is that "Kings shall fall down
before Him; all nations shall serve Him." The provisional
fulfillment of this was the wise men coming to bow down
before the infant Christ and bestow their gifts upon Him.
This shows us the trajectory of the new age that Jesus has
brought in with His saving rule over the nations.

"Of the increase of His government and peace there
will be no end" (Isa. 9:7). *The kingdom is expansive in its
very nature* and every image given of the kingdom of God
in Scripture is of something that grows. Matthew 13:31-32
records Christ's parable of the mustard seed:

> The kingdom of heaven is like a mustard seed,
> which a man took and sowed in his field, which
> indeed is the least of all the seeds; but when it is
> grown it is greater than the herbs and becomes a
> tree, so that the birds of the air come and nest in
> its branches.

In this parable, the kingdom of God is described as a
tiny mustard seed. When this seed is planted in the ground,
it grows to be the biggest tree in the garden such "that the
birds of the air come and rest in its branches."

The parable of the mustard seed tells us about the *extensive* growth of the kingdom of God in history (Ezekiel
17, Daniel 4). The kingdom grows, but it is not instant

growth, as we are conditioned to expect in our "microwave" culture. The mustard seed grows into the largest of all trees gradually and slowly. Jesus is assuring His disciples that even though the kingdom looks small and insignificant in the beginning, it is going to grow to be the greatest of all kingdoms. It is going to fill the earth.

The parable of the mustard seed is paired with the parable of the leaven in Matthew 13:33. If the parable of the mustard seed describes the extensive growth of the kingdom, filling the earth, over the millennia, the parable of the leaven describes the *intensive* growth of the kingdom, as it permeates, restores, and transforms all of human life and culture. The two parables together give us a comprehensive view of what the kingdom will accomplish in history, converting and discipling the nations.

The Shift to Pessimism

Jesus includes in the Great Commission a promise of success. Contemporary culture is defined by cynicism, pessimism, and nihilism, and in many ways the church is as well. Over the last two centuries, in the American church especially, this hopeful vision of the future which animated and inspired Christians for so many generations has been "left behind." It has been replaced by a very pessimistic and bleak outlook for the kingdom of God in history.

Much of this trend can be traced to a theological movement called dispensationalism, which arose in the 1800s and departed from the church's traditional covenant theology. While dispensationalism should be credited with taking the Bible seriously, it was largely cut off from the way the church had historically read the Scriptures. Historically, the church had read the Scriptures with a covenantal understanding, seeing the Bible as one big story with God's one plan for His one people throughout all ages. There were different stages and covenantal administrations, but they were all tied together by God's promise to redeem the world through Jesus (cf. Eph. 2:12, which speaks of a plurality of covenants tethered to a singular promise).

Dispensationalism took a new approach, sharply separating old covenant from new covenant and Israel from the church. Instead of seeing old covenant and new covenant as chapters in a single story, they were set against each other. Instead of seeing the church as the Israel of God in new covenant form, they view Israel and the church as disconnected entities. Adherents to this theology believed that the kingdom does not exist in the present; we live in the church era, not the kingdom era, with the church and kingdom having no connection. According to the dispensationalists, all the prophecies about the kingdom growing apply to a different era. The effect of this viewpoint among dispensationalists is to take a very pessimistic and short-term view of the future, believing that Jesus might come back any minute. This belief in the imminence of Christ's return became a defining feature of certain dispensational proponents. They wrote books like *88 Reasons Jesus is Coming Back in 1988* (which is obviously obsolete now) and *The Late Great Planet Earth* and said that we should live as if we are not going to be around here much longer. Once the prophecies of Christ's imminent coming are properly interpreted as having occurred at A.D. 70, we no longer have to place an emphasis on Jesus's imminent return. Jesus will not return until the mission is fulfilled (1 Cor. 15:23-

28) and will then hand the kingdom over to His Father. We should therefore have a long-term view of mission and plan accordingly. (For a more extensive treatment of Jesus's words in Matthew 24:1-35, see chapter 7.)

Pessimism about the future of the church has now become "orthodoxy," and the standard view among many Christians. While this error of pessimism and defeatism is prevalent in our day, there also is an opposite error in shallow triumphalism. Shallow triumphalism accurately understands that the Bible promises victory to the church in Christ and that the kingdom of God will spread throughout the world in history. But just as certain defeatists deny such victory and focus only on the weakness and suffering of the church, shallow triumphalists forget the role of suffering and martyrdom in the advance of the kingdom of God. The kingdom is established through the suffering of Jesus Christ in His cross. The kingdom advances as we take up our crosses and are willing to suffer and sacrifice for the kingdom as well. As Tertullian said, "The blood of the martyrs is the seed of the Church." But we must understand that this pessimism is a new development. Historically, the church has not held this view. The defeatism that is so prevalent in the church today is simply unbiblical. Unbelief in the promises of God is promoted as authentic Christianity, in a way that would salute the ten spies sent into Canaan that came back in fear of the giants and great walled cities. The two faithful spies, Joshua and Caleb, trusted God's promises and knew that they could take God at His Word. The lack of trust in God's promises on the part of His people became a self-fulfilling prophecy. Because of their lack of faith, the Israelites were forced to wander the desert for a generation before entering the Promised Land (Num. 13-14). Likewise, the church today has abandoned trust in God's promises, and we see the fruit of this lack of faith in the self-fulfilling prophecies of a shrinking kingdom of God.

Pessimistic thinking, in which we believe things are supposed to get worse and worse, does not challenge the evils of our day. If we believe that God is not interested in changing the world and that it is God's plan for Christianity to decline, we are not going to be motivated to engage the world around us, because we do not think it will make any real difference. Against this spirit of pessimism and defeat, Oswald T. Allis, Old Testament professor at Westminster Seminary in Philadelphia, said:

> My studies in this and related fields have convinced me that the most serious error in much of the current prophetic teaching of today, is the claim that the future of Christendom is to be read not in terms of revival and victory, but of growing impotence and apostasy, and that the only hope of the world is that the Lord will by his visible coming and reign complete the task which He so plainly entrusted to the Church. This claim is rendered formidable and persuasive by the all too obvious fact of past failures and present feebleness of the Church. But it is pessimistic and defeatist and I hold it to be unscriptural. The language of the Great Commission is world embracing and it has back of it the authority and power of One who said, "All power is given unto me in heaven and in earth, go ye therefore

and make disciples of all nations." The duty of the Church is to address herself to the achieving of this task in anticipation of her Lord's coming and not to expect Him to call her away to glory before the task is accomplished.[37]

Hope for the Kingdom

Jesus gave us a vision of His kingdom which ought to fill us with an irrepressible joy and hope. This vision laid out by Jesus is a vision of gospel prosperity for the people of God and success for the kingdom of God. On a global, long-term scale, the church is just getting started discipling the nations. Like any massive undertaking, there have been and will be setbacks, which requires us to have a long-term view. The church must recover a multi-generational vision of the spread of the gospel, because the discipling of the nations will not happen in an instant. It will take generations and centuries of God working through the church. God has chosen to grant His church victory "little by little," just as the Israelites slowly drove the Canaanites out of the promised land (Deut. 7:22). But God's promises are sure and the successful advance of the gospel is sure because, ultimately, the discipling of the nations is God's mission and purpose. God will bring His mission to fruition. God will not fail.

As Christians, we can take the long view because time is on our side. But unfortunately far too many modern

---

37. Oswald T. Allis, foreword to *Israel and the New Covenant* by Roderick Campbell (Tyler, TX: Geneva Divinity School Press, [1954] 1981), ix.

American Christians have taken a short-term view of history, assuming that the end of the world must surely be right around the corner. There is a kind of chronological snobbery involved in this view; it assumes that we must be living in the most important and climactic moment in all of history. But the Bible suggests a different way of reckoning time. God has promised to show mercy to thousands of generations (Deut. 5:10; cf. Deut. 7:9). If God spoke those words through Moses in approximately 1500 B.C., and a generation is typically 40 years, then we have more than thirty-six thousand years of history to go—and that's assuming faithfulness to only one thousand generations, not *many* thousands of generations! Christians in the past looked at time not in terms of years or even decades but centuries and millennia. Think of all those Christians who started work on the medieval cathedrals, knowing they would not live to see their completion. An early version of the Anglican *Book of Common Prayer* included tables for calculating the date of Easter out to A.D. 8400. The contemporary view that Jesus could come at any moment, and probably will very shortly, is out of step with our fathers in the faith and is probably one reason why they accomplished more than we do, despite having fewer resources and fewer comforts.

Again: The Great Commission is a daunting task! But the church has been equipped with every resource she could ever need to accomplish this mission. We have the presence of Jesus: the one who has all authority in heaven and on earth is with us. We have the presence of the Holy Spirit, who outfits the church as a spiritual army, prepared for this spiritual warfare. We have the Word of God, which is called God's hammer (Jer. 23:29) and God's sword (Heb. 4:12). If we believe that Jesus Christ is now presently King of Kings and Lord of Lords, that He is presently reigning and ruling from His Father's right hand, then we must believe that Christ's mission is being fulfilled.

As John 3:17 says, "For God did not send His Son into the world to condemn the world, but that the world through Him might be saved." When we look at what the Scriptures have to say about the sum total of human history, it teaches us that Christ is saving the world and His kingdom is growing to fill the earth. This growth may be slower and more gradual than we would like, but it is happening. His kingdom is displacing and replacing Satan's kingdom. "The light shines in the darkness, and the darkness has not overcome it" (John 1:5, ESV).

Chapter 10

The Church is Community

Community: The Image of the Triune God

The story of Christian community begins, as every Christian story does, in the Garden of Eden. Adam was created in knowledge, righteousness, and holiness. He was created in perfect covenantal fellowship with the triune Lord. No sin stood in the way of communion with God, as the Creator and creature loved one another in fullness. Moreover, Adam did not have to earn anything: God had freely and graciously blessed him. He had all the privileges of divine sonship. The Lord had, in the most intimate way, breathed life into Adam, imparting his own Spirit to the first man (Gen. 2; cf. John 20). The Lord gave him access to the Tree of Life and a fatherly warning to avoid the Tree of the

Knowledge of Good and Evil until the time was right. Of course, implicit in the Tree of Knowledge was a promise of a promotion to an even higher level of glory and kingship if he remained faithful and matured over time. The Lord gave Adam meaningful labor, as he was to serve and guard the garden the Lord had planted for him. Adam had abundant food and a beautiful environment in which to live, worship, and play. All creation was his, as God's vice-regent. And yet, the Lord evaluated the situation at the midpoint of the sixth creation day and said, "It is not good that man should be alone" (Gen. 2:18).

Alone? Adam was emphatically *not* alone at his creation. He enjoyed friendship with the Father, Son, and Holy Spirit. He was in fellowship with the triune family. What more could he need? We'd expect the text to read, in harmony with the rest of Genesis 1-2, "And the Lord God said, 'It is good for man to be *with me*, to have *me* as his friend." But that is not what the inspired narrative says. The way God created Adam, his pre-fall communion with the Father, Son, and Holy Spirit was *not enough*. God made man for *more than* fellowship with Himself. To be complete, satisfied, and fully realized as a creature made in God's image, Adam needed fellowship with other humans. He was not only created, as Augustine said, with a Trinity-shaped void in his heart that only the Father, Son, and Spirit could fill; he was also created with a human-shaped void that only other people could fill.

This is part of what it means to be made in God's image. God is not merely a single individual. He is a community of three distinct persons, bound together in an absolute oneness of love and fellowship. For man to *image* this kind of God requires a plurality of humans in fellowship with one another. An isolated individual is not a full image of the plural Godhead. Thus, in a very real but qualified sense, *God is not enough*. People need other people to be complete.

We were made for each other. Because we are made in God's image, God is the model for humanity. We have to be careful here; the Trinity is utterly unique and aspects of the Trinity cannot be replicated in any way within the creation. Calling the Trinity a "community" or a "family" runs the risk of tritheism since the oneness of the three persons is not just volitional but metaphysical. Nevertheless, Scripture does provide some warrant for speaking of God's triune life as a model for man's communal life in some real way. At the very least, we can say the economic Trinity—the Trinity at work in creation and redemption—provides a pattern for human life and relationships (cf. John 17:20-26; 1 Cor. 11:3). The Father, Son, and Spirit mutually indwell one another; even so, we are to indwell one another (John 13-17). C. S. Lewis compared the three persons moving in oneness to a kind of divine dance. The idea is that the three persons of the Godhead "dance around" or "dance within" one another. Their lives are totally intertwined. They move in lockstep with one another because they abide within one another. This is precisely how we are to live in Christian community. We are to open our lives to others so they can indwell us, but we are also to seek to "move into" the lives of others, abiding in them. In this kind of community, as we indwell one another, we image the life of the triune God in some faint way.

Obviously, the claim "God is not enough" is hyperbolic. This should not be understood in an idolatrous fashion. In an ultimate sense, God *is* enough for man. We can and must still speak of the *absolute adequacy* of God. It is God, after all, who provided all Adam's needs. It is God who created Eve and gave her to Adam as the crown of His other gifts. It is God who ultimately completes Adam. But the point here concerns God's creation design. God designed humans to live in community with one another. God made us in such a way that vertical fellowship with the divine would be insufficient; we also need horizontal fellowship with other humans. God did not just make us for Himself; He made us for each other.

To look at things from another angle, God made the world in such a way that His presence would be mediated from one human to another. God dealt directly with Adam, but for the most part God deals indirectly with us. He speaks to us, disciplines us, molds us, and transforms us in the gospel, through the agency of others. God works through means, especially the means of humans made in His image.

Community is inescapable. Each one of us came into existence only because two other people "communed" (so to speak) in just the right way. Our bellybuttons are proof that we came from community and we need community. After birth, we would perish in days, if not hours, if others did not care for us. We learn every social skill we possess (or do not possess) from others—language, manners, games, and proficiencies. And this need for others is not something we outgrow. It is more obvious in the case of infants but just as real in the case of adults. No man is an island and no man is self-sufficient.

Thus, the pessimistic dictum of existentialist philosopher Jean Paul Sartre, "Hell is other people," is exactly backwards. Hell is the *absence*, not the *presence*, of other people. In fact, in hell, the wicked will be utterly alone, apart from an all-too-personal, all-too-close relationship with the God they utterly despise. Contrary to existentialism, other people do not stifle our freedom or get in the way of our self-actualization. Rather, it is precisely *in community* that we are free to find and be our true selves.

We are not self-made, but God- and others-made. Heaven and the new creation are precisely what Sartre dreaded, but in a form he could not imagine. Heaven is, as Jonathan Edwards put it, a society of love.[38] It is not the absence of other people, but precisely their presence that makes heaven so heavenly. The saved community is marked out even in the present by this mutual love (John 13). Our love for one another shows that the power of God's new creation is already at work in the world. This love will be perfected in the resurrection.

The Gospel is Social

Salvation itself must be understood in communal terms. Just as sin wrecked our fellowship with God and with one another (e.g., Adam and his wife turning on each other in Genesis 3 and Cain murdering Abel in Genesis 4), so in redemption our fellowship is restored. Psalm 133 spells

------

38. Jonathan Edwards, *Heaven: A World of Love* (Pensacola, Florida: Chapel Library, 1998).

out the connection between salvation and community in beautiful, poetic terms:

> Behold, how good and how pleasant it is
> For brethren to dwell together in unity!
> It is like the precious oil upon the head,
> Running down on the beard,
> The beard of Aaron,
> Running down on the edge of his garments.
> It is like the dew of Hermon,
> Descending upon the mountains of Zion;
> For there the Lord commanded the blessing—
> Life forevermore.

Brothers dwelling together in unity is likened to the precious anointing oil flowing down Aaron's beard to the edge of his garment. The priest's body and robe become symbolic of the oneness of the community. The body of the priest is now the body of Christ (cf. 1 Cor. 12). The oil—usually symbolic of the Spirit in Scripture—covers the body from head to toe. The psalmist goes on to compare fellowship among the redeemed to the refreshing dew of Hermon flowing down Mount Zion. This is an interesting picture, since Hermon was in northern Israel and Zion in the south. The Spirit, now symbolized by the dew, unites things disparate in space and even culture. The conclusion is remarkable: "For there the Lord commanded his blessing—life forevermore." That is to say, *eternal life* takes the shape of *community life*. The structure of the psalm itself makes the point: Just as the inner sections of the psalm match (oil and dew, priests and mountains), so the outer sections match (brothers dwelling together in unity and eternal life).

The gospel is irreducibly social. Liberals in the late nineteenth and early twentieth century used the label "social gospel" to refer to their heretical program. They erroneously substituted deliverance from poverty and ignorance through state-mandated welfare and educational programs for salvation from sin and damnation through the cross and Spirit. Theologian H. Richard Niebuhr characterized the social gospel of liberalism as a God without wrath, bringing men without sin into a kingdom without judgment through a Christ without a cross. Obviously, that is a total distortion of biblical teaching. But, if we properly define the terms, we could benefit from restoring and redeeming the label "social gospel." The gospel is social through and through. Traditional Christian teaching claims that outside the church there is no ordinary possibility of salvation.[39] That is to say, forgiveness from sin and incorporation into Christ's body go hand in hand. Salvation includes a new status (justification) *and* a new community (the church).

Salvation is ecclesial, not individualistic. To be saved is to experience the salvific presence of Christ in His church, through the means of grace, by the work of the Holy Spirit. Salvation is not merely a matter of individuals "getting right with God" individually. It also is about the restoration, healing, and transfiguration of human life, especially human relationships. Indeed, the whole creation will be included in the scope of God's redemptive plan (cf. Rom. 8:17ff; Eph. 1:9ff; Col. 1:15ff). Biblical religion is not just

---

39. Westminster Confession of Faith, 25.2

doctrine, but a holistic, communal form of life. It is *incarnational.*

The whole Christian life can only be lived out in the context of the church community. The New Testament authors presuppose that followers of Christ will be discipled in the matrix of an ecclesial community (cf. Acts 2:42ff). Numerous apostolic commands only make sense in this light. For example, we are told to love one another, pray for one another, bear one another's burdens, confess to one another, forgive one another, and so on. In other words, we are to "one another one another," as James B. Jordan has put it.[40] But this can only happen in the environment of a church body. It cannot be done in isolation.

Practically, this means we live in submission to those whom God has appointed to rule over us in the church, we invite one another into our homes for fellowship, we participate in various Bible studies and prayer meetings as opportunity allows, and we learn how to carry on deep, loving friendships with people who may be very different than ourselves. We are certainly not looking to create a church in which everyone has the same skin color and economic status; our churches should generally reflect the diversity of creation and providence as much as the particular geographic locales they inhabit. This is the day-to-day life of the church, the pattern of living we are called to exhibit from one Lord's Day to the next.

---

40. James B. Jordan, *Trees and Thorns: Studies in the First Four Chapters of Genesis* (West Monroe, LA: Theopolis Books, 2020), 118-119.

American Individualism

American Christians struggle with the social nature of the gospel because of our heritage of individualism and dislike for authority (including church authority). To be sure, there are certain aspects of American individualism that are positive goods and are consistent with the gospel. Individual initiative and responsibility, individual innovation and invention, and appreciation for individual uniqueness are all wonderful things. But many Americans have become so hyper-individualistic, we are isolated from one another in unhealthy ways. We have lost important connections with others. Christians have not been immune to these problems.

Community always entails some level of sacrifice, whether of individual privacy or rights or goods. Community means we have to accommodate ourselves to things we wish could have been done differently. We have to learn to "give a little," and to be flexible. It means we have to learn that life together involves becoming vulnerable at times, admitting weaknesses and needs. It also means meeting needs and showing strength on behalf of others at times. Communal life in the church means we are willing to submit to the brethren, especially those God has put in charge of us through ordained office.

But whatever the costs, it is imperative that we learn to live in community once again. We must learn to deal with our differences in a Biblical manner (Phil. 2:1-11). We must learn to live under authority (Heb. 13:7, 17). We must learn to work together on the common project of building God's kingdom. We must learn to live as an organic body, in which every part of the community cares for every other part. We must learn what it means to be the communion of the saints, as we confess from the early church creeds. We must rediscover what it means to live shared lives of generosity, mercy, friendship, and hospitality. Many of the virtues the ancient church excelled in have been lost on us.

American spirituality often treats church community as a "tacked on" extra to a personal relationship with Jesus. There is a tendency to put "me" above "we." In other words, we often act as if God alone is enough, and other Christians are quite unnecessary. "Quiet times," in which the individual gets alone with God, have replaced the church's corporate gathering as the pinnacle means of spiritual growth. But the Bible points us in a different direction. Remember Adam: life alone with God is not the divine plan for us. God alone is not enough, in a profound sense. We must live in fellowship as one body with other believers if we are to grow and mature as God's people. As Augustine suggested, the essence of God's plan for humanity is mutual fellowship with Himself. We are called to share a common life with the Trinity and with one another. God meets our needs by giving us each other, and together we are called to mirror His life—the life of triune community.

Our low ecclesiology has radically deformed our faith. We must recover the robust, church-centered faith of the patristics, medievals, and Reformers. Georges Florovsky brilliantly summarizes:

> Christianity entered history as a new social order, or rather a new social dimension. From the very beginning Christianity was not primarily a "doc-

trine," but exactly a "community." There was not only a "Message" to be proclaimed and delivered, and "Good news" to be declared. There was precisely a New Community, distinct and peculiar, in the process of growth and formation, to which members were called and recruited. Indeed, "fellowship" (*koinonia*) was the basic category of Christian existence. Primitive Christians felt themselves to be closely knit and bound together in a unity which radically transcended all human boundaries – of race, of culture, of social rank, and indeed the whole dimension of "this world."[41]

The church lives because she is united to the living God in and through Christ. In the church, we've been restored to fellowship with God and with one another.

Community Formation

Through Word and sacrament, God forms us into His covenant community and maintains our standing as His treasured people. The gracious action of God in the weekly liturgy, when received by faith, generates the rest of our life together as the covenant people. As Augustine pointed out, men could not be bound together in a religious body apart from common sacraments and communal practices, distinguishing them from the world:

---

41. Georges Florovsky, "Empire and Desert: Antinomies of Christian History," *CrossCurrents* 9, no. 3 (1959): 233–53. http://www.jstor.org/stable/24457097.

Our Lord Jesus Christ has knit together the company of new people with sacraments, few in number, easy of observance, explicit in meaning, such as baptism in the name of the Trinity, the sharing of his body and blood [in the Eucharist], and whatever other practice is commanded in the canonical Scriptures.

Both Aquinas and Calvin relied on this statement from Augustine in developing their own sacramental theologies. Like Augustine, they had a deep regard for the horizontal, social significance of the sacraments. God created man in community. For man, just as for the persons of the Godhead, "to be" is "to be in relation." The fall wrecked this harmonious community, but did not completely eradicate it. In redemption, it is restored. But redemption apart from sacraments, that is, apart from communal practices, would not restore the social dimension of human existence. It would give us a Gnostic, privatized, individualistic salvation. A sacramentally mediated salvation implies the full restoration of community. A salvation that comes through external means is a social salvation. One example will suffice: No one is ever baptized alone. The church—at least in the person of the baptizer—is always present. It is an inescapable communal rite. It is not surprising that those forms of Christianity that have degraded the sacraments have tended to become very individualistic.

Through God's ordained rites, the means of grace, we are congealed together into Christ's new society. Therefore, as an outflow of the liturgical sacramental gathering each week, we begin to experience real community with our fellow Christians. Human community is not something we create from scratch; it is the gift of God. Friendship and fellowship do not come naturally in a fallen world; these blessings must be bestowed from above. When God redeems a person in Christ, He begins to teach that person a new grammar: no longer "I" but "we"; no longer "mine" but "ours."

The church is not merely an adjunct to the gospel, tacked on as an afterthought or an unnecessary append-age. Rather, as Calvin says, "the one effect resulting from [Christ's death] is, that there is a church."[42] One of the pur-poses of the gospel is the existence of a people living in restored fellowship with God and in harmony with one an-other. The church is nothing less than God's new humanity and new creation. At the heart of the gospel and the life of grace, the community of the church is forming us into the people of God.

---

42. *Genevan Catechism of 1545*, Question 94

Chapter 11

Discipleship and the Visible Church

Jesus Christ commissioned His church to make disciples. The church's motherly, nurturing role as disciple-maker is indispensable. John Calvin begins his discussion of the church with this summary statement:

> Because it is now our intention to discuss the visible church, let us learn from the simple title "mother" how useful, indeed how necessary, it is that we should know her. For there is no other way to enter into life unless this mother conceive us in her womb, give us birth, nourish us at her breast, and lastly, unless she keep us under her care and guidance until, putting off mortal flesh, we become like the angels. Our weakness does not allow us to be dismissed from her school until we have been pu-

pils all our lives. Furthermore away from her bosom one cannot hope for any forgiveness of sins or any salvation.[43]

The ancient saying is true: One cannot have God for his Father unless he has the church for his mother. The church, like Noah's ark, may stink on the inside, but it sure beats drowning in the wrath of God on the outside. Throughout the New Testament, abandoning the covenant community is equated with forsaking Christ (Heb. 6:4-6; 10:24-25). We simply cannot live without the nourishment God provides through the church.

To be a disciple is to be a follower of Christ, being transformed by the Spirit evermore into His likeness. Discipleship involves education: we should be students of the Word of God. Yet, to be a disciple involves more than receiving information. The very word "disciple" sounds similar to the word "discipline"—formation through training. Disciplines are the repeated communal practices through which we are conformed to Christ's image within the context of the church. Indeed, the church is the school of discipleship. We are enrolled in her school in baptism, educated in the Word by her pastors and teachers and fed at her table in the weekly covenant renewal service.

The Nature of Discipleship

The church's educational ministry is varied. After all, Jesus called upon His first ministers to teach disciples *everything* He had commanded them (Matt. 28:19-20). This holistic

---

43. Calvin, *Institutes of the Christian Religion*, IV.1.4

discipleship begins with the proclamation of God's great work of salvation in the death and resurrection of Jesus Christ. And though we never stop learning the glories of what Christ has done for us, we have other things to learn as well. The Bible addresses all life, and thus the church's teaching ministry must be wide ranging. Far too many churches today have narrowed the scope of their preaching and teaching, leaving their members to be "discipled" by the world in most areas of life. But the Bible deals with public matters, as well as private, and so the faithful pastor must as well.

True discipleship includes learning God's will for family, business, and society, as well as the practical skills needed to live the Christian life (e.g., how to pray, how to be a peacemaker, how to share and defend the faith, how to apply Biblical principles to one's calling, how to use and enjoy the things of the world without becoming "worldly," etc.). Through preaching, teaching, and catechesis we are educated in God's glorious truth. We become a people saturated in the whole counsel of God's wisdom-imparting Word. We learn how to be *in* the world without being *of* the world.

Yet we must also remember that discipleship can never be reduced to a matter of ethics or values. C. S. Lewis once pointed out the whole purpose of the Gospel is to deliver us from morality. Morality, after all, is still something the world can deal with. Discipleship, therefore, is not *mere morality*. Rather, it is a matter of what the apostle Paul calls the "obedience of faith," or "faith's obedience" (Rom. 1:5, 16:26).

Faith and obedience are not two separate ways of relating to God, as though we had faith for justification and works for sanctification. Rather, faith-filled obedience is the holistic, full-orbed response to God's grace that the gospel calls for and calls forth, by God's Spirit. The obedience of faith is nothing less than eschatological life—the life of the new age, the life of the world to come—already experienced in some measure by virtue of our union with the resurrected and glorified Christ. Obviously, this eschatological discipleship is not a matter of becoming "moral." In fact, countless millions of "moral" people are in desperate need of genuine discipling.

The School of Discipleship

In addition to confusing discipleship with morality, many Christians think of discipleship as taking place everywhere except the church. Discipleship means having daily devotions or family prayer. Or it means attending a Bible study after school or on lunch break at work. These activities are well and good, but we must never lose sight of the centrality of the church as the chief agent of discipleship.

The privatization of Christianity in the modernized, secularized world has made the church seem irrelevant for many Christians. The key thing, they think, is to be part of the "invisible church." After all, the visible, institutional church has all kinds of problems and may even be detrimental to spiritual growth. But the book of Acts points us in a different direction. Think about Pentecost in Acts 2. When the Holy Spirit is poured out, what kind of institution does He form? Or does He shed the "husk" of institutional forms and practices, leaving only a naked spirituality? We find that Christ poured the Spirit out upon a *visible* community of saints, indwelling an identifiable body of people.

The new temple is just as visible as the old. Peter—an officer in the community (cf. Acts 1:20)—preached publicly, announcing in unmistakably political terms that the world had a new king and emperor, the crucified and risen Jesus (2:36). He called on those who desired salvation to repent and submit to the public, external rite of baptism (2:38). At the end of the chapter, we find that the disciples are countable—they are not free floating individuals, but have been bonded together in an organized, formal, institutional community (2:41). Moreover, we find they practice various bodily, corporate rituals together, such as the Lord's Supper and prayer (2:42-45). Through these means, they knew Christ continued to be present with them; through these means the invisible Spirit worked visibly to grant forgiveness and new life. In short, Acts 2 shows us that to be saved is to be added to the visible church (2:47).

Later in Acts, we see that the disciples gathered for scripted, prayer-book style intercession. Acts 4:24 seems to indicate their prayer was verbalized in unison. They formally elected officers and commissioned missionaries (Acts 6, 13). Their leaders assembled to make authoritative decisions on behalf of the body (Acts 15). The earliest Christians clearly did not lodge ultimate religious authority in the individual's private conscience nor did they think institutional structures could be discarded in the new, Messianic age. Pentecost did not mark the founding of a new, de-publicized, de-ritualized, disembodied religion. If anything, it intensified these features of the old covenant pattern of religion by calling for their worldwide application.

The entire New Testament is clear: God works in and through the ordained, public, communal practices of the church. Even a form of church polity is God-established, albeit loosely. The Spirit is not opposed to structure, but rather creates structure out of chaos (cf. Gen. 1). Now, the core of God's work is in the Word and sacraments, applying the once and for all redemption Christ accomplished. God gives us Himself in and through these means. God has made Himself publicly available—*He's there for the taking*, if I may put it crassly—in the church's means of grace. As Luther said, "Neither angel nor pope can give you as much as God gives you in your [local] parish-church."[44]

Insofar as we have privatized biblical religion, we have made God virtually impossible to find. So would-be disciples end up turning inward, and that's when things get weird. Luther described the essence of sin as the state of being curved in upon one's self. But if Jesus is not found with confidence in the means of grace, where can He be found? Where should aspiring disciples go to find Him? As Puritanism drifted further and further from its Calvinistic moorings, this was just the problem it faced. God became progressively hidden and assurance became increasingly impossible. Emily Dickinson's poem about the elusive Puritan Jesus sums up the matter:

---

44. Martin Luther, *An Open Letter to The Christian Nobility*, Project Wittenberg, https://www.projectwittenberg.org/pub/resources/text/wittenberg/luther/web/nblty-06.html

At least – to pray – is left – is left –
O Jesus – in the air –
I know not which thy chamber is –
I'm knocking – everywhere –
Thou settest Earthquake in the South –
And Maelstrom in the sea –
Say, Jesus Christ of Nazareth –
Hast thou no Arm for Me?[45]

She looks everywhere, but nowhere in particular. She cannot find Jesus because He has been vaporized into thin air! He is not present in the communal practices of the church, so He is nowhere to be found. She looks and grasps for the strong arm of the Savior, but finds nothing. No wonder Dickinson believed it was fine to forsake the church and worship God through nature. This is how Luther would answer Dickinson's search, pointing seekers to the place where Christ has promised to be found:

Therefore, he who would find Christ must first of all find the church. How would one know where Christ and his faith were, if one did not know where his believers are? And he who would know something of Christ, must not trust himself, or build [his] own bridges into heaven through his own reason, but [he must] go to the Church, visit,

---

45. Emily Dickinson, *The Complete Poems of Emily Dickinson*, ed. Thomas H. Johnson (Boston: Little, Brown, 1960), No. 502, 243-44, quoted in Phillip J. Lee, *Against the Protestant Gnostics* (New York: Oxford University Press, 1987), 178-79. This line of argument owes a great deal to Lee's book.

and ask of the same . . . for outside of the Christian
Church is no truth, no Christ, no salvation.[46]

Thus, a Christian can no more be discipled apart from
the church than a fish can live outside of water. If we want
to grow and thrive, we must inhabit the basic means entrusted to the body of Christ, especially preaching and sacraments. We come to know God through these practices.

But we must also avail ourselves of corporate prayer
and the authoritative accountability of church discipline.
Other aspects of traditional church life, such as the ecclesiastical calendar and hymnody, are useful discipleship aids
as well. This is also why things like vestments and church
architecture are important. They are further ways of making
the church—and therefore God's presence—*visible* in and
to the world. When officiating the liturgy, pastors need to
dress like pastors (not businessmen or hipsters), and whenever feasible our church buildings need to look like sacred
houses of worship (not shopping malls or concert halls).

We will not find God, or ourselves, by turning inward but by attending a faithful church. In the gathered
assembly, we corporately enter God's Most Holy Place, His
heavenly sanctuary. He gives Himself to us through His
means and we offer ourselves back in body and heart. Together, we are discipled by the master teacher, Christ Himself, through His ordinances. The body of Christ, especially
in her liturgical gathering, is the engine that drives true

---

46. R. L. Greaves, "Luther's Doctrine of Grace," *Scottish Journal of
Theology*, 18, No. 4 (1965), 394, quoted in Lee, *Against the Protestant
Gnostics*, 59.

discipleship. Personal piety and devotion flow out of this assembling together.

The Purpose of Discipleship

Discipleship is never merely for our own sake. The community of disciples exists to serve the world. The church is not a cozy, privatized community, but an open-faced, outward-moving army. Our mission is to conquer in the sign of the cross and the power of divine love. As Luther said, the mission of each Christian is to be a christ (with a small "c") to his neighbor, replicating in a miniature way the mission of Christ (with a capital "C") to the world. But this is also true of the church corporately. We are sent even as Jesus was sent (cf. John 20:21). Our calling is to be a cruciform people, dying for the life of the world, pouring ourselves out that others may be filled. Discipleship that never reaches further than one's own personal piety is a travesty.

While disciples certainly enjoy community with one another within the comfort of the church walls, they must never lose sight of their calling to minister to the stranger and the alien in God's world, namely the unbeliever. This is *our* world (cf. Matt. 5:5; Rom. 8:17ff; 1 Cor. 3:21-22) and we must be good hosts. Discipleship has an inescapably public dimension. It means the church must serve the common good, not merely by inculcating private piety (as important as that is), but by acting in the public square in a Scripture-shaped fashion.

Creating "safe havens" to protect ourselves from a hostile culture simply will not cut it. Increasingly, even privatized Christianity is being encroached upon by the world. A strategy of retreat fundamentally misses the heart of the church's calling—to be the face and hands and feet of Jesus to a hurt and broken world. The purpose of discipleship is not the establishment of warm and fuzzy centers of community that have their backs turned to the world. Rather, it is the creation of a host of servants willing to live in and die for the world. When Jesus said that He would build His church and the gates of hell would not prevail against it (Matt. 16:18), He was not promoting a defensive strategy. He was saying that the church would go on the offensive and the gates of hell would not be able to withstand her march forward.

The church's discipleship tasks, both inward and outward facing, must be viewed in an eschatological frame. We must allow biblical theology to grind out and shape the lenses of discipleship, or else everything will be out of focus. Without a proper awareness of ecclesiology and eschatology, we are bound to fall short of the goal, no matter how doctrinally pristine our soteriology is. The church, as a community of disciples, living under the sign of the cross and in the power of Christ's Spirit, is a signpost pointing ahead and above to the world to come. The church, in short, is a colony of heaven on earth, living the life of the future in the present and living the life of the new creation in the midst of the old. The church is the foothold of the world to come in the present age.

N. T. Wright has made the point that Paul's mention of "heavenly citizenship" in Philippians 3:20-21 is likely intended as a contrast to the Philippians' Roman citizenship.[47] A Roman citizen in Philippi knew his hope was not

---

47. N. T. Wright, *Surprised by Hope* (New York: HarperCollins Pub-

"going to Rome when he died." Rather, their hope was bringing Rome—that is, Rome's way of life, Rome's culture, Rome's governance—to Philippi while he lived. In the same way, heavenly citizenship is not a free pass to check out on worldly culture, becoming so "heavenly minded that you're no earthly good." The point is not to dream of harps in the sky while the world slowly teeters into hell. Rather, the point of "heavenly citizenship" is to bring heaven—the life of heaven, the culture of heaven, the rule of heaven—to earth. Our citizenship above shapes our citizenship—and everything else—here below.

Most of our talk about the Christian life (and the church!) is far too mundane. We must envision grasping once again Paul's eschatological consciousness that declares to the church body, "The kingdom age has come! You are a new creation! Live accordingly!" (Rom. 6). And as we do so, we will become more and more like Christ and create a culture that in appropriate ways previews the world to come.

_____

lishers, 2008), 293.

Chapter 12

Covenant Renewal Worship

When modern evangelicals consider how to transform our culture, to have dominion over our land (Gen. 1:28), what kind of things do they usually promote? Many Christians turn to politics: "We need to get the right candidates in office, get laws changed, then everything will get fixed." Others go another route: "If we could just influence Hollywood to make more family friendly movies, that would do it." Some say, "If we could just tone down the liberalism on college campuses or maybe have our own faithful Christian colleges, then our culture would change."

The reality is that all of those are very worthy goals. These are efforts we should pursue. We do not need to stop doing those things altogether, but we need to understand that they are not central. These efforts are not the fountain from which the rivers of cultural transformation flow. For such an outcome we have to go further upstream to the very source.

If the people of God want to disciple our nation and see other nations discipled, if we want to shape society in a distinctively Christian way, where do we start? What is the center of it? We should not begin with the Capitol building, the movie studio, or the college campus, but with the church. We want all society to be touched and transformed by the gospel, individuals and institutions to be reached by the grace of God. But in order to be effective in that mission on a grand scale, we have to start with the church. We have to start with the liturgy and the other marks and ministries of the church.

But here is the problem: *when Christians today talk about cultural transformation, they seem to talk about everything but the church. They talk about everything except Lord's Day worship.* Covenant renewal liturgy on the Lord's Day is the first step in God's plan of renewing and re-ordering and re-creating the world. Liturgy drives mission. The Lord's service on the Lord's Day drives cultural transformation. Faithful worship unleashes the Spirit's work in the world and transforms the nations.

As we, the church, are gathered together and lifted up into the heavenly presence of God's Most Holy Place by the Spirit and through Jesus, to meet God the Father, God is at work to renew and re-order our lives and to transform the world. Our families are torn apart and put together in a more glorious way each Sunday. We are cut up by the priestly sword of the Spirit so we might become a living sacrifice. The nations are renewed and refreshed by the living waters that flow out of the sanctuary.

Until faithful worship is restored, all of our cultural activity will amount to very little. The Scriptures give the people of God a blueprint for cultural transformation. And this is a very different plan than what you find in most Christian circles today. It is a church-centered blueprint. The first step is getting God's house in order, for *liturgical reformation drives cultural transformation.*

Biblical Pattern: Worship, then Dominion

When God set up the world, He built it with three zones. These zones are apparent in Genesis 1-3. There is the garden, the land, and the world; specifically in Genesis there is the Garden of Eden, the land of Eden, and the outer lying lands. The garden is the sanctuary where man relates to God and serves as a priest. The land is his home where men relate to one another, where we do family life, and where man serves as a king. The world is the place where man works, carries out his mission, and acts as a prophet. Just as in Genesis the rivers flowed through the Garden of Eden, out to the land and world, so what happens in the sanctuary flows out to the family and the world. The sanctuary is at the heart of transformation and dominion.[48]

One thing Genesis shows us is that if we corrupt these zones, we lose them. In Genesis 3, Adam sinned against God in the sanctuary Garden of Eden, and he was exiled from it. In Genesis 4, Cain sinned against his brother in the land, and he was sent out of the land into the wilderness of the world. In Genesis 6, all of humanity sins in the

---

48. Many of these points are deeply indebted to James Jordan's work.

world, as the godly line intermarried with the daughters of men, and so they lost it all in the Flood.[49]

Anytime God wants to restore and rebuild a world, anytime God wants to bring life, renewal, healing, and dominion to a culture, the first thing He does is restore proper worship because everything is going to flow out of the altar. Renewal in the land and the world are downstream from the sanctuary.

God promised a land to Abraham. He promised to give this land to Abraham's descendants, as a place where they could build a godly civilization as a model for all the other nations. They would conquer the pagan culture there (the Canaanites) and set up a culture that would be a light to all the world (Deut. 4). But before they can set up this godly civilization, what has to happen first? Abraham treks through the land, "conquering" it liturgically. It may not look like much of a conquest, but if you follow Abraham as he travels throughout the land, he goes through the land in a proto-conquest, laying the groundwork for what his descendants will later do in their cultural, political, and military conquest. Everywhere he goes in the land, Abraham sets up wells and builds altars. He is setting up places of worship all throughout the land. Those very spots become key places a few generations later, when Joshua fights battles against the Canaanites and wins. Why does Joshua win culturally and politically? Fundamentally, because Abraham had already laid the groundwork through faithful

---

49. This same three-fold pattern happens with Israel in the book of Judges. Saul repeats it in his own life in the book of 1 Samuel. He has a three-fold fall, loses the three zones, and the whole kingdom is taken from him. It happens again and again in Scripture.

worship. The land had to be conquered liturgically before it could be conquered politically. It had to be conquered in prayer and praise before that cultural transformation could come. God is showing through Abraham that liturgy is the tip of the spear. Liturgy is the cutting edge of the kingdom, the alpha form of the kingdom, the nursery of the kingdom. It is where Christian culture and Christian civilization begins.

In 1 Kings 22-23, when the godly King Josiah could see that Judah was a complete mess and needed reformation in every way, what did he do? Virtually all his reforms were liturgical reforms. They were directed toward renewing the sanctuary and the liturgy. He restored the Temple that had fallen into disrepair. He tore down the idolatrous altars in the high places. He reinstituted the Passover. Josiah faced major military and political threats to his kingdom. It might have seemed that a wise king would focus all his energy elsewhere, to deal with those threats head on. But Josiah knew the divinely ordained order of cultural renewal must start with the temple. It must start with worship.

In Ezekiel 47, the prophet has a vision of a gloriously rebuilt temple and a river of living water flowing out of this temple. The river of living water does not flow out of the king's palace. The river of living water does not flow out of the capitol building. The river of living water flows out of the temple, bringing renewal and transformation to the land and to the world. It restores everything.

In our day, we think that the church as an institution, including her ministry of worship, is irrelevant to what happens in the culture and in history. But nothing could be further from the truth. If the church in America is not having the cultural impact that she should, it is because we are focused on having a cultural impact in the same way unbelievers have a cultural impact. We have neglected the worship of the Lord; the Lord's house has fallen into disrepair.

We can keep trying to change the culture the way the pagans try to change culture. That is directly, by force, by majority vote, by lobbying, by military power, or by proposing new candidates and new laws. But none of these things will actually work so long as the Lord's house is in disrepair. If Christians are really serious about making our nation godly, we must start with the Lord's house because this is where it starts for every nation. If we want to see the nations discipled, it cannot happen apart from faithful churches worshiping the Lord in the beauty of His holiness. Scripture is clear that judgment begins with the house of God (1 Pet. 4:17). Reformation and transformation begin with the house of God as well.

If we do not make worship central, we are basically practical and political atheists, thinking we are the ones who can change the world in our own strength. Making worship central to cultural transformation is a way of confessing our own impotence. It is a way of confessing that the Lord alone can give us the nations as discipled kingdoms.

Our cultural pursuits are worthwhile, but we have to get the order and emphasis correct. Cultural activism can and should exist alongside liturgical activism, but the liturgy serves as the basis for cultural dominion. In our day, it is safe to say that the Lord's house is in ruins all over our land. The teaching of the Word is eclipsed by all kinds of entertainment. The Lord's Supper—our new covenant Passover meal—has been neglected, at least at most churches on most Sundays. Even churches that do the Supper frequently rarely do it according to the biblical pattern. We have to get serious about worship—about prayer, about preaching, about the Psalms, about the Scriptures, about tithing, about feasting weekly in the Lord's Supper.

In this chapter, we will highlight some areas where most modern evangelical worship is insufficient and offer directives from the Scriptures. Modern evangelicals conceive of worship as the "work" of ascribing worth to God. We will argue here that the liturgy is, at its center, God's service to us rather than our service to him. Modern evangelicals see no biblical basis for an order of worship. But there is an order of worship given to us in the Bible. Modern evangelical worship tends to focus on the internal—the mind, heart, and soul, but we believe worship should be about the whole person, including the body. Modern evangelical worship is often individualistic and passive, but biblical worship is corporate and participatory. Last, modern evangelical worship fails to recognize that worship takes place in heaven, but the heavenly context is the key to resolving the "worship wars" that have afflicted the church for a generation or more.

Grace First: We Receive in Order to Give

When we use the term "the Lord's Service" for our Lord's Day gathering, are we describing our service to God or God's service to us? The phrase "the Lord's Service" has a built-in ambiguity to it. Ultimately it is both, but the divine service is first and foremost God giving gifts to His people. In the liturgy God is at work: He opens His heavenly sanctuary to us, invites us in, and gives us the treasures of His kingdom. We respond by giving Him thanks and praise, but note that even our response is empowered and animated by the grace of our union with Christ, who is the great high priest leading His people in worship. Christ delivers the Father's gifts to us, and He delivers our praise to the Father.

The working definition of *worship* for most modern evangelicals is a personal expression of thanks and praise to God. But this is only half the picture, and the back half at that. Jeffrey Meyers says:

> Our fathers in the faith considered God's service to us (the forgiveness of sins, the ministry [service] of the Word, the Sacraments, etc.) as primary and our service to Him as secondary response. But this emphasis is exactly what is lost when we call our corporate, Sunday assembly "worship." This term comes to us by way of the Anglo-Saxon word "worth-ship," which simply meant to accord someone his proper worth. What we appear to be emphasizing with this term is not God's gifts and ministry to us through His Word and Sacraments, but our ascribing "worth" to Him…. We are too ready to accept the misleading definition of liturgy as "the work the people," which…is a severely truncated view of what happens in the Divine Service. What

happens on Sunday is the continuation of the service of the ascended Lord Jesus for His people.[50]

It sounds more pious to say we come to worship to give: *our* praise, *our* thanksgiving, *our* adoration, *our* gifts. But the reality is that we are needy creatures, and we need God's grace in order to return praise to Him. Before we come to *give,* we must come to *get.*

In the liturgy, whose action takes priority? Who calls us to worship? Who cleanses us and declares us forgiven? Who sets the table and feeds us? Who speaks wisdom to us from the Word? The priority in the Lord's service is on God's gracious action.[51] It's all about God—His action, His grace, His initiative. God works through human instruments and physical means to give us spiritual blessings. We do have a role to play. We are to receive God's gifts by faith and we are to return those gifts to God in the form of thanksgiving and praise, as our corporate response. But we only serve God because He has first served us. To really understand what is happening in the liturgy, we must see what God first does for us.

---

50. Jeffrey J. Meyers, *The Lord's Service* (Moscow, Idaho: Canon Press, 2003), 99-100.

51. This is why Presbyterians ought to love liturgy. It is embodied Calvinism. To deny the priority of God's gracious action in the liturgy is to move toward Pelagianism. Calvin's own theology (like Augustine before him) combined God's sovereign grace in salvation with a high view of the tangible, physical means God uses to apply his salvation. Some contemporary Calvinists mistakenly believe sovereign grace must be unmediated and immediate but Calvin himself certainly did not believe that.

We are gathered by God each Lord's Day so that God can renew covenant with us by giving us His gifts. We return those gifts to God by giving Him thanksgiving and praise. This means that if you miss church, you miss out on God's gifts. Imagine God spoke to you from heaven, "I have gifts I want to give to you. Come and get them! Show up with your church community on Sunday morning and I will give you these gifts." It would be a real insult to reply to God, "You know God, this Sunday, I'd rather sleep in." Or, "You know God, Your gifts sound great, but I'd rather play golf this week." Gathering is about receiving the gifts of God. When you come to an understanding of what is happening in the liturgy, when God meets with His people in the Lord's service, how could you miss the assembly unless you were providentially hindered in some way? We ought to place a high emphasis on church attendance, not merely because it is our duty and obligation, but because our reception of the gifts of God are our very life. If you want life, wisdom, and glory, receive these gifts in the means of grace.

Compare the triune biblical God with false gods. Other gods require you to give and serve first, and so you hope you've done enough to appease the idol and earn its gifts. Other gods demand you give your gifts, and they are never satisfied. Paganism was always about trying to satisfy the wrath of the deity on your own.

The "Lord's Service" turns worship upside down. We do not give gifts to satisfy God's wrath. God gave us the gift of His Son to do that. We do not give gifts to God or worship Him hoping that perhaps He will serve us in return, or answer our prayers, or do what we need. Rather, God serves us and it is His service to us that actually enables us to serve

Him in return. We come to God empty handed—"Nothing in my hands I bring, simply to thy cross I cling"—but He fills our hands, and now we have something to give to Him and to others.

When we recognize that corporate worship is primarily about God giving gifts to His people, and that this all takes place in Christ, we can clearly see that the service is primarily for the people of God. It is the "gifts of God for the people of God." When some churches organize the Sunday service around the unbeliever, they are inverting God's pattern. The Lord's service is about God serving His people, so that they can go out into the world in mission. Seeker-sensitive services, on the other hand, are about drawing unbelievers into the Sunday service so they can hear an evangelistic message. Liturgical discipleship is displaced by evangelism. Therefore, the seeker-sensitive service does not have enough emphasis on feeding, discipling, and transforming the people of God. Over the long run, this leads to deformation within the body of Christ. Without being fed solid food in the Word and in the sacrament, the people of God will not have the stamina to continue on the mission of God, which is to disciple the nations. A thin liturgy leads to a malnourished church.

The Biblical Order of the Lord's Service

In regards to the worship service, Paul says in 1 Corinthians 14:40, "Let all things be done decently and in order." From this commandment alone, we can clearly deduce that we should not have chaotic and unorganized gatherings. *But how is the worship service supposed to be arranged?* If we only look in the New Testament epistles, we do not obtain a lot of information. From the characterization of early church practices in Acts 2:41-42, we can see that "those who gladly received his word were baptized; and that day about three thousand souls were added to them. And they continued steadfastly in the apostles' doctrine and fellowship, in the breaking of bread, and in prayers." This gives insight into what is called the "elements" of the worship service: the sacraments of baptism and the Lord's Supper, prayer, and ministry of the Word. This leads some to focus on the "elements" of worship, leaving the order and flow of the service up to local churches and pastors to determine.

To see a biblically-prescribed order of worship, we must look at the whole Bible, not just the New Testament. God actually *did* give to Israel a pattern for worship. If we go back to the Old Testament book on the basics of worship—Leviticus—we can indeed see the pattern that God intends for worship, especially in Leviticus 9.

At this point in Israel's history, the Tabernacle had just been built (Exod. 40), and the priests were now ordained (Lev. 8). The laws describing the rituals for various types of sacrifices had been given in the early chapters of Leviticus. Now in Leviticus 9, the priestly ministry begins, with the first corporate worship service at the Tabernacle. This serves as a paradigm for all subsequent worship services at the Tabernacle, and later at the temple. It is a template for corporate worship.

Significantly, the sacrifices come in a particular sequence. Every time that covenant renewal occurs in the rest of the Old Testament, the sacrifices always occur in the same order seen in Leviticus 9. When we come to worship, God is renewing covenant with us, and we are renewing covenant with Him. Therefore, it is fitting that we follow the order of worship, based on the sacrificial system given in the Old Testament, within our weekly covenant renewal service of worship.

Jesus fulfilled the whole sacrificial system in which all the animal offerings pointed to the offering of Jesus on the cross (Heb. 9:11-15). However, these sacrifices do have ongoing application to the life of the church, providing a liturgical pattern for us to follow. All throughout the New Testament when worship is described, sacrificial language is used (Heb. 4:12, Heb. 13:15, Phil. 4:18, 1 Cor. 16:2, Rom. 15:16). In the new covenant, we no longer offer animals; instead we offer ourselves.

What the old covenant priests did to the sacrificial animals, Jesus now does *with us* in the liturgy. Animal sacrifices have ended, but sacrificial worship has not. Animals are no longer offered in God's presence. Instead of dead animals, people are offered as living sacrifices to God in the midst of the liturgy. Romans 12:1 says, "I beseech you therefore, brethren, by the mercies of God, that you present your bodies a living sacrifice, holy, acceptable to God, which is your reasonable service."

To understand the meaning of New Testament sacrificial language, we must look at the original context in the Old Testament. Once we understand the sacrificial system and what the different offerings mean, we can translate that into new covenant categories.

Leviticus 9 is the first corporate worship service at the Tabernacle with the ordained priesthood. It begins with a call to worship, as the people are called to assemble at the Tabernacle (Lev. 9:3-5). It ends with a benediction (Lev.

9:23), presumably the Aaronic benediction of Numbers 6:24-26, "The Lord bless you and keep you; the Lord make His face shine upon you, and be gracious to you; the Lord lift up His countenance upon you, and give you peace." In between the call to worship and the benediction, there is a series of offerings, and the order of them is of utmost significance.

First, there is the *sin offering* (Lev. 9:15). The sin offering highlights our sin and God's forgiveness. Liturgically, this corresponds to confession and absolution. We offer to God a broken spirit and a contrite heart (Ps. 51), confessing our sins and sinfulness. God then declares us forgiven in the blood of Christ.

Second in the sequence of Leviticus 9 is the *ascension offering* (Lev. 9:16). This is sometimes mistranslated as the "whole burnt offering," but the word doesn't mean "whole" or "burnt." It means "to go up." The emphasis is on our ascension into God's presence. This ritual points to our total consecration to God as we are accepted into His presence, and the transformation that God brings about in us, especially through His Word. This corresponds to the part of the service where God speaks to us through His Word as it is read and preached. The pastor, as a priestly servant, uses the sword of the Word to cut us up so we can be transformed by the fiery Spirit and ascend to the Lord as a sweet smelling aroma in Christ.

The third offering is called the *tribute offering* (Lev. 9:17), as the word for "grain" really describes "tribute." What is unique about this offering is that it is not an animal offering, but a bread offering. The grain is baked on the altar fire and turned into bread. The same word used for the grain offering is used elsewhere in the Old Testament to describe tribute that a people give to their king. In new covenant times, this corresponds to the collection of tithes and offerings. We are giving to God the fruit of our labors *on the basis of* a blood sacrifice already offered. To offer our works (our tribute) without first being cleansed by the blood of a substitutionary sacrifice would result in rejection (like Cain's offering in Genesis 4). But on the basis of a prior blood offering, God can accept both us and our good but imperfect works.[52]

The last offering is the *peace offering* (Lev. 9:18-21). The other sacrifices God Himself eats, but in the peace offering, God shares His own table with us. This translates into the covenant renewal meal, the new covenant Passover, the Lord's Supper. God is inviting us to His table to eat and this means that we are at peace with God and one another.

When we put all of this together, this is the biblical order of the covenant renewal service:

1. Call to worship
2. Sin Offering: confession of sin and absolution
3. Ascension Offering: praise and hearing of God's Word
4. Tribute Offering: collection of tithes and offerings
5. Peace Offering: Lord's Supper
6. Benediction: sent out with God's blessing

---

52. See chapter thirteen, in which we delve into the topic of good but imperfect works more fully.

If you look at the historic liturgies of the church, you will find they generally follow this order of worship.[53] Throughout church history, there has been a basic consensus regarding the structure and order of the service. At the time of the Reformation, when Luther and Calvin began putting together revised liturgies for their churches to use, this is essentially the order they followed.

In the Lord's service, we do not want Scripture to simply determine the content of the liturgy, in the sense that we want the sermon, prayers, and hymns to be biblical, but Scripture also should determine the shape, structure, and flow of the service. This order of service makes gospel sense. It is the gospel embodied liturgically, moving from God calling us, to confession and cleansing from sin, to consecration, to collection of our Spirit-wrought works, to communion with God, to being commissioned to go and spread the good news. Week after week, as God's people move together through this pattern of gospel liturgy, they are built up into a spiritual house. As 1 Peter 2:4-5 says:

> Coming to Him as to a living stone, rejected indeed by men, but chosen by God and precious, you also, as living stones, are being built up a spiritual house, a holy priesthood, to offer up spiritual sacrifices acceptable to God through Jesus Christ.

Embodied Worship for Embodied Creatures

We must be reminded from the Scriptures that our bodies matter. Jesus said, "And you shall love the Lord your God

---

53. See *Beyond Smells and Bells* by Mark Galli.

with all your heart, with all your soul, with all your mind, and with all your strength" (Mark 12:30). We must love God, serve Him, and worship Him with every aspect of who we are. Loving God "with all your strength" includes the use of your body. In 1 Corinthians 6:19-20, Paul corrects false views of the body:

> Do you not know that your body is the temple of the Holy Spirit who is in you, whom you have from God, and you are not your own? For you were bought at a price; therefore glorify God in your body and in your spirit, which are God's.

At the end of history, Christ will raise us to eternal life in our resurrection bodies: "We also who have the first-fruits of the Spirit, even we ourselves groan within ourselves, eagerly waiting for the adoption, the redemption of our body" (Rom. 8:23).

The biblical word that is translated "worship" in English literally means "to bow down" or "to kneel." It describes a bodily action. Psalm 95:6 says, "Oh come, let us worship and bow down; let us kneel before the Lord our Maker." We may read this verse in our worship service, but do we actually follow it? Note that the text does not say to "bow down in your hearts" or "bow down in your minds." Any honest interpretation of this text shows us we must use our bodies in worship, and bow down on our knees before God. John Calvin showed this connection between the heart and the body. In his commentary on Acts 20:36, he wrote:

The inward attitude certainly holds first place in prayer, but outward signs, kneeling, uncovering the head, lifting up the hands, have a twofold use. The first is that we may employ all our members for the glory and worship of God; secondly, that we are, so to speak, jolted out of our laziness by this help. There is also a third use in solemn and public prayer, because in this way the sons of God profess their piety, and they inflame each other with reverence of God. But just as the lifting up of the hands is a symbol of confidence and longing, so in order to show our humility, we fall down on our knees.

Worship is not a disembodied, gnostic event. It involves the whole person.

James K.A. Smith's *Desiring the Kingdom* series shows the connection between the human body, desires, and habits. While he has compromised his theology in many areas, in this regard Smith is quite correct: biblical liturgy requires a holistic, embodied response to God and His Word. As human beings, we are not just thinking beings, we are desiring creatures inhabiting bodies. Humanity's first sin involved both heart/desire and the body: "When the woman saw that the tree was good for food, that it was pleasant to the eyes, and a tree desirable to make one wise, she took of its fruit and ate" (Gen. 3:6). Thus, redemption requires both a reordering of the heart's desires toward God and a reshaping of how we use our bodies. For the Christian, there is a war between righteous living and sinful living that involves the whole person: "For the flesh lusts against the Spirit, and the Spirit against the flesh; and these are contrary to one another, so that you do not do the things that you wish" (Gal. 5:17).[54]

As bodily creatures, how do we reshape our desires to be oriented toward the kingdom of God, to be sanctified unto righteous living? This transformation takes place in a unique way in the Lord's service, through the rituals prescribed by God in the Scriptures, week after week. Worship practices done according to the Scriptures aid in the transformation and reshaping of our desires, so that we long for the kingdom above all else.

We must drop the assumption that "ritual" is a bad word, conjuring in our minds only dry, rote, dead orthodoxy. Liturgy and ritual will be unavoidable in weekly worship services. At almost every church's service, there are particular events every week: a prayer, a sermon, an offering, and singing. These are rituals: repeated, established, and prescribed procedures. Rituals in and of themselves are not unspiritual, cold, or empty. When rituals are appointed by God in His Word, they are spiritual and life giving.[55]

---

54. We should note that "flesh" here in the Scripture is sinful flesh, not bodily existence. It is not as if we are trying to escape our bodies into a purely spiritual realm. Rather, through the Holy Spirit, we are enabled to reshape our bodily desires from sinfulness to sanctification. Paul puts a major emphasis on bodily holiness (Rom. 6).

55. The sacramental rites of the Lord's Supper and Baptism are means of grace. The Westminster Larger Catechism, 161 says, "The sacraments become effectual means of salvation, not by any power in themselves, or any virtue derived from the piety or intention of him by whom they are administered, but only by the working of the Holy Ghost, and the blessing of Christ, by whom they are instituted."

Peter Leithart describes it this way:

> Ritual reflects and shapes individual life and the order of a community. It is at the heart of Christian *paedeia*.
>
> For individuals, Christian ritual trains the body and soul in suitable posture and movement. By moving us through a series of spiritual and physical postures, liturgical ritual imposes a choreography on us. Patterned by rituals of worship, we begin to live life before God *as* kneeling to confess, *as* standing to hear, *as* singing and clapping in praise, *as* sitting to eat and drink. Worship trains us in the steps for walking, for dancing rightly through life. Christian [worship] trains us in the protocols of life in the presence of God, and thereby, since all life is in the presence of God, acclimates the worship to Christian culture.
>
> For groups, ritual depicts the world as it ought to be, the real world as it is believed to be, especially the social and political realities of the world. Christian ritual displays the world as we believe and hope it one day will be. Ritual displays to public view who goes where, how each of us fits into the whole, how the members of the body are knit into one while yet remaining many, how the melodic lines of each individual life harmonize into a communal symphony. By repeated display, ritual reminds us again and again that this is the real world, objectively real outside our imaginations,

and encourages us to live on the confidence that this is the real world.[56]

The rituals of the Lord's service shape us into people of the kingdom. Ritual itself is not magical, but rituals that are rooted in Scripture become a training ground for the Holy Spirit to shape our desires to follow God in discipleship. Kneeling down for confession and rising to hear absolution, week after week, frees us from disordered desires. We are trained in humility and proper contrition. For those who are ungrateful, receiving the Eucharist meal and dining in God's presence leads to thanksgiving. The ritualized pattern Jesus gave us for the communion meal requires not one but two prayers of thanksgiving—one over each of the elements. This pattern reverses the failure of Adam to give thanks before eating in garden and trains us to thank and glorify God as we were created to do (cf. Rom. 1:18ff). For those struggling with greed, giving to God in the collection can be a helpful reminder that our money is not our own. Money is reduced from Mammon—the almighty dollar—to mere money, when brought into the presence of the living God. For those struggling with joy, the lifting of our hands in the doxology can help elevate the soul. We do not wait until we feel joy or thanksgiving or charity or self-control before we come to worship. As we participate in the liturgy, God often works through our bodies to get our souls back on track. The patterns and rituals of biblically shaped liturgy flow over us and mold us, often subtly

---

56. Peter J. Leithart, *Against Christianity* (Moscow, Idaho: Canon Press, 2003), 82.

and imperceptibly, like water currents flowing over rock in a river bed. The Spirit uses the liturgy to ingrain godly habits into us by repeated rituals, knitting the language and imagery of Scripture into the very fabric of our being. C. S. Lewis encapsulates the topic of liturgy well:

> Every service is a structure of acts and words through which we receive a sacrament, or repent, or supplicate, or adore. And it enables us to do these things best—if you like it, it "works" best— when, through long familiarity, we don't have to think about it. As long as you notice, and have to count the steps, you are not yet dancing, but only learning to dance. A good shoe is a shoe you don't notice. Good reading becomes possible when you need not consciously think about eyes, or light, or print, or spelling. The perfect church service would be the one we were almost unaware of; our attention would have been on God.
>
> But every novelty prevents this. It fixes our attention on the service itself; and thinking about worship is a different thing from worshipping. The important question about the Grail was "for what does it serve?" "'Tis mad idolatry that makes the service greater than god."
>
> A still worse thing may happen. Novelty may fix our attention not even on the service but on the celebrant. You know what I mean. Try as one may to exclude it, the question "What on earth is he up to now?" will intrude. It lays one's devotion waste. There is really some excuse for the man who said, "I

wish they'd remember that the charge to Peter was feed my sheep; not Try experiments on my rats, or even Teach my performing dogs new tricks."

Thus my whole liturgiological position really boils down to an entreaty for permanence and uniformity. I can make do with almost any kind of service whatever, if only it will stay put. But if each form is snatched away just when I am beginning to feel at home in it, then I can never make any progress in the art of worship. You give me no chance to acquire the trained habit—*habito dell'arte*.[57]

Worship that is Corporate and Participatory

In the previous section, we discussed the use of our bodies in worship. Have you ever wondered why charismatics relish raising their hands in worship? Perhaps it is because they get to use their bodies: they lift their hands rather than sit on them. We do not necessarily advocate spontaneous and individual lifting of the hands when you "feel the Spirit" as a remedy to overly cerebral approaches to worship. Such an individualistic approach has other potential problems, including not doing things "decently and in order" (1 Cor. 14:40) or trying to bring attention to oneself. An important point to stress is that in the Lord's service, we do these bodily practices *together* as a church body. It is not as if we can say, "You kneel if and when you like," or "You can raise your hands if that helps you get in touch with God." That misses the entire point of worship being a *corporate*

---

57. C. S. Lewis, *The Joyful Christian* (New York: MacMillan Publishing, 1977), 80-81.

experience. *We* lift *our* hands up to the Lord—and we all raise our hands *together* and sing the doxology *together*. In 1 Timothy 2:8, we read, "I desire therefore that the men pray everywhere, lifting up holy hands." Psalm 28:2 says, "Hear the voice of my supplications when I cry to You, when I lift up my hands toward Your holy sanctuary." This corporate practice gives all of the benefits of the charismatic expression, without the pitfalls of disorder or individuals drawing attention to themselves. The bodily postures and gestures of the liturgy—kneeling, raising hands, standing—are done together as one body.

We are not spectators in the worship service. We are a priesthood. We are actively engaged in the worship, together offering God a sacrifice of praise. The Corinthian church went overboard with so much individual participation that it was disorderly (1 Cor. 14:26-33). In general, today's church has the opposite problem: we have too little participation. Today people would rather be passive, listening to a concert instead of singing along. They would rather watch a video clip on a screen than hear a message that requires effort to think about. We live in an entertainment driven culture that disciples us in passivity.

In one of her works, Marva Dawn talks about a church service she went to where the congregation was not expected to do anything. They were mere spectators. There were no corporate prayers or creeds to say together. All the singing was performed at the front by professional musicians. The only thing expected of the congregation was to drop a check in the plate when it came around. This is not a biblical liturgy nor the kind of participatory worship that Scripture calls us to.

We are called to engage God with every action in the service. We do not just read the prayers. We *pray* the prayers. We do not just mumble our way through the creed. We use those ancient words that the church has always used to confess our faith from the heart. We do not just sing mindlessly. We use our voices to praise God while we are meditating on the lyrics. If we leave Sunday a little tired from having worshiped, that is acceptable because worship requires effort. The fact that worship requires effort does not contradict the earlier emphasis on worship as receiving grace. The apostle Paul in 1 Corinthians 15:10 shows that grace and effort belong together. It is grace that produces the effort, including effort within the Lord's service. "But by the grace of God I am what I am, and His grace toward me was not in vain; but I labored more abundantly than they all, yet not I, but the grace of God which was with me."

Whatever the occasion in worship, we are to throw our whole selves into it. Worship is not just an action of the intellect, it includes our bodies as well. Our whole persons—mind, emotions, and body—are to be engaged in worshipping the Lord. This is because biblical religion is not just an "ism" or an ideology. It is not just about ideas and doctrines, as important as those things are. We cannot have biblical religion without true doctrine, but biblical religion also involves practices as well. It involves a transformed way of life in the community of the church, and this transformation becomes more and more a reality as we gather together as Christ's body each week. As Hebrews 13:15 says, "Therefore by Him let us continually offer the sacrifice of praise to God, that is, the fruit of our lips, giving thanks to His name."

Heaven: Where Our Worship Takes Place

Thus far, we have described how and what our worship should be like in order to be more fully biblical, and why this is important. But we have not talked about *where* worship takes place. By this reference to location, we are not referring to the choice of church, or the church building in which we worship. In worship done according to the biblical pattern, in our union with the risen and ascended Christ, we actually ascend up into the heavenly presence of God (Heb. 12:22-24). There in heaven, we join the continual worship that is taking place around God's throne.

This biblical reality of going to heaven in the Lord's service ought to have a "heavy" regulative principle effect on how we worship. If we really realized that we were going into the throne-room presence of the thrice-holy God on the Lord's Day, some of the trite gimmicks and nonsense that we call "worship" in the modern church would quickly fall by the wayside. In fact, we would have Josiah's reaction upon hearing the long-lost Word of God read: "Thus it happened, when the king heard the words of the Law, that he tore his clothes" (2 Chron. 34:19).

In authentic new covenant worship, we do not go to an earthly temple on a mountain in Jerusalem as the old covenant worshipers did. Rather, we come. . .

. . . the city of the living God, the heavenly Jerusalem, to an innumerable company of angels, to the general assembly and church of the firstborn who

are registered in heaven, to God the Judge of all, to
the spirits of just men made perfect, to Jesus the
Mediator of the new covenant, and to the blood
of sprinkling that speaks better things than that of
Abel (Heb. 12:22-24).

There is a lot to unpack in these verses, but it is clear
that in the Lord's service, we are in the presence of angels,
those who have gone before us in the faith, and indeed the
very presence of Jesus the mediator. We enter into heaven,
the heavenly Jerusalem. The apostle John, for example, also
is called up into the heavenly worship service on the Lord's
Day (Rev. 1:10)

This ought to be mind-blowing, even for those who
are familiar with this truth! Jesus is the bridge between
heaven and earth. The eternal God came from heaven to
earth to save us, and now has ascended back to heaven so
that we too may ascend into heaven. As Jesus said to Na-
thanael, "Most assuredly, I say to you, hereafter you shall
see heaven open, and the angels of God ascending and descending upon the Son of Man" (John 1:51).

At Jesus's death, "the veil of the temple was torn in
two from top to bottom" (Matt. 27:51), a sign that God
was giving all of His people access to the true and heavenly
Most Holy Place. When we join together in the Lord's service, we are no longer simply on earth, but we have entered
into the heavenly throne room of God (Heb. 10:19-22).
The earthly tabernacle was a copy of the heavenly original.
In the new covenant, we are no longer worshiping God at
a shadowy sanctuary on earth. We are entering the true

sanctuary above. Obviously this is a mystery, but by faith we know it is a reality.

When we proclaim in the Lord's service that we are worshiping "with angels and archangels, and with all the company of heaven," we really mean it.[58] This isn't just metaphorical or symbolic speech, but a real life, glorious event each week. We may not be able to see it with our physical eyes, but with the eyes of faith, we experience the heavenly presence of God.

On the Lord's Day, we are called to heaven by our resurrected and ascended king, in order to receive His gifts. God renews covenant with us, and cleanses us from all our sins because of the sacrifice of Christ. God feeds His people and nourishes us with His Word and sacrament, and sends us back into the world to serve as the people of His kingdom in our vocations.

---

58. The language of worshiping "with angels and archangels and all the company of heaven" comes down to us from Hippolytus, one of the church fathers, probably the oldest post-apostolic liturgy that we have.

Section 3

Kingdom Living: Vocation

Chapter 13

Kingdom Living

We gather on the first day of the week because worship is of first importance. But not every day is a Sunday. What are the other days of the week for? Does God care about the rest of our life? In Colossians 3:17, the apostle Paul answers these questions for us: "And whatever you do in word or deed, do all in the name of the Lord Jesus, giving thanks to God the Father through Him." He answers again in verse 23, "whatever you do, do it heartily, as to the Lord and not to men." This is what the other days of the week are about. Whatever we are called to do is to be offered to the Lord. Work is a form of worship.

Whatever we do Monday through Saturday is to continue and flow out from what we do on Sundays. At the end of the Lord's service, in the benediction, the congregation is blessed by God. This blessing is not for ourselves only. We are blessed in order to go out and be a blessing to the world. Theologians refer to this as the "liturgy after the liturgy." This blessing of the world will primarily take place within the context of our vocations. Vocations are our callings from God through which we serve in the world. Vocations include our work and much more. Your vocation is the sum total of the responsibilities God has given you.

Paul uses the phrase "whatever you do" twice within a few verses in Colossians 3. For Paul, there is no divide between sacred worship and secular living. Worship on Sunday is meant to transform the rest of the week and the rest of life. There is no wedge between the so-called spiritual and secular aspects of life. The Christian life is an integrated, seamless whole. For the Christian, even the most mundane physical actions are shot through with spirituality. This is why Paul says in Galatians 2:20, "the life which I now live in the flesh I live by faith in the Son of God, who loved me and gave Himself for me." The whole of Paul's life was dedicated to God by faith. Whether he was preaching or making tents, Paul lived by faith in Christ.

The Logic of Luther

The Protestant Reformation's major contribution was a return to justification by faith alone. But connected to this was the re-capturing of the priesthood of believers.[59] The logic of the Lutheran Reformation has often been summarized in one sentence: *"God does not need your good works, but your neighbor does."*

---

59. Gene Veith, *God at Work* (Wheaton, Illinois: Crossway Publishing, 2002), 18.

The first half of that statement—"*God does not need your good works*"—is *justification by faith alone*. God does not need our works to satisfy His justice or earn His favor. He justifies us apart from those things through Christ. Christ already made propitiation and secured God's good will toward us. All that Christ did on our behalf, offered to us in Word and sacrament, is received by faith alone. Works have no place in bringing about the transition from wrath to grace, or in moving us from a state of condemnation to a state of justification. God does not need our works. He rescues us by the work of His Son.

The second half of the statement—"*your neighbor does [need your good works]*"—is the *priesthood of all believers*. Since we are no longer focused on doing good works to try to earn justification or quench God's wrath, we are now set free to serve our neighbors in love through our daily vocations. Good works take on a horizontal focus. We serve God as priests by serving one another, doing something useful and oriented to the public good. We do not do good works to *earn* salvation before God, but to *demonstrate* salvation before our neighbor.

Before Luther, monks were kept busy doing "good works" like climbing the castle stairs on their knees or saying five hundred "hail Marys" to try to assuage an angry God. But such works did not do anything to help neighbors. They were completely privatized and, in a sense, selfish, because they focused totally on the salvation of the self. After the Reformation, Christians came to know the issue of God's wrath was settled at the cross, and so good works could become genuinely *good*, by focusing outwardly and publicly on the needs of others. The gospel turned loose love for neighbor. Since our relationship with God has been restored by Christ through faith, we can get to work restoring relationships with our neighbors through love. In this way, Luther's rediscovery of the gospel unleashed human energies and potentialities not seen since the generation of the apostles. When man no longer has to futilely expend energy climbing a ladder into the heavens, he can get to work transforming the earth. Thus, the Reformation has done more to fulfill the dominion mandate and the Great Commission than any other movement in history.

Calvin was getting at the same thing when he said in his famous letter to Cardinal Sadolet, "It is certainly the duty of a Christian man to ascend higher than merely to seek and secure the salvation of his own soul." That higher calling—*higher than even securing your own salvation*—is glorifying God in the world through service to neighbor. The Bible identifies the great enemy of this kind of love and service as the self. Because of sin, love for self competes with love for neighbor. The self gets in the way, and we live in a culture obsessed with the self (a "selfie" culture). If you go into any bookstore, there is a huge section of books labeled self-help. But you will never find a section called "others-help."

The old self, in Adam, focuses more on what I deserve than how I can serve. Scripture tells us this old self must die if we are going to truly live a life of love. We have to get out of ourselves and into our neighbors. To paraphrase Luther's summarizing statement from his booklet, *Freedom of a Christian*: "A Christian lives in Christ and in his neighbor. The Christian ascends by faith to receive Christ's righteousness. The Christian descends in love to serve his neighbor. Each Christian should be a Christ to his neighbor." Just as God in Christ found you and loved you and provided everything you lacked, so we ought to show mercy to our neighbor in the same way. This is what love looks like: do unto your neighbor as God has done unto you. We are to imitate God in how we love our neighbor. Indeed, as God pours His love into us, that love overflows to others, so we love our neighbor with the same love with which we have been loved. The source of our neighbor-love is not our hearts but God's heart. While God's love for us is the pattern for our love toward our neighbors, we should obviously remember that we are creatures and not deities. Therefore, we will always face creaturely limitations. Our loves must be ordered by various realities. Our highest obligation is always to love God. Our love of neighbor will generally move in concentric circles from those naturally, spiritually, and geographically closest to us. For example, Scripture stresses caring for one's own family or fellow church member above others. Understanding these boundaries on our obligations protects from false guilt. We should love everyone, but obviously we cannot love everyone in the same way, nor do we have the exact same duties toward everyone.

In present day society, in which God is banished from the public realm, even Christians are tempted to live as practical atheists or deists from Monday to Saturday. A major way of fighting this temptation is to acknowledge that God is working in and through us in our vocations. God works through means such as Word and sacrament. But He also works through means in our vocations, in which we serve the world. Through our callings from God to our particular place in the world, God enables us to love and

serve our neighbors, in order to transform the earth. Gene
Veith summarizes this well:

> When we pray the Lord's Prayer, we ask God to
> give us this day our daily bread. And he does. The
> way he gives us our daily bread is through the voca-
> tions of farmers, millers, and bakers. We might add
> truck drivers, factory workers, bankers, warehouse
> attendants, and the lady at the checkout counter.
> Virtually every step of our whole economic system
> contributes to that piece of toast you had for break-
> fast. And when you thanked God for the food that
> he provided, you were right to do so.[60]

This means that we receive God's blessing through the
callings of others, but God also works *through us* in our
callings. Veith adds, "For a Christian, conscious of vocation as the mask of God, all of life, even the most mundane
facets of our existence, become occasions to glorify God."[61]
God delights to work through the ordinary. He can do miracles of course, but his usual pattern is to work through
the mundane. Our love for our neighbor is actually the
love of God working in us and through us, reaching out to
embrace our neighbor, so that they can experience the love
of God. Our love for others should be practical and earthy,
not abstract. This should be the kind of love that changes
lives and meets needs.

---

60. From article by Gene Veith, "Our Calling and God's Glory,"
Modern Reformation 16, no. 6 (November/December 2007).

61. Veith, "Our Calling."

Justification by Faith,
Union with Christ, and Good Works

One struggle facing Christians who embrace Reformation teaching is wondering whether Christians can actually do good works that are pleasing in God's sight. Is it true that our lives are so tainted by sin that all we do is sinful? While acknowledging that those apart from Jesus are totally unable to please God, is it also true that those who are in Christ are unable to please God?

Indeed, there is no work that humanity in Adam can do that will please God. Jesus said in John 15:5, "without Me you can do nothing" and the apostle Paul reiterated this truth in Romans 8:8, "those who are in the flesh cannot please God." Mankind, apart from Jesus, cannot please God. As Calvinists point out from Scripture, man is totally depraved, sinful in all his parts and faculties. This is why salvation must be entirely a work of sovereign grace.

But what about the new humanity in Jesus, equipped and empowered by the Holy Spirit? Are Christians—those who have been made alive in Christ and brought to faith in him—also totally depraved? No, certainly not. While Christians still sin and will continue to sin until the time they go to be with the Lord in glory, the believer is not under sin's dominion in the same way as the unbeliever. He has been set free from the penalty and even the power of sin (in principle). In the future, he will be set free from the presence of sin. The Christian life is expected to be one of growth and maturation in obedience.

Many Christians have a far too pessimistic a view of the Christian life. The Christian life is a battle with the world, the flesh and the devil. We are constantly dealing with temptation that comes from within (the flesh) or from without (Satan). We will often fall into sin, sometimes grievously. Christians can struggle with all kinds of sinful desires, and sometimes we will lose those battles. But we also can gain the victory. And this is an important point. Many pastors find it is just as difficult to convince the non-Christian he is actually a slave to sin as it is to convince the Christian he is not a slave to sin. Christians can actually do good works. Non-Christians are totally depraved, but Christians are being renewed in the image of Christ. We can actually do things that please our heavenly Father, thanks to the intercession of Christ and the indwelling of the Holy Spirit.

Those who are in the Son, filled with the Holy Spirit, should joyfully recognize that God has made them into saints who are able to please their heavenly Father. We no longer have to wallow in our sinfulness but can revel in our sainthood. Of course, saints remain sinners in this life but the Bible makes clear our union with Christ is the dominant reality in the life of the believer.

Our whole salvation is enclosed in Christ. He *is* the gospel. He *is* our salvation. He *is* our righteousness. When we are brought into union with Him, which happens subjectively by Spirit-wrought faith and objectively in the sacrament of baptism, we are made sharers in all that is His. We are united to Christ by faith alone. Faith receives Christ as He is offered to us in the gospel. When we are united to Christ, we share in His new resurrection life; union with Christ is transformative. Likewise, we share in His judicial status. Union with Christ has a legal, or forensic element.

It is particularly important to understand how union with Christ relates to justification in the present and final judgment at the last day. When we are joined to Christ by faith, His righteous status as the *justified one* before the Father becomes ours. Jesus was condemned by humanity on the cross, but in his Resurrection, the Father reversed the verdict of the earthly court and vindicated Him. His justification and vindication is now our justification and vindication. Jesus was without sin but died a sinner's death as a substitute, taking upon Himself the curse we deserve because of our sin. In His Resurrection, Jesus was declared righteous. We share in the declaration because we are united to Him. This is why Paul says there is now no condemnation for those who are in Christ Jesus.

But what is interesting is that the same Bible which teaches justification by faith alone (because of union with Christ by faith alone) also teaches we will be judged according to our works at the last day. For example, 2 Corinthians 5:10 says, "For we must all appear before the judgment seat of Christ, that each one may receive the things done in the body, according to what he has done, whether good or bad." What can this mean? How do these truths of justification by faith alone and a judgment according to works fit together? To be more specific: How does *initial* justification by faith fit together with our *final* justification at the last day according to good works?

The most important answers to these questions come from Scripture, of course. But because these issues can become controversial, it should be noted that the Westminster Standards teach that even as we are justified by faith alone, the faith that justifies produces fruit in the form of good works, and those good works play a role in the final judgment.[62] Thus, faith must bear "fruit," which has as its end "eternal life" (Westminster Confession of Faith 16.2). Forgiveness is only given to the repentant (WCF 15.3). Initial justification is inseparable from sanctification, perseverance, and good works (WCF 10-18). God requires repentance if we are to escape His wrath and curse (WSC 85). Holy obedience is not only evidence of salvation, but the *way* of salvation (Westminster Larger Catechism 32). Our good works are "accepted" by God in Christ, so that He, "looking upon them in His Son, is pleased to accept and reward" them (WCF 16.6).

All of this, of course, reflects Biblical teaching and reminds us that salvation, from beginning to end, in all its legal and transformative elements, is a gift of grace. Further, following Scripture, the Westminster Confession teaches that all men will be judged at the last day, with the result that each will "receive according to what they have done in the body, whether good or evil." This eschatological, forensic judgment can only result in two possible outcomes: "For then shall the righteous go into everlasting life. . . but the wicked, who know not God, and obey not the Gospel of Jesus Christ, shall be cast into eternal torments." In view of this coming judicial examination, we should "shake off

---

62. The Westminster Confession of Faith (WCF) came together in the 1640s after many years of deliberation, with the purpose of creating new doctrinal standards in Protestant, Reformational England. Along with the Confession, there is the Westminster Shorter Catechism (WSC), Westminster Larger Catechism (WLC), and other documents pertaining to the life of the Church. Many Reformed and Presbyterian denominations subscribe to the Westminster Standards.

all carnal security, and be always watchful" (WCF 33.1-3). While the language of justification is missing here, the conceptual apparatus of justification is certainly present.

The same is true of Westminster Shorter Catechism question 38. The "benefits. . . believers receive from Christ at the resurrection" include being "openly acknowledged and acquitted in the day of judgment." "Judgment" language reminds us this is a forensic event, issuing forth in either justification or condemnation. At that day, God will do more than "openly acknowledge" that believers have *already* received acquittal. He will actually acquit them *in* the day of judgment. While some might want to quibble over the precise term used here, no legitimate argument can be mounted against the notion that "acquittal" is a virtual synonym for "justification." To be acquitted is to be found "not guilty" in a court of law; the word describes a judicial deliverance in which the one on trial is freed from all charges. This acquittal/justification should be the eschatological expectation of all believers. The proof texts to the Westminster Confession and catechisms show us how the Westminster divines read Scripture. In this case, the divines cited Matthew 25:23, "His lord said to him, 'Well done, good and faithful servant.'"

Scripture is clear that we are already justified, but there is another phase or application of our justification still to come, when we will be found worthy and blameless in His sight. Here are a few verses from Scripture that are consistent with this teaching:

- For we must all appear before the judgment seat of Christ, that each one may receive the things

done in the body, according to what he has done,
whether good or bad (2 Cor. 5:10).

- Finally, there is laid up for me the crown of righteousness, which the Lord, the righteous Judge,
will give to me on that Day, and not to me only
but also to all who have loved His appearing (2
Tim. 4:8).

- And I saw the dead, small and great, standing before God, and books were opened. And another
book was opened, which is the Book of Life. And
the dead were judged according to their works, by
the things which were written in the books (Rev.
20:12).

- Then I heard a voice from heaven saying to me,
"Write: 'Blessed are the dead who die in the Lord
from now on.' " "Yes," says the Spirit, "that they
may rest from their labors, and their works follow
them" (Rev. 14:13).[63]

It is crucial to note that the good works which play a
role in the final judgment are not meritorious. They do not
earn anything. They are the product of God's grace at work
in us, as we obediently work out what God works in (Phil.
2:12-13). Good works are necessary for our salvation, precisely because they are evidence of our faith and union

---

63. See also Matthew 12:37; Romans 2:1-16; 2:26-29; 5:9-10; 8:33-
34; 14:10-18; 1 Corinthians 1:8; 4:2-4; Galatians 2:17; 5:4-5; Philippians 3:9; Colossians 1:22; 1 Thessalonians 3:13; 2 Thessalonians 1:5;
2 Timothy 4:8, 16; Revelation 22:12-14.

with Christ. As Hebrews 12:14 says, without holiness, no one will see the Lord. But how exactly can a holy God be pleased with our good, but admittedly imperfect, works?

The good works that Christians do by the power of God's Spirit and offered through the mediation of Christ are acceptable and pleasing in our Father's sight. In the Last Judgment, God will say to you, "Well done, good and faithful servant" (Matt. 25:23). When God makes that declaration, He will be crowning His own work. This is because He works all of our good works in us: "you, however, are not in the flesh, but in the Spirit" (Rom. 8:9). The Holy Spirit empowers this obedience of faith. Christ's intercession, based on His once-and-for-all atoning death on the cross, covers whatever imperfections remain. Justification by faith alone in the present is the Father's approval of the Son's work *for us*. Final validation of our lives at the last day is the Father's approval of the Spirit's work *in us*. Our salvation is Trinitarian, as Father, Son, and Spirit work together as one to redeem us.[64]

God's Pleasure in Our Obedience

To recap the argument thus far: By grace through faith in Christ, we share in Christ's righteous status, apart from our works. We are justified right now, in the present moment, by faith alone in Christ alone. God declares believers righ-

---

64. Rich Lusk, "Future Justification: Some Theological and Exegetical Proposals," in *A Faith That Is Never Alone*, ed. P. Andrew Sandlin (Kerygma Press, 2007). For more historical background, see also Rich Lusk, "The Reformed Doctrine of Justification by Works," *Obedient Faith: A Festschrift for Norman Shepherd*, ed. P. Andrew Sandlin (Kerygma Press, 2012).

teous in His Son. We share in the same status as Christ Himself. Justification is forensic and declarative. It is a verdict the Father passes over us when we are united to Christ. Jesus was condemned by human courts when He was tried and crucified, but in reality He was taking the condemnation His people deserved. In His Resurrection, the Father overturned the verdict of the human court and vindicated Him, declaring Him to be in the right. By faith, we participate in His resurrection righteousness. We have the same status and legal standing that Jesus Himself has. This is why Paul says there is no condemnation for those who are in Christ (Rom. 8:1).

But Scripture plainly teaches that we are not only justified in God's heavenly law court in the present by faith alone. We will also be openly justified—publicly acquitted and vindicated—at the last day, in the final judgment. And in that final judgment, our works will play a role not because they are meritorious in any way but because they are signs and evidences of our faith in Christ.

God accepts our persons in Christ right now. At the last day, He will accept the grace-empowered, Spirit-wrought good works we have done. This is the biblical pattern: there is an initial justification by faith alone in the present day followed by a judgment according to works at the last day. When we stand before the judgment seat at the last day, the Spirit's work in us, offered through the mediation of Christ, will be approved in the Father's sight. Salvation is by grace alone through faith alone, but this truth does not conflict with a final judgment according to works because grace not only forgives sins, it also transforms sinners. Ephesians 2:8-9 clearly declares, by grace we have been saved, through faith, not by works. Yet, the very next verse says, "we are His workmanship, created in Christ Jesus for good works, which God prepared beforehand that we should walk in them." This doctrine is a safeguard against both legalism and antinomianism. The final judgment is not a terror to the people of God. It is a gospel comfort (cf. Rom. 2:16).

God accepts us as we are, welcoming sinners into His fold, but He does not let us stay that way. Salvation is a seamless work that includes both legal and transformative elements. Again, God's grace not only forgives sin, it also transforms us. Faith not only justifies, it also produces fruit. To be abundantly clear, this *does not* mean that at the last day that our works will become the *ground* of our acceptance with God. Rather, they are *evidence* of our faith. Christ paid for our salvation with His blood. Now the good works that the Spirit works in us are evidence that we are in Christ. Our works are acceptable to God only because we are in Christ and thus our works are presented to God through Christ's intercession and mediation.

Granting that only the Spirit can work in us good works, the reality is that all of our good works in this life are still stained with sin. Our works may be good, but they still are not perfect. Even the most mature Christian is still a sinner, struggling with sin even in blatant ways.[65] We must

---

65. See the Westminster Confession of Faith 16.6: "Notwithstanding, the persons of believers being accepted through Christ, their good works also are accepted in Him; not as though they were in this life wholly unblamable and unreproveable in God's sight; but that He, looking upon them in His Son, is pleased to accept and reward that which is sincere, although accompanied with many weaknesses and imperfections."

remember that to whatever degree our sins are exposed at the Last Judgment, they will be sins that have already been covered by the blood of Christ. They will not be brought up to condemn or shame us, but to magnify the grace and mercy of God. The good yet imperfect works which the Spirit has wrought in us will be approved and rewarded.

In Ecclesiastes 9:7, the preacher says, "Go, eat your bread with joy, and drink your wine with a merry heart, *for God has already accepted your works.*" What a comfort it is to know that God has accepted our works and is pleased with us! Why do we as Christians not talk more about pleasing God? This is something that does not seem to be part of the ordinary Christian's vocabulary. It is as if we are simply scared to talk this way because we know that everything we do is still tinged with sin.

The apostle Paul, while certainly acknowledging the depth of sin even in the life of the believer, also talked about pleasing God a great deal. In 2 Corinthians 5:9, before discussing the judgment seat of Christ, Paul says, "Therefore we make it our aim, whether present or absent, to be *well pleasing to Him.*" In Philippians 4:18, he thanks the church for having sent a financial offering that is "a sweet-smelling aroma, an acceptable sacrifice, *well pleasing to God.*" In Colossians 1:10, Paul prays for the church, "that you may walk worthy of the Lord, *fully pleasing Him,* being fruitful in every good work and increasing in the knowledge of God." In 1 Timothy 2:3, Paul says that prayer is, "good and acceptable in the sight of God our Savior." In 1 Timothy 5:3-4, Paul says that caring for widows is, "good and acceptable before God." Isn't it an encouragement to know that God our Father smiles and delights over these efforts that He is working in us? God is pleased with us when we give generously, pray to Him, care for widows, or share with those in need (Heb. 13:16). God takes pleasure in our efforts to do right, our baby steps of obedience. It has been said God is hard to satisfy but easy to please. This is helpful: even as God calls us to ever greater acts of obedience, He is pleased with the progress we have made. Even as we have a long way still to go, He delights in the direction we are traveling.

When we are honest with ourselves, we acknowledge that our obedience to God is not what we wish it was. We can become disappointed and frustrated with ourselves. Sometimes our consciences can accuse us even as Christians in our struggle with sin. But if we have a desire to please God, no matter how imperfect or flawed the expression of that desire is, it is a sign that God is at work in us, causing us to bear fruit. When we seek to obey God, He smiles upon His children. This brings joy to our heavenly Father. This is how John Calvin put it in his *Institutes*, 3.15.4, 3.17.3:

> [When God] examines our works according to his tenderness, not his supreme right, he therefore accepts them as if they were perfectly pure; and for this reason, although unmerited, they are rewarded with infinite benefits, both of the present life and also of the life to come. For I do not accept the distinction made by learned and otherwise godly men that good works deserve the graces that are conferred upon us in this life, while everlasting salvation is the reward of faith alone. On the other

hand, so to attribute to the merit of works the fact that we are showered with grace upon grace as to take it away from grace is contrary to the teaching of Scripture. . . . Whatever, therefore, is now given to the godly as an aid to salvation, even blessedness itself, is purely God's beneficence. Yet both in this blessedness and in those godly persons, he takes works into account. For in order to testify to the greatness of his love towards us, he makes not only us but the gift he has given us worthy of such honor.

Finally, while they [the Roman Catholic sophists] repeatedly inculcate good works, they in the meantime so instruct consciences as to discourage all their confidence that God remains kindly disposed and favorable to their works. But we, on the other hand, without reference to merit, still remarkably cheer and comfort the hearts of believers by our teaching, when we tell them they please God in their works and are without doubt acceptable to him . . .

[T]he promises of the gospel. . . not only make us acceptable to God but also render our works pleasing to him. And not only does the Lord adjudge them pleasing; he also extends to them the blessings which under the covenant were owed to observance of his law. I therefore admit that what the Lord has promised in his law to the keepers of righteousness and holiness is paid to the works of believers, but in this repayment we must always consider the reason that wins favor for these works.

Commenting on Romans 3:22, Calvin says,

Having been made partakers of Christ, we ourselves are not only just, but our works also are counted just before God, and for this reason, because whatever imperfections there may be in them, are obliterated by the blood of Christ; the promises, which are conditional, are also by the same grace fulfilled to us; for God rewards our works as perfect, inasmuch as their defects are covered by free pardon.

This truth of God being pleased with our Spirit-empowered obedience isn't merely an abstract point for theologians to expound upon or argue about. It has significance in our daily living. As we go about living in the kingdom, in our vocations, we should be assured that God is with us in our struggles and His Spirit is at work bearing fruit among us. As we seek to live faithful, sacrificial lives for the sake of others, we can know that the smile of God our Father is upon us.

A final pastoral point before moving on: There is a kind of latent antinomianism that pervades a lot of Reformed, evangelical preaching and worship music today. Preachers and songwriters tell church members they are "nothing but sinners" and "hell-bound rebels" who can do nothing right. The Christian is reduced to his faults and Jesus is reduced to exclusively being a Savior from sin's penalty. In other words, there is no sense of the Spirit's power indwelling and transforming the believer so he can do genuinely good works, and no sense of other roles Jesus plays in our lives, such as king, rescuing us from sin's reign so we can submit obediently to His authority. Over time, this can create a sense that Christians are so wretched they should not even bother trying to be obedient—and all that effort and striving for obedience is probably a sign of legalism anyway. The result of this teaching is a weak, immature church, vulnerable to compromise with the world. Christians who do not have much hope for transformation in their own lives or in the world are easily manipulated and misled by influences from the culture; they are short on courage and long on shame. They eventually ask themselves, "Why bother?" If nothing can really get better in this life and in this world, why try? This is why the teaching we have offered in this chapter is so vital to recover. We need to know God not only forgives our sins, but crushes them under His and our feet. While we should be realistic about remaining sins and weaknesses in our lives, we should also be triumphalistic. We should approach each day in a spirit of triumph because we are assured of victory in Christ our Lord. We should not wallow in sin and shame. We should rise up and pursue obedience because the Lord is with us.

Dominion through Service

If we believe the gospel of the kingdom, we will live as faithful subjects of the King of Kings. This means we will work toward the fulfillment of the mandate He has given us. The mandate, originally given in Genesis 1 as the command to rule and fill the earth, has been republished for a fallen world in the Great Commission of Matthew 28. The creation mandate and the Great Commission fit together and reinforce one another. The only way the original mandate can be fulfilled now is through the fulfillment of the Great Commission. Today we multiply and fill the earth not only by having and discipling covenant children, but also through "spiritual multiplication" that happens when we evangelize the lost. And only disciples can produce the kind of godly civilization the original mandate called for. When the nations are discipled, in terms of the Great Commission, the creation mandate will be completed.

Just as Adam and Eve's original charge was to "fill the earth and subdue it" and "have dominion" (Gen. 1:28), the church has been "co-missioned" to extend God's kingdom (Matt. 28:18-20). Kingdom dominion comes first through worship, but at the benediction in the Lord's service, the royal priesthood of God is given God's blessing to go and serve in the world. The way of kingly dominion is the way of service: King Jesus knelt before His disciples and washed their feet (John 13:1-17).[66] In his book, *The Kingdom and the Power*, Peter Leithart rightfully notes:

> Christians exercise earthly dominion by loving their neighbors as themselves.... Service is not a *means* to earthly dominion. It is not as if we serve our neighbor so that we can gain sufficient influence and opportunity to dominate and exploit him. For the Christian, service is the *form* of dominion.

---

66. Leithart, *The Kingdom and the Power*, 181.

Through our callings, God enables us to serve our neighbors. Workers serve their employers and customers, parents serve their children, husbands and wives serve one another, employers serve their employees, and so on. As the apostle Paul said, all this is to serve God, for "whatever you do, do it heartily, as to the Lord and not to men" (Col. 3:23). When we serve in a Christ-like way, we become living icons of Christ for all the world to see. When we embody this kingdom love through service, the church becomes a colony of heaven on earth.

In the following chapters, we will focus on several areas of vocation through which Christians are called to serve the world and extend God's kingdom: singleness, marriage, parenting, and work.

Chapter 14

Singles: Serving in the Church Family

The vocation of celibacy, or singleness as it is sometimes called, is a complex topic to address in the church. Partly, this is because there are many types of singleness. Those who are single by divine calling, or gifting, are generally joyful and contented about being single. They embrace their status as an unmarried person as a gift. Burdened singles see their singleness as a problem that brings suffering. They have been deprived of a gift (marriage) they wish they had or still wait to receive. Some are not burdened by their singleness who should be. They have rejected God's vocation of marriage, often because they have fallen into sexual sin and have rejected the mature responsibilities of normal adulthood. These singles should be married by now. This category is far larger than it should be in our day. Disabled singles are single because of some kind of physical problem that prevents them from marriage. Seasonal singles see their singleness as a season that prepares them for marriage. Everyone who eventually gets married experienced a season of singleness on the way there. Previously-married single people are those who have been either widowed or divorced. In addition to these categories of singles, men and women experience singleness differently. Single parents have a different experience than singles who are not parents; and young and old experience their singleness differently.

Jesus and Paul on Singleness

In Matthew 19:1-12, Jesus is asked by the Pharisees whether it is lawful for a man to divorce his wife for any reason. Jesus's reply begins where we must always begin: with the creation order. God's original design was for one man and one woman to be joined together in marriage as a covenant bond for life. After the Fall, and with the coming of the law of Moses, divorce was permitted but only in cases of covenant breaking, such as adultery (Deut. 24:1ff) or extreme deprivation tantamount to desertion (Exod. 21:10-11). Jesus's disciples heard this and, living in a culture much like ours with liberal views of divorce, did not like the binding nature of marriage. They wanted loopholes that would allow them to justify exiting an unhappy marriage. In Matthew 19:10 they say, "If such is the case of the man with his wife, it is better not to marry." Jesus responds by pointing out that the single life has challenges as well. Marriage is for better or for worse, but singleness is for better or for worse, too. There are pains and pleasures that come with both states of life.

Jesus goes on to identify three legitimate categories of singles. First, there are those who are born eunuchs, who have some deformity (or lack of desire) that would prevent them from ever being able to marry. Second, there are those who are made eunuchs by men. Taken literally, this likely referred to men who served in royal courts who were made eunuchs so they could be trusted to oversee the royal women. More broadly and metaphorically, this is talking about anyone who is made a eunuch not so much by choice but by providential circumstances. The opportunity to marry has just never presented itself. They have been called to singleness, perhaps not so much by a clear sense of calling, but by default. Third, Jesus talks about voluntary eunuchs: those who willingly renounce marriage for the sake of the kingdom of heaven. They give up marriage with its blessings and benefits for the sake of kingdom service. They choose to serve God in a way they could not do as a person married with children. Their natural desires are subordinated to a greater end—God's kingdom. They are gifted in a way that enables them to live contentedly without marriage and sex. But that does not mean it is always easy.

For most singles who remain celibate (as they should), not being married is a costly deprivation. It means that certain needs and longings go unmet. The blessings and joys of marital and family life are sacrificed. This is a hard path, and Jesus acknowledges that it is difficult by saying not all can accept His teaching, but only those to whom the gift has been given (Matt. 19:12).

Some have said that singleness is "the gift no one wants," but this clearly is not Jesus's or Paul's attitude toward singleness. The Bible describes a certain kind of celibacy or singleness as a gift from God. The same kind of language that is used for singleness is used for other spiritual gifts. In 1 Corinthians 7:7, Paul says, "But each one has his own gift from God, one in this manner and another in that." In the context, Paul is dealing with problems with marriages within the Corinthian church. Paul affirms the goodness of marriage and sexuality within marriage. In effect, he issues an ultimatum: if you cannot live without sex, you must marry. If sexual temptation is a major issue for you, you do not have the gift of singleness and need to do what you can to marry (in the Lord, of course). In 1 Corinthians 7:9, Paul says, "but if they cannot exercise self-control, let them marry. For it is better to marry than to burn with passion." Sexual desire and temptation serve as a way to test whether or not one is gifted in this way. The obvious implication is that the vast majority of people need to marry.

Yet at the same time, Paul affirms the legitimacy of a single life *for those Christians who are called to it*. He even suggests that in certain ways and in certain circumstances (like the coming persecution he references later in 1 Corinthians 7), there are advantages to being a single Christian. As a single man himself, Paul says, "For I wish that all men were even as I myself."

It is useless to debate whether the married life or single life is spiritually superior. This is a debate that has gone on for much of church history, but it misses the point. The issue is not "Which kind of life is better?" The question is, "What kind of life has God called me to? How has He gifted me?" Those called to marry should marry. Those called to celibacy should embrace and use it. The test given in 1 Corinthians 7—whether or not one "burns" with sexual desire—is at least one way to decipher one's calling in this area. Sadly, when many people today say they want to remain single, they do not mean they want to be celibate. But for the believer a life of chaste singleness or a life of marital faithfulness are the only options.

Today, we have an odd situation in the church. Many Christians who *ought* to be getting married are not doing so. They are delaying marriage—and in doing so, they might be violating the seventh commandment according to the Westminster Larger Catechism, which forbids the "undue delay of marriage." In some cases, people are delaying marriage because they want to play. They want to avoid responsibility. They want to extend adolescence. In many cases, they are able to extend singleness not because of some gift but because they are sinning sexually, whether through pornography or with other persons. Sexual purity would put pressure on them to marry, but they release that pressure through unlawful sexual activity. People who should marry but put it off are causing themselves (and the person they should be married to) incalculable damage. If you are not gifted with celibacy—if you "burn" with passion and find sexual purity a struggle—then you should seek to get married as soon as you can do so responsibly. This is not to say marriage will solve all your problems with sexual temptation. But, as the *Book of Common Prayer*'s beautiful wedding liturgy acknowledges, one of the reasons God calls us into marriage is that it might be "a remedy against sin, and to avoid fornication; that such persons as have not the gift of continency might marry, and keep themselves undefiled members of Christ's body."

Many pastors are to blame for this situation with Christian young people because they either paint marriage in such a poor light and emphasize the challenges and difficulties of family life to the extent it appears unattractive, or they treat singleness as a neutral life choice rather than a divine calling that requires a special gift. Singleness becomes an option rather than a vocation as though it is something we choose for personal reasons (some of which might be selfish) rather than a status God assigns to a few for kingdom purposes. The reality is that the gift of celibacy is not common. For the vast majority of people, marriage is normative. Falling marriage rates (as we see in our culture right now) should greatly alarm us: something is going terribly wrong. Does God call some people to the celibate, single life? Yes, Matthew 19 and 1 Corinthians 7 are clear about that. Did God suddenly start giving more people this gift in the last few years? That is not likely. And that means something else is going on.

Some pastors today are also to blame for the singleness crisis in the church because they have warned that marriage (and family life) have become idols. It is certainly possible to make marriage into an idol, just like anything else in creation. There are no doubt some people who have done this, either by wanting to get married so much that they compromise morally, thinking it will secure marriage for them, or they place completely unrealistic expectations on their marriage, thus expecting things of their spouse (or children) that only God can give. But in general, marriage should be seen as natural and normative for most people. Desiring marriage is thus no more idolatrous than desiring food, clothes, and shelter. Sexual desire can be perverted, certainly, but it was part of God's good original design for men and women, and Scripture gives plenty of examples of what holy, redeemed sexual desire looks like (Prov. 5:17ff). Sexual desire should not be pathologized or demonized. It should be disciplined and channeled toward marriage where it can be satisfied in a glorious and guilt-free way (Prov. 5:19ff).

What Singles Teach the Church

What does faithful Christian singleness have to teach the church? How is singleness a sign of God's kingdom? There are at least three ways that God uses singleness to display His kingdom. First, singleness is an eschatological lifestyle, prophetic of what is to come. Second, singleness helps believers to remember that our ultimate and eschatological family is the church. Third, faithful Christian singleness witnesses against our contemporary idolatry of sexual autonomy. The biblical vision of singleness is about kingdom service and mission—and thus it is a form of fruitfulness. All three of these points taken together teach us the same thing: whether you are married or single, live for the glory of God.

Christian Singleness: An Eschatological Lifestyle

Human marriage is a temporary institution, belonging only to the pre-resurrection age. Thus, the Christian single lives a uniquely eschatological lifestyle. Eschatology has to do with the last things and especially with resurrection life. The single life is, to some degree, a prophetic preview of the life of the world to come. It is a reminder to all of us that our hope is not to be placed in the things of this world. It is a sign to us that the age to come has already broken into the present age (though not yet consummated).

This is what Jesus indicated in Matthew 22:30, where He says that marriage as we know it will not exist in the resurrection state. Marriage will not exist because God designed our marriages in history to be temporary symbols that will point us to the ultimate, eternal marriage of Christ and the church. At the end of history, when Christ returns, marriage will go away and the shadow will give way to reality. The only marriage left will be our corporate marriage to Christ. Those gifted with singleness already live that way in the present. They point us to that final union of the bride, the church, to her husband, the Lord Christ.

Singles remind us that eternal marriage is found in Christ and in the church. Jesus and Paul presented a view of singleness in their day that was radically counter-cultural. They lived in a culture that tended to make family life the highest created good. Virtually no other religion had ever validated an unmarried, chaste life in the way Jesus and Paul did. The thought that a single life could be a "kingdom life" was unheard of. In most ancient cultures, status was entirely linked to family. Your only possible legacy was tied to your physical heirs. The gospel proclaimed that believers could find true family in the church and the true meaning of marriage in union with Christ. Single Christians continually bear witness that our biological families are not ultimate in God's purposes. The church family is ultimate because the church is Christ's spouse. As part of the body of Christ, single men and women have the opportunity, through evangelism, to become spiritual mothers and fathers.

Christian Singleness:
Christ, Singleness, and the Family

Building on what we have just seen about singleness as an eschatological form of life, and closely related to it, is the ecclesial nature of the single life. The gift of singleness not only witnesses to resurrection life, it also points us to the centrality of the church as our true family. In this way, faithful and contended Christian singles can expose the idolatry of the family. While "idolatry of the family" is often invoked improperly, it is a possibility, as noted above. This is not a matter of loving fellow family members a great deal, but giving your family a different priority in your life than it has in God's purposes. In many traditional cultures, family was regarded as an absolute. Blood and marriage were everything. There was a duty to get married, and if you did not get married and have children, you were nobody. But then along came Jesus, who never got married or had children, yet lived the most significant life in history.

The apostles and the early Christians asserted that singleness, for those so gifted, was an equally valid form of life for those called to it. This was not totally unexpected, given prophecies of Messiah's kingdom. The prophecy of Jesus in Isaiah 53 says that He shall "see his offspring and be satisfied." For Jesus, this was not fulfilled through marriage and biological children. His offspring are His disciples. Single Christians belong to Jesus's family and can become fruitful themselves by making disciples.

Further, Isaiah 56:4-5 tells us:

> To the eunuchs who keep My Sabbaths, and choose what pleases Me, and hold fast My covenant, even to them I will give in My house and within My walls a place and a name better than that of sons and daughters; I will give them an everlasting name that shall not be cut off.

This was radical, set against the backdrop of the rest of the Old Testament. Old covenant Israel existed to bring the promised Messiah into the world. Israel kept the promised seed line going. This required marriage and procreation. Thus, barrenness was devastating in a way beyond the pain normally experienced by an infertile couple today. But now that has changed. Singles can have purpose, mission, and even family, through union with Christ and His church in a way that was not possible before.

Jesus inaugurated the kingdom, which ultimately takes precedence over the family. Family is no longer the central institution in society. The church is now seen to be the ultimate, central, eternal institution. As Christians, our primary goal is not building up our family names but building up Christ's name (though these can be connected and the former can serve the latter). We are still concerned with family life and physical multiplication, of course, but the Spiritual multiplication of disciples is central to the mission Christ has given the church. In the eyes of many in the ancient world, the church was the enemy of the family since the gospel sometimes divides families (cf. Matt. 10:16-23). The family could actually become a rival to Jesus and to His church. There are many people who have been forced to make a very difficult choice—family or Jesus? There are many who have been abandoned by their spouses and disinherited by their parents because they chose Jesus over family. But Jesus promised a new family to all who are forced to leave their old family behind (cf. Matt. 19:29).

Jesus prioritized Himself over our biological families. In Mark 3:34-35, Jesus redefined the family around Himself: "Here are My mother and My brothers! For whoever does the will of God is My brother and My sister and mother." He said, "let the dead bury their dead" (Luke 9:60). The family is dead to Jesus unless it is remade and enlivened in Him through baptism and faith. The unmarried person must remember that no matter how great a gift from God a spouse would be, a spouse would not meet his or her deepest needs. Having singles who are gifted to live fulfilled, satisfied, joyful, contented lives in our midst is a reminder to married Christians that they should not look at their families for ultimate fulfillment and satisfaction. One reason many married people become bitter and disappointed is because they are looking to their familial relationships for ultimate meaning rather than to Christ. The family is not designed to carry those burdens and fulfill those expectations. Only Christ can do that for us.

Paul was a single man but described his ministry in fatherly and even motherly terms. Consider 1 Corinthians 4:15: "For though you might have ten thousand instructors in Christ, yet you do not have many fathers; for in Christ Jesus I have begotten you through the gospel." He described himself as a mother in labor, giving birth to the Galatian church (Gal. 4:19). Writing to the Thessalonians, he says, "we were gentle among you, just as a nursing mother cherishes her own children" (1 Thess. 2:7). Four verses later, Paul changed the language from that of a mother to that of a father: "as you know how we exhorted, and comforted, and charged every one of you, as a father does his own children." Paul described himself as a mother and a father in the church, and there are many single Christians who are mothers and fathers in the church today. Isaiah 54:1 says,

> "Sing, O barren, you who have not borne! Break forth into singing, and cry aloud, you who have not labored with child! For more are the children of the desolate than the children of the married woman," says the LORD.

How can the barren woman have more children than the married woman? The answer is that the family has been re-defined in Christ. Involvement in the mission of the church—evangelism and discipleship—is an opportunity for singles to be fruitful and multiply. (This also is true for married couples who are unable to have biological children.)

None of this disparages the natural family. Even if the supernatural family of the church is more ultimate in the purposes of God, the natural family is crucial to God's work in the world. The terms of the creation mandate to be fruitful and multiply still stand. Most people do have a duty to marry and have children. There will not be spiritual disciples unless there are natural children. The Great Commission has not replaced the creation mandate, but presupposes it. The point here is that singles are not excluded from the great work God is doing in the world. They have a role to play in the ongoing mission and growth of the church even though they do not have physical children.

Christian Singleness: Against the Contemporary Idolatry of Sexual Autonomy

Christian singleness witnesses against several contemporary idolatries, especially the desire for sexual autonomy. Traditional societies perhaps led people to overvalue marriage and family, but in our contemporary culture we have a tendency to undervalue marriage and over-value personal freedom. Contemporary culture views singleness as a time to live for yourself. This is an utterly false view of singleness. The gift of singleness, for however long someone has it, is not the absence of a spouse, but it is the presence of Christ with the single Christian to carry forward the mission of the church in a special way.

Singleness, whether as a permanent or temporary state, can be used for kingdom purposes. But there is something else to note. For some in our day, sexual identity has become the lens through which they view themselves and the whole of life. In our culture, one's sexual desires, distorted from God's design in myriad ways, have become the most important thing about you. But in a culture that has made sex the dominant aspect of human life, what happens to the person who is celibate? That person must be less than fully human in the eyes of the world. In this situation, the faithful, chaste Christian single bears witness against our culture's idolatry of sex. Christian singles demonstrate it is possible to live a fulfilled and fully human life as a chaste person. In this context, the celibate Christian becomes an important counter-cultural member of the church. The celibate Christian challenges and subverts the most central and powerful idol in our culture.

There is a movement within the church, attempting to Christianize the worldly notion of sexual identity. They argue that the phenomenon of persistent sexual desires are so central to their being that it is a part of their identity.[67] These groups will declare that you can be a "gay Christian" so long as you remain celibate. Does this fit with Jesus's teaching and the rest of Scripture? This movement misses the mark in several ways. First, illicit sexual desires, which Paul calls "vile passions" in Romans 1, are incompatible with the Christian life and to be repented of. Second, throughout the New Testament, Christians are called saints and holy ones. It is true that Christians can struggle with same-sex attraction even as they struggle with a multitude of other sins. But this struggle is not so much a part of the Christian's identity as it is the *contradiction* of his true identity. We find our identity as saints in union with Christ. Last,

---

67. Wesley Hill, quoted in Denny Burk and Rosaria Butterfield, "*Learning to Hate Our Sin without Hating Ourselves*," (July 4, 2018), https://www.thepublicdiscourse.com/2018/07/22066/. Hill says, "Being gay colors everything about me, even though I am celibate…. Being gay is, for me, as much a sensibility as anything else: a heightened sensitivity to and passion for same-sex beauty that helps determine the kind of conversations I have, which people I'm drawn to spend time with, what novels and poems and films I enjoy, the particular visual art I appreciate, and also, I think, the kind of friendships I pursue and try to strengthen. I don't imagine I would have invested half as much effort in loving my male friends, and making sacrifices of time, energy, and even money on their behalf, if I weren't gay. My sexuality, my basic erotic orientation to the world, is inescapably intertwined with how I go about finding and keeping friends."

Jesus's teaching on those who are eunuchs for the kingdom shows their purpose is to display that His church is our true family, even more important than any other tribe or group we can belong to. But this "gay Christian" movement seeks to have one foot in the LGBTQ+ tribe and one foot in the church. A community formed around sin, temptation, and sinful desires is never really a model situation. In reality, the LGBTQ+ tribe is a rival and counterfeit of the true and faithful community—the church. Christians cannot have one foot in that community any more than they could have one foot in the Islamic community and the other in the church, or one foot in Mormonism and the other in the church.

Contented Christian singleness, or celibacy, is for those who are not burning with passion, as Paul describes in 1 Corinthians 7. To live in such a manner is to display to the world that the gospel and the kingdom—not one's sexual desires—are paramount.

Singles in the Church: Community, Discipleship, and Mission

Singleness clearly bears witness to the church as God's new and true family. The church must be a place that nurtures singles either by preparing them for marriage and encouraging them to pursue marriage, or by giving them the family and community life they need as a celibate person. To be single does not mean you are alone. Singleness need not be solitariness. Christian singles are part of the covenant community and should not be floating around without attachments, commitments, or family-like connections.

This is especially true of older singles, such as widows and widowers.

In a healthy church, singles will be included in warm fellowship and friendship throughout the life of the church. They will be given opportunities to use their singleness to serve. They will not be sequestered from the rest of the church as part of a singles' group, but will be mixed in with the rest of the body. There are many churches today that design everything around the family. In light of 1 Corinthians 7, we can see that churches must not be so centered on family that singles are completely marginalized. What if the apostle Paul was a member of your church? Where would he fit in as a single man? Churches must find ways to include and involve singles. Remember, some singles will be widows and justly divorced persons. There must be a place for them, too.

Singles need encouragement with the inevitable periods of loneliness that come. We should encourage singles to remember that God's Son was single throughout His earthly life and that He can sympathize with singles. He has experienced an even greater loneliness than anyone else when He died on the cross. Singles who want and need to be married should not live life only waiting for marriage, but should do something with their lives in the meantime, serving God and neighbor with their gifts. Singles should remember that God promises to compensate them for whatever earthly blessings are withheld from them if they serve Him faithfully and fruitfully. For example, if you give up wealth to serve the kingdom of God, then God becomes your wealth. If you give up a potential spouse and children in order to serve God, then all these sacrifices are paid back a hundred fold (Matt. 19:29).

Singles should remember that as long as they are fixated on their singleness, they are focused on themselves. It is easy to get curved inward, which inevitably leads to misery. In 1 Corinthians 7, Paul is calling singles to live outward facing, mission-oriented lives. While the married have many blessings that singles do not have, singles have many blessings that the married do not have. The single person has much more flexibility with time and money, whereas the married person has more worldly cares. There are more mouths to feed, more people to consider and factor in whenever making a decision: life is simply more complicated. The single person is less vulnerable to persecution.

Singles must remember that they do have a wedding day coming. The groom has proposed, and as a part of the bride of Christ, they will be a part of the happiest marriage the cosmos has ever known. This will be the only marriage that will exist when Jesus returns in the fullness of His glory. As a single, your calling now is to prepare to meet Him by serving Him faithfully.

Chapter 15

Marriage: A Picture
of Christ and the Church

The story of the Bible begins and ends with a wedding. All history is enclosed by two wedding celebrations. At the beginning, in the book of Genesis, Adam and his bride were joined together in holy matrimony. At the end, in the book of Revelation, it will be the marriage supper of the Lamb, as the New Jerusalem descends from heaven. History ends with Christ consummating His marriage to His bride as He becomes one with His church in the fullest way. Contrary to the feminist assertion, the future is not female, but the future is most certainly marital, as it ends with a covenant union of groom and bridegroom.

History does not end with a whimper or a bang but with the sound of wedding bells and the laughter of a wedding feast. All throughout Scripture, a wedding feast is used to image the kingdom of God. Human marriage is celebrated in the Bible because it symbolizes what history is all about. God's plan for the whole creation can be summed up in marriage. Thus, marriage is of the utmost importance and if we do not understand what marriage is designed to be, we will struggle to understand the gospel since the gospel takes marital shape.

The Scriptures teach that marriage is the best symbol we have in the creation and in history of what the kingdom of God is all about. Christ is the king, the church His queen, and together they rule creation. Every marriage is a miniature picture of that kingdom. The husband is the king, the wife is his queen and together they rule their domain, the home. His love for her is to mimic and picture Christ's love for His bride. Her reverence for him is to mimic and picture the way the church submits to Christ. The kingdom-household they build together extends the kingdom-household of Christ.

Knowing that marriage pictures the Gospel gives marriage great honor, value, worth, and beauty. At the same time, knowing that marriage is only a picture, reminds us that there is something greater than marriage. In the resurrection, our marriages will fall aside to make room for the one marriage that will endure for all eternity, the marriage of Christ and His bride. What we must know is that the fundamental purpose of marriage is gospel embodiment, or gospel symbolism. Everything else that the Bible wants us to know about marriage flows out of this foundational purpose. Marriage exists to point to a greater reality. Symbolism is not added to marriage; it is the heart and ground of marriage.

Note how different this view of marriage is from what is typically found in our culture. Today, marriage is seen as a social construct, a human invention that is malleable. We can change the permanence of the institution with no-fault divorce laws. We can change the sex of the participants to create "same-sex marriage." We can change the numbers of participants, denying monogamy. We can change the core of what marriage is about by permitting sex outside of marriage. But if marriage is recognized as a divinely ordained, divinely designed institution, it has certain objective features. Denying these features will only hurt those who rebel against the way God made the world.

Because God designed marriage to symbolize the relationship of Christ and the church, deviations from God's instructions for husbands and wives end up "preaching" a false gospel. It is crucial for Christian marriages to showcase the Christ and church relationship by how husbands and wives relate. The gospel is a love story and every marriage should echo that love story, as husbands take their cues from Christ and wives take their cues from the church.

Men and Women: Equal, but Different by Design

Marriage brings together a man and a woman. The man and woman are, in a fundamental way, equals. They equally share in the image of God and the creation mandate. They have equal worth and value. They have equally important roles to play. They are equally fallen into sin, in that they are dead in sins and trespasses, and, if they are believers, they are equal heirs of eternal life in Christ. But while the man and woman are equal in these ways, they are unequal in others. They have different roles to play in the marriage relationship. To be sure, it makes no sense biblically to talk about whose role is better or worse, harder or easier. There should not be any doubt that the difficulties and blessings of the husband's role and the wife's role are also equal. Each role has unique benefits and burdens. It is useless to talk about whether it is more difficult to be the head or the body, the leader or the follower, in the marriage. But in the modern world, a false notion of equality has led many to think the differences between the man and woman must be flattened out. The only way to have equality is if the man and woman are interchangeable pieces. This is false, and such an understanding will corrupt our view of marriage. The truth is that God ordained the equal partners in the marriage to exist in a hierarchy. Marriage is not a democracy, and a democracy of two is impossible anyway.

Marriage has a God-given structure in which a husband's glory is found in sacrificial headship and the woman's glory is found in submitting to that headship as a helper. It may seem offensive to modern ears to describe a wife as a "helper," but in Scripture "helper" is used most often to describe God. This means that, properly understood and applied, there is nothing degrading or second-best about the role of helper. It is a God-like role to be a helper. If the wife is going to help at all, she is going to help from a position of strength. It is clear that Adam has certain deficiencies and is not a self-sufficient being. He has built-in designed deficiencies that need to be met by the strengths of a woman. She can only be a helper if she can do things that he cannot. She can only be a helper if she has insights and perspectives on reality that Adam lacks. The masculine and the feminine need one another and are drawn to one another.

The different roles assigned to the man and the woman in marriage are not arbitrary but are rooted in our creation design. Scripture shows us there are deep differences in men and women, going back to the way the man and woman were created. The man is to be the protector and provider. His wife is his glory and his helper. The man is made from the earth and is oriented to the earth and therefore to dominion over the earth. The woman is made from the man and is therefore oriented toward the man and relationships.

Social and scientific studies back up these generalizations, but most of us are familiar with them from daily life. Boys like to play with things—guns and trucks. Girls like to play with dolls. This is not simply due to nurture. It is hardwired into us by nature. Men's bodies are designed for conquering created reality. Women's bodies are designed for nurturing children. Obviously there is more to manhood and womanhood than these realities. We should not be reductionistic as if persons were nothing more than their core roles. But these roles do matter because they derive from and flow out of our creational design.

While it is clear that the roles which God has assigned men and women to play are not arbitrary, but are based on our natural, creational design, that does always mean that these roles will be easy for us to fill. After all, we are now fallen, and sin has corrupted our ability to fulfill God's design. But growing into our understanding of what God calls us to be and do can help. The man is the head of the marriage because he was made for headship. The woman is called to be in submission to her husband because she was designed to respond to masculine leadership and to help him.

But here is the problem: In the modern world, God has been rejected and so we have begun to lose touch with God's design. Today, it is common to view gender and sex as completely fluid. There are no givens. Everything is malleable. Men and women can be whatever they feel like being. According to the reigning transgender ideology, a man can even turn himself into a woman and a woman into a man. And because sex and gender are fluid in the modern world, marriage must be fluid too. What does the Bible say about this?

Biblically, just as men and women have God-given natures and God-given design, so marriage is a relationship with certain objective features. Marriage is not anything we want it to be. It is what God created it to be. And we should desire for our society to adhere to God's norms for marriage as much as possible, for the good of all. Deviations from God's design bring pain and suffering because when we fight the way God made the world, we always lose.

The Covenant of Marriage

Biblically, marriage between a man and a woman can appropriately and properly be described as a covenant (Mal. 2:14). In Scripture, a covenant is a defined and structured relationship with fixed promises, obligations, and roles. To say that marriage is a covenant is to say that marriage is a promise made in public, with attendant blessings for keeping the covenant and curses for breaking the covenant.

Marriage is fundamentally not about feelings or self-fulfillment. The traditional Christian wedding service bears out these truths in the vows. The bride and groom do not say touchy-feely romantic things to one another in their wedding service. They do not express their feelings in that moment because those feelings will fluctuate over time. Rather, they make promises to one another that commit them to act lovingly into the future, for as long as they live and no matter how they feel in any given moment. They are bound together by the promises they make; marriage hangs by a promise. Dietrich Bonhoeffer said:

> Marriage is more than your love for each other. . . . In your love you see only the heaven of your own happiness, but in marriage you are placed at a post of responsibility towards the world and mankind. Your love is your own private possession, but marriage is more than something personal—it is a status, and office. . . .

> As you gave the ring to one another and have now received it a second time from the hand of the pastor, so love comes from you, but marriage from above, from God. As high as God is above man, so high are the sanctity, the rights, and the promise of love. It is not your love that sustains the marriage, but from now on, the marriage that sustains your love.[68]

---

68. Dietrich Bonhoeffer, *Letters and Papers from Prison*, ed. Eberhard Bethge (New York: Macmillan, 1967), 27, quoted in John Piper, *This Momentary Marriage* (Wheaton, Illinois: Crossway Books), 15, 19.

It is not your love that holds the covenant intact. It is the covenant that holds your love together. Certainly, marital love should ordinarily include romantic and affectionate feelings between the husband and wife, but for most couples there is some ebb and flow in feelings of affection. Our feelings are not a trustworthy guide in marriage. Feelings are not stable enough or reliable enough foundation to build a marriage upon. Marriage obligates you to act in a loving way toward your spouse, whether you feel like it or not. Of course, acting in a loving way toward your spouse when feelings have waned can actually rekindle feelings. When a couple gets married, each spouse makes a promise to be there for the other physically, emotionally, spiritually, socially, sexually, and in every way. Remember that love, biblically defined, includes feelings of affection in its fullest form, but it is fundamentally a matter of treating others according to God's Word.

The covenantal view of marriage, with marriage based on a promise, can be contrasted with the predominant view in our society, which is a consumerist view of marriage. In the consumerist view of marriage, people approach the relationship as though it were some kind of commodity that exists for their personal happiness and self-fulfillment. If you take this attitude with you into your marriage, you will be looking for a relationship in which you can get more than you have to give. You want a good deal, after all. You are going to want all of the other person, without having to give yourself up. You will use the other person as an object, as a means to fulfilling your own desires and wants. In this sort of marriage, you essentially say to the other, "I will be a good spouse and do what you want me to do, to the extent that you are being good to me and do what I expect you to do." This kind of approach is a marriage killer and this is why 50 percent of marriages in our society fail. If the purpose of marriage is happiness, why not leave when you are no longer happy—or when you find someone else who you think can make you even happier? The only way to make marriage work is to commit yourself to keeping covenant with your spouse no matter what. You must commit yourself to being a promise keeper even when, indeed especially when, your spouse disappoints you or frustrates you.[69]

If you see marriage as a covenant that exists for the purpose of symbolizing and embodying the Gospel in the world, you will be who God calls you to be within the marriage whether your spouse is or not. The covenant will hold your marriage together even when your romantic feelings or self-fulfillment are not there. Martin Luther described marriage as a school for character, an arena for sanctification and discipleship. He understood that in marriage we are called to do the right thing, even when we do not feel like it. Marriage requires us to habituate ourselves to do our duty without regard for our personal feelings. He knew this was not easy: "It takes courage to enter both marriage and tournaments." By tournaments, he was referring to medieval jousting in which two combatants on horseback would drive at each other with lances. Of course, marriage at its best will generally be a happy and fulfilling relationship. But we must not make personal happiness and fulfillment the main purpose of marriage. Otherwise, we come to view

---

69. Of course, there are Biblical grounds for divorce, but it is beyond our purpose to discuss them here.

our unhappiness as a reason for getting out of the marriage. More is at stake in your marriage than just whether or not your needs get met. When you understand your marriage in light of the gospel, you see that the whole point of your marriage is not your self-fulfillment, but demonstrating and building the kingdom of God. Of course, this includes the process of our own sanctification. Your spouse's failings provide an opportunity for you to grow in Christ-like grace. You love and honor the other unconditionally.

In our day, faithful Christian marriages and happy, holy families might be one of the most powerful arguments for the gospel we can offer. As family life disintegrates, society itself unravels. Progressivism, feminism, socialism, and other idolatrous "-isms" have made people lonely and miserable. We are now isolated atoms, and the secular worldview offers no way to bond us together. Sure, people might use one another for sexual pleasure, but there is no lasting happiness in that. A marriage where the husband and wife know and embrace their distinctive roles, where the man and woman seek to please one another as a way of pleasing God, where sacrificial love reigns, where all sexual desire is focused on one's spouse—that kind of life is a compelling apologetic for the gospel because only the gospel can create that kind of life.

The Marriage Crisis

Only the church can lead the culture in recovering God-given, God-ordained, God-designed archetypes for the masculine and feminine. The modern West has been captivated by a false notion of equality that would make men and women androgynous interchangeable pieces. But this kind of equality kills romance. It destroys the sexual division of labor that is necessary for civilization and human thriving. It leaves us confused and directionless, without a clear sense of what our duties and responsibilities are. When a man and woman come together in the covenant of marriage in the way God designed, his masculinity symbolizes the initiative, responsibility, authority, and love of Christ. The wife's responsiveness, receptivity, respect, and submission symbolizes the calling of the church. She is the garden, the field, the earth. He is the water from above that nourishes her, the farmer who cultivates her, and together they become fruitful. He will give himself to her. She will receive from him, and in receiving, she gives herself to him, just in a different way. No, there is not equality by the world's standard or understanding, but there is most certainly mutuality. And that should be the goal. In a Christian marriage, the focus is not on "keeping everything equal," as that leads to scorekeeping and rivalry, but on doing what God has called each to do within the marriage covenant.

In our day, it is common to point out that there is a crisis of masculinity. Some have suggested that all forms of masculinity are toxic. Others push back with a kind of hyper-masculinity that obviously caricatures what God calls men to be. The key is to recover a fully biblical, Jesus-shaped vision of masculinity—a man who combines the best of so-called "alpha male" and "beta male" qualities: he is tough and tender, confident and humble, strong and kind, decisive yet deliberate, calm yet passionate. Like Jesus, he is both lion and lamb, a kingly ruler who lays down his life for others. That's true masculinity. Masculinity requires discipline, especially sexual self-control. Men must know their weaknesses and guard themselves accordingly.

But while the crisis of masculinity is readily seen by many, the equally dire crisis of femininity has not gotten similar attention. And yet, women are just as confused about womanhood as men are by manhood. This is to be expected, given that men and women are really all in the same boat. We will sink or swim together. It is impossible for one sex to flourish while the other sex flounders. Women, like men, face a dizzying array of voices telling them what they ought to be. As with manhood, it is crucial to avoid caricatures. While femininity is especially focused on a woman's highly relational nurturing qualities, biblical models of womanhood are not just frilly, they can also be fierce. Mary nurtured baby Jesus, but she also wrote the stinging words of the Magnificat (Luke 1-2). Jael was obviously a homemaker, but she could turn her domestic tools into weapons when needed (Judg. 4). Beware of all cardboard cutout versions of femininity. The biblical reality is more complex.

Completion within Marriage

The husband's calling is to sacrifice for his wife. The wife's calling is to give her husband something worth sacrificing for. At least, that is one way to look at what should happen in marriage. Marriage is a dance of headship and submission, in which one leads and the other follows. The one who leads has one type of glory. The one who follows another type of glory. The marriage thrives because there is synergy between the man's masculine energy and woman's feminine energy. Together, they are able to accomplish things they never could on their own. This is God's design—a marriage that enables the man and the woman to thrive.

It is really important that we derive our understanding of marriage from creation, before the Fall of man into sin. (Starting with creation rather than the Fall is a theme we have highlighted elsewhere in this book.) Marriage is clearly not man's invention, but is God's institution. God designed marriage to be an exclusive covenantal relationship between one man and one woman who are joined together in a one-flesh partnership for life. As the man and woman build their kingdom together, they extend God's kingdom in the world.

In God's created order, men and women are different from one another in ways that ultimately complement and complete one another. When we talk about the differences between men and women, we are not describing how one sex is better or worse than the other. The sexes are equal, yet different. The Bible confirms an intrinsic equality between men and women. Men and women are equal in worth and significance, in creation and redemption. Even though our callings and our orientations are diverse, there is this basic equality. This equality and diversity is intended by God to be a reflection of the economic Trinity. The Father and the Son and the Holy Spirit are equally God, but they have different roles to play in the economy of redemption. The incarnate Son submits to the Father, but if this leads us to think He is in essence inferior to the Father, we are heretical. Likewise, if we say that because Paul tells wives to submit to their husbands, that this must mean they are inferior, our view of marriage will embody a Trinitarian heresy (See 1 Cor. 11:3.). Both men and women are made in God's image, but we image God in different ways. Maleness and femaleness are not just biological realities, but are a matter of essence. It is not as though we have androgynous souls placed into gendered bodies. A person is either male or female all the way down to the very deepest depths of his or her being. These differences mean that gender is basic to human existence and is relevant to everything we do. They are irreducible. Even in the resurrection, we will still be male or female. Men and women are not interchangeable. The differences between the sexes did not come into the world with the Fall of man into sin, but are built into creation by God from the beginning. We see this in the creation account in Genesis 1:27, "God created man in His own image; in the image of God He created him; male and female He created them."

God gave the whole human race, men and women, a task in the beginning. This job description is summed up with a handful of verbs in Genesis 1:26-28: man is made to *have dominion* over the earth, to *subdue* and *rule* the earth, and to *be fruitful* and *multiply* and *fill* the earth. This is known as the creation mandate. It basically breaks down into two components: ruling and multiplying. Man is to build a God-glorifying civilization out of the raw materials of the earth, and through having children, he is to extend that civilization to the ends of the earth.

Man: On A Mission

Men and women are different in their being and in their roles. But their being and their roles were meant to mesh together. Men, in general, are oriented toward work and subduing the earth, toward dominion. This involves risk-taking and accomplishing a mission. Men tend to be goal and task oriented. Generally, women are more orient-ed toward relationships; they tend to be more nurturing, more agreeable, and more risk-averse than men.

This is overly simple and a generalization, but it cap-tures something important about the sexual division of labor God has built into the human race: Men produce, women reproduce. Men build civilizations, women make people. Obviously accomplishing any of these things re-quires teamwork and cooperation of men and women with each other, especially through the covenant of marriage. But each sex has a particular emphasis and it is important to understand what it is. We are all familiar with this. For example, if a bunch of guys get together to watch a movie, it is likely going to feature a man (or group of men) on a mission and will involve blowing up lots of things. The movie's protagonist may be defeating the bad guy or res-cuing the damsel in distress, or both, but the storyline is going to be mission and goal-oriented. When a group of women get together to watch a movie, they are likely to watch a "chick flick"—a movie in which the guy/girl re-lationship is the heart of the plot. These preferences (even if influenced by sin) reveal something about who we are designed to be as men and women.

Camille Paglia, a lesbian feminist who occasionally offers strong insights, once said, "If civilization had been left in female hands we would still be living in grass huts." More fully, she explains why even the most committed feminist should recognize the importance of men in build-ing and maintaining civilization:

History must be seen clearly and fairly: obstructive traditions arose not from men's hatred or enslavement of women but from the natural division of labor that had developed over thousands of years during the agrarian period and that once immensely benefited and protected women, permitting them to remain at the hearth to care for helpless infants and children. Over the past century, it was labor-saving appliances, invented by men and spread by capitalism, that liberated women from daily drudgery…. After the next inevitable apocalypse, men will be desperately needed again! Oh, sure, there will be the odd gun-toting Amazonian survivalist gal, who can rustle game out of the bush and feed her flock, but most women and children will be expecting men to scrounge for food and water and to defend the home turf. Indeed, men are absolutely indispensable right now, invisible as it is to most feminists, who seem blind to the infrastructure that makes their own work lives possible. It is overwhelmingly men who do the dirty, dangerous work of building roads, pouring concrete, laying bricks, tarring roofs, hanging electric wires, excavating natural gas and sewage lines, cutting and clearing trees, and bulldozing the landscape for housing developments. It is men who heft and weld the giant steel beams that frame our office buildings, and it is men who do the hair-raising work of insetting and sealing the finely tempered plate-glass windows of skyscrapers fifty stories tall.

Every day along the Delaware River in Philadelphia, one can watch the passage of vast oil tankers and towering cargo ships arriving from all over the world. These stately colossi are loaded, steered and off-loaded by *men*. The modern economy, with its vast production and distribution network, is a male epic, in which women have found a productive role —but women were not its author. Surely, modern women are strong enough now to give credit where credit is due![70]

As Doug Wilson has said, civilization is built by men with mouths to feed. Men were designed to build, to explore, to invent, to conquer, to provide, to protect. It is true that men make more money than women—a fact offensive to many feminists.[71] But women spend more household income than men. The reasons are not hard to figure: Men work to provide, while women are more devoted to caring for the household. Accordingly, most advertising is

---

70. Camille Paglia, "It's a Man's World, and It Always Will Be," *Time*, December 16, 2013, http://ideas.time.com/2013/12/16/its-a-mans-world-and-it-always-will-be/

71. Diana Furchtgott-Roth, "The Gender Wage Gap Is a Myth," Manhattan Institute, (July 26, 2012), https://www.manhattan-institute.org/html/gender-wage-gap-myth-3786.html. When men and women do the same job with the same experience and qualifications, studies show they make about the same amount. It is true that men make more money overall, but that is because men and women make different career and life decisions. For example, men tend to pursue more demanding fields with longer hours while women tend to choose more family-friendly and nurturing-oriented professions.

directed toward women, who account for 85 percent of all purchases, spending some $5 trillion, more than half the U.S. GDP. Men have often paid a great price in their pursuit of economic provision for the women and children they love. They die earlier, often from overwork, and many more men than women die or get injured on the job (e.g., over 90 percent of work related deaths happen to men).[72] Men thrive most when they are clearly needed. Men rise to the occasion when there is a clear need for their masculine qualities (like storming the beaches at Normandy). But a society that treats men as unnecessary or expendable, or a society full of "strong, independent women" who say they do not need a man any more than a fish needs a bicycle (as one feminist put it), or a society that brands conventional male qualities as "toxic," will be full of disengaged, disconnected men. This is what we are seeing today: Mission-less men become a scourge to society. Their masculine energy becomes predatory rather than productive.

When it comes to understanding manhood, sometimes a distinction is made between "being a good man" and "being good at being a man." Being a good man has to do with character—a man must have traits such as integrity, diligence, faithfulness, purity, gentleness, discipline, and humility. Being good at being a man has to do with competence—a man must be confident, skilled, strong (whether intellectually or physically), decisive, able to lead, possessing gravitas, and so on.

---

72. Gray Babbs, "Men Hard at Work," Public Health Post, June 9, 2020, https://www.publichealthpost.org/databyte/men-hard-at-work/.

In our day, many men feel as if they must choose between Christianity and masculinity. They can either be good men or be good at being men, but not both. Some of this is due to caricatures of masculinity that have infiltrated the church. The good man, many think, is mousy, while the man good at being a man is macho. But this is wrong on both counts. The key is to integrate virtue with virility. Men maximize their dominion when they have high character and well-developed competencies. These are the kinds of men who can do what men are designed to do—build a God-glorifying civilization that ensconces women and children. And frankly, these are the kinds of men women are most attracted to. By God's design, women are drawn to men who demonstrate genuine masculinity. Good character is essential, but purpose and strength (manifested in the ability to protect and provide, thus fulfilling the part of the creation mandate that especially belongs to them) is essential in men. Women do not go looking for future husbands in unemployment lines. Women want a man who can bear the load of protection and provision.

Woman: Nurturing Life-Giver

By contrast, women are life-givers and nurturers. Women have been given the incomparable privilege of bringing new life into the world, and every healthy society is designed around this fact. This is central to the glory of femininity: A woman can actually contain another human inside her body. She can keep another human alive with her body. Women may largely operate in the background instead of the foreground of history. But women still shape history. "The hand that rocks the cradle rules the world," as the saying goes. Women's contributions can go far beyond having babies, but nurturing children is the most uniquely distinctive feminine task women undertake. If men are primarily oriented toward dominion, women are primarily oriented toward multiplication. In Genesis 3, the man is cursed in the realm of work. Thorns and thistles will get in the way of his labor as he seeks to make provision for his family (Gen. 3:18). The woman is cursed in her primary domain and role, that of child-bearing and child-rearing (Gen. 3:16). The curses are gender specific and hit each sex precisely in that area where each sex is called to contribute most fully to the fulfillment of the creation mandate.

Femininity reaches its fullest expression in maternity. Motherhood, like fatherhood, is not limited to biology. There are ways for women who cannot have children of their own to become "spiritual mothers." But physical motherhood helps us understand spiritual motherhood. Women have the great privilege of bringing new life into the world. But in our day motherhood is despised by many. Many have pointed out the problems of widespread fatherlessness and the resultant father hunger. And, indeed, many social ills have fatherlessness as the common denominator. But mother hunger has become a reality as well. Many mothers have abdicated their role as the nurturers of children and have instead chosen to pursue a career. There is nothing inherently wrong with a woman working outside the home. Women can and should use the full range of their gifts. But women are instructed to be anchored to the home (cf. Tit. 2:3-5). And when they have small children, if at all possible, moms should devote as much time and energy as possible to caring for those children. There is no substitute for a mother's care and attention. Sadly, many mothers want to do anything and everything except spend time with their children. Secular social worker Erika Komisar's book, *Being There*, makes many interesting claims about the importance of motherhood, especially during the early years of a child's life.[73] While she gets some key things wrong, she also gets a lot right. Relying on science, sociology, psychology, and a good deal of common sense, she argues that mothers need to be fully devoted to their children for at least the first thousand days of the child's life. I would lengthen that time considerably, if possible. But the main argument that Komisar makes is that motherhood (at least when children are young) cannot be outsourced or easily combined with other vocations. It requires undistracted devotion to the child's nurture and development.

The results speak for themselves, as Komisar demonstrates. Children who get more time with mom in those early, foundational years have better relational bonding abilities, fewer behavioral issues (because moms will discipline in ways daycare workers will not and cannot), fewer emotional issues, fewer neuroses, and are overall healthier and better equipped to grow into mature, productive adults. In short, *motherhood matters*. No daycare worker can do what moms do. Even close relatives are not the same as mom. *And the reality is that both mother and child know this.* The mother knows this, even though the feminist environment in which we all live pressures her to deny it and to justify outsourcing the nurture and care of her child so she can

---

73. Erika Komisar, *Being There: Why Prioritizing Motherhood in the First Three Years Matters* (New York: TarcherPerigee, 2017).

get back to the office. The child (even as an infant) knows when he is with a stranger rather than with mom, and as Komisar shows, this can cause irreparable harm and trauma to the child if it goes on too long or happens too regularly. Obviously not all moms get to be with their children, and God can compensate for that. But in a culture that pushes women toward a focus on career over family, it is up to the church to push back by giving mothers their due.

Of course, motherhood is not the only controversial aspect of the woman's calling in today's world. Modern culture is especially offended by the Biblical teaching that wives should submit to their husbands (Eph. 5:22, 24; Col. 3:18; 1 Pet. 3:5-6). The fundamental issue here is not simply whether a wife trusts her husband enough to submit to him (though that is a crucial issue). The real question is whether or not the wife trusts God's design for her marriage. Does God know what He is talking about or not? Obviously, since this submission is in the Lord, it is qualified. No human authority in family, church, or state is absolute. Wives should never follow their husbands into sin. And husbands who commit adultery or act abusively violate the terms of the covenant and forfeit their right to rule their homes. Further, men are nowhere told to force their wives into submission. They can teach their wives to submit to them as part of "cleansing her by the washing of water with the Word" (Eph. 5:26). This is one way he can be her spiritual leader. But her submission is a voluntary act on her part. Submission is virtuous only if it is freely chosen.

Completion

Husbands should remember that in the beginning it was "not good" for man to be alone. He has been given his wife by God as a companion and helper. Note that even though Adam had perfect fellowship with Father, Son, and Spirit, he was still lacking something that only a woman could provide. Adam was lonely, in need of a companion, and alone, in need of a helper. The woman met both needs. Further, the creation of the woman is the apex of the creation story. God saved his most glorious creation for last (cf. 1 Cor. 11:7). In the woman, the man found a God-given helper perfectly suited to him. They would fit together perfectly and become one. She was made for him. They were made for relationship with each other. Their relationship (a paradigm of all subsequent marriages) would be the core of human life, enabling humanity to fulfill God's purpose as revealed in the creation mandate. The two of them share one purpose, one mission, one life.

The woman can only complete the man because she is equal to him, bearing the same imprint of the divine image, while also being different from him, with different qualities, different proclivities, and a different role to play in the great drama of history. We see this filled out in later Scripture. Two examples will suffice.

First, the woman is identified with wisdom in the book of Proverbs. Indeed, the whole book of Proverbs is a kind of courtship story, with the young man urged to eschew Harlot Folly (despite her attempts to seduce him) and pursue Lady Wisdom. The book ends with the young man making Lady Wisdom his wife, as depicted in the virtuous wife of Proverbs 31. It is true that the man is the head of his wife and indeed the whole household. It is true that he is the final earthly authority in the home. It is true that he is fully and finally responsible for the household. This is why God came to Adam first in Genesis 3, calling on him to give an account. But precisely because the man is responsible to rule his home in wisdom, he simply must be in continual consultation with his wife. Only a fool of a man would neglect to seek out what his own personal Lady Wisdom might have to say. This is not to suggest a man's wife is infallible. There is a ditch on the other side, in which we see men following their wives into sin, and the accusation comes, "Because you listened to the voice of your wife..." (Gen. 3:17; cf. Gen. 16, where Abraham repeats Adam's error). But men who want to lead their families honorably will listen to their wives and accept their insight, perspective, and advice as part of their decision-making. The fact that the wife must submit to the husband does not make her a doormat. It does not mean the husband is the "boss" who always gets to do what he wants to do. A husband who treats his wife as a maid or slave or beast of burden is clearly a fool. The husband should never use his position as head to his own selfish advantage. At the same time, wives should recognize that the command to submit to a husband is not degrading or dehumanizing. Indeed, there is a kind of glory in humble submission, as the model of Jesus submitting to His Father revealed. The man must see his wife as his closest confidant and advisor. If he has married well, her wisdom will be worth more than gold and rubies.

The second example is found in 1 Timothy 5:14, where Paul describes the wife as an *oikodespoteo*, meaning something like "house guide" or "house master" or "house manager." While the man rules the household (1 Tim. 3:5), she manages the household. This obviously means she carries out her household authority in submission to the authority of her husband. But it also indicates she has real authority herself. She is expected to be competent and to exercise agency in her domain. She does not need to be micromanaged by him. She needs to be set free to flourish and fulfill her tasks in the domestic sphere. Of course, Proverbs 31 is an excellent illustration of what a woman looks like when she wisely and virtuously guides her house. She makes decisions, she has agency, and she is required to be intelligent and strong in her own feminine way. Again, we see that a man would be a fool to not accept all the help his wife has to offer him. In the past, especially before the Industrial Revolution, being a "home manager" was a huge task because the home was a source of productivity. The modern household has been largely hollowed out, which led to the bored housewife of the 1950s and then the rise of career-oriented wives who wanted to adopt the life plan of men as their own. One of the great challenges facing Christians in the twenty-first century is how to recover the productive household, and with it, the full meaning of the wife's role as house manager.

The upshot of all this is that the man is to see his wife as a helper who completes him, a helper who is suited to him in every way. She is not given to him merely to meet sexual needs or to make reproduction possible. She is not given merely to provide a set of services, like making his sandwiches or folding his laundry (though her domesticity equips her well for those tasks). She certainly brings beauty to his life but she is not a mere ornament or decoration. She is a whole person—body and spirit, mind and emotion. She should be valued by him for who she is. She is his helper physically, sexually, socially, and emotionally because she brings wisdom, insight, knowledge, creativity, energy, and glory to the relationship that he does not possess. He needs her, and she needs him. They are mutually dependent. While the man and woman each bear God's image, in a very real sense, they complete one another when they are called into the marital covenant, and thus they image God more fully together than they could apart (cf. 1 Cor. 11:3).

Creational Design

The early chapters of Genesis explain most everything about human life. Virtually everything traces back to Genesis 1-3. These chapters give us the archetypes and paradigms we need to understand the world and our place in it. Today our society is wracked with what have become known as the "culture wars." But I think they could be better called the "Genesis wars" because virtually every issue we fight over in our culture goes back to these foundational chapters in Genesis. The definition of marriage, the roles of men and women, the place of children, the importance of work in an economy, stewardship of the environment, and much more—it's all there, in those chapters. Our focus here is on men and women in the covenant of marriage.

Young men would do well to consider the paradigm of Adam's creation, calling, and marriage. There is a pattern set up in the creation account that can help young men (and by implication, young women) plan out their lives. Note that Adam is given a job before he is given a wife. In some sense, the creation mandate (dominion and multiplication) belonged to Adam from the moment of his creation. Of course, he will need a woman as his helper to complete the task, but the task belonged to him before he has a wife, and he comes to see his need for a wife in this way. What might a young man glean from this? Before he takes a wife, he needs to have some idea of the mission God has assigned him. Mission comes before marriage. He seeks a wife to help him fulfill his already-established life mission. A young woman's father might tell the young man, "You are a fine young man and I know you want to marry my daughter, but how are you going to provide for her?" The father is asking the young man to put mission before marriage. And he is right. "Mission" here is being used primarily in the sense of vocation, or one's life work. Obviously a man's mission can and should evolve over the course of his life. But he needs to be on a trajectory toward doing something meaningful and profitable with his life before he contemplates marriage. For the man, it is "mission before marriage"; for the woman, it is "marriage before (sub)mission," since she finds her mission in terms of her husband.

The woman is made from the man. She will be oriented to him in the same way he is oriented to the garden. The woman was given to him to enable him to do his job. She will tend to the gardener as the gardener tends to the garden. For the woman, the relationship comes first. The first woman was married within moments of being created and thus did not know life apart from her marriage relationship. He was made outside the garden. She was made inside the garden, and in some way is identified with it. All this suggests the woman will typically find her true mission inside the marriage relationship as she lives in sub-mission to her husband. Contrary to feminists, women must understand that they can have value even if their life plan does not look the same as a man's.

Again, note that in Genesis 3:16-19, after the man and woman have sinned and turned away from God, they were cursed in their respective roles and domains. The man was cursed in the realm of his work and the woman was cursed in the realm of motherhood. These sex-specific curses are crucial to understanding our respective natures and callings as men and women. While men and women both experience the curse across the whole of life, the curses most directly impact each sex within each sex's special domain.

In the beginning, Adam and his wife would have related to one another perfectly. They were naked and unashamed. They knew one another. Their nakedness was certainly physical but it also indicated they were open and transparent to one another. They had nothing to hide from each other. There was no friction between them, no shame. They each played their role within the marriage perfectly, complementing and completing one another, as they collaborated in the work God gave them.

Men and women have now been corrupted by the Fall, but our hope through the gospel is that we are being restored to true manhood and true womanhood by the grace of God. The redemption that comes through the gospel works within the structures of creation, including marriage. While men and women are now both under the curse—the generalized curse of death itself as punishment for sin and the sex-specific curses we find in Genesis 3—in Christ we can be forgiven and restored to to live life the way God intended. We do not have to have a perpetual "battle of the sexes," in which the sexes become rivals and competitors rather than complements. By grace, we can have harmony in marriage, as the husband and wife each fulfill their roles, completing the other and thus ultimately completing the creation mandate.

Marriage: Christ and the Church

Representing Christ to his wife, the husband accepts the difficult calling of headship, nourishing and cherishing his wife, as he lovingly leads her (Eph. 5:29). Nourishing is supplying needs; cherishing is looking after and guarding. Husbands are protectors and providers. This is the kind of leadership that the husband is to give his household, and it is the very opposite of male chauvinism, tyranny, abuse, and oppression. A husband who is harsh with his wife is not exercising his headship, he is denying it. He is contradicting what he is supposed to be, which is an icon of Christ.

Ephesians 5:25 is the key verse, "Husbands, love your wives, just as Christ also loved the church and gave Himself for her." Headship expresses itself in the home through sacrificial love. The husband gives himself for his wife. In marriage, the husband is the head who wears a crown, but it is a crown of thorns. Headship does mean authority and leadership, but it means exercising that authority in a Christ-like manner. What husbands cannot do is abdicate their role by becoming passive, sitting back and simply watching family life happen rather than actively directing it and leading it where it ought to go. Wives typically do not find marriage to a passive, abdicating man a very fulfilling experience. How can she follow if he does not lead and isn't going anywhere? How can she be in submission if he has no clearly defined mission in life? Husbands must lead in a Christ-like, sacrificial way, and as they do so, they will generally find their wives responding to their initiative. If a man wants his wife to respect him, the best thing he can do is live a respectable, admirable life. He should seek to be the best man she knows.

Loving her as Christ loves the church does not mean always giving her her way. She will actually feel more secure if she knows that he has the backbone to stand up to her when the situation warrants. She does not want a husband who will replicate Adam's abdication in Genesis 3, when he stood by and watched as his wife was led astray by the serpent and then followed her into ruin. She will be much happier with a man who can act like Jesus in John 6, where we see Jesus acting resolute and remaining confident in his mission, even in the midst of crisis as the crowds abandon Him.

At the same time, husbands should dote upon their wives enough to make them feel special. He should know her desires, her preferences, her joys, and should seek to regularly indulge her. He should make her laugh. He should listen to her. A good and godly man will want to lay the world at his wife's feet. He will not only be willing to die for her, he will live for her daily. He will often sacrifice his wants to meet her needs and even her preferences. He will make sure, as much as possible, she enjoys their sexual relationship. He will make sure she gets rest. He will not burden her unnecessarily. He will seek to relieve her anxieties rather than increase them. In short, he will take good care of her in every way. He will be a safe space for her.

Representing the church to her husband, the wife accepts her role of respectful submission to her husband. If men were designed for leadership in the home, women were designed to respond to and help that leadership. Note that submission does not mean that all women submit to all men. Paul ends the passage with Ephesians 5:33, "let the wife see that she respects her husband." The wife is commanded to submit precisely within the marriage relationship, to her own husband. I don't get to tell your wife what to do just because I am a man; she submits to you, not me. Likewise, submission does not mean that a wife must give up thinking for herself, or never seek to persuade her husband. There are respectful ways of doing so. First Peter 3 describes a situation in which a Christian woman is married to a non-Christian man, and indicates that unbelieving husbands "may be won by the conduct of their wives." Peter assumes that she is going to try to change him, and seek his conversion to the faith. Obviously the wife can think for herself if she has become a Christian, despite her husband's unbelief. Peter shows her how to go about winning her husband in a submissive way, consistent with her role. The wife is to honor and respect her husband in his position as head and leader of the family. She must respect him because she must respect the architecture God has built into the marriage relationship; in honoring him, she honors what he represents. Wives who try to win rebellious husbands by rebelling against God's order are trying to make water flow uphill. It will not work.

A godly wife will seek to know and understand her husband just as he does her. She will seek to understand what makes him feel respected and disrespected. She will seek to please him by how she speaks and dresses. She will seek to please him sexually. She will never follow him into sin, but otherwise she will seek to be obedient to him. She will not talk publicly about his failings. In short, she will seek to build him up and gain his trust.

The husband rules *over* the home and his wife rules *within* the home. He is the head of the home, she is the heart (cf. Ps. 128). This is what marriage is all about. The husband and wife come together in a mutually beneficial relationship, where they complete one another according to God's design. Through her and only through her, can man fulfill the calling that he has been given by God in Genesis 1:28. The fulfillment of the creation mandate hinges on the man and woman, each playing their part.

God designed men and women to join together in fulfilling the mandate that He gave to the human race at the beginning. Women cannot multiply without men and men can't take dominion, as they are called to, without women. In the marriage relationship, the two become one flesh, and their different strengths and weaknesses fill in one another so that together they are complete in a way they would not be otherwise. When this happens as God intended, it is beautiful.

While our look at marriage has stressed the specific roles of husband and wife, we must always beware of reducing the husband and wife to a simplistic or formulaic role. It is not that simple, and certainly not that rigid in real life. A husband and wife have roles because they are living within a drama, a story—the Gospel story, to be precise. But there is plenty of room for improvising within those roles, given the messiness of life. A husband and wife in a good, healthy marriage will constantly be seeking out ways to serve one another and serve the household. There is a kind of built-in flexibility that allows them to continually compensate for one another. The broad pattern of God's design for marriage is set forth very clearly in Scripture. But the specifics in any given marriage have to be worked out in a way that suits the strengths and weaknesses of the spouses in each particular marriage.

Children

How do children fit into the purpose of marriage? In Genesis 1, we see that God made man in His image, male and female. And He blessed them, commanding them to be fruitful and multiply and have dominion over every living thing. In Genesis 2, God brought the first man and woman together in the relationship of marriage. In principle, marriage, sex, and children all belong together as part of one package.

There is no doubt that God's grace always meets us where we are and compensates for our deficiencies when we cry out to Him. Those who are barren should realize that they can be fruitful in other ways, even if biological fruitfulness is impossible. Those in single parent situations or with other difficulties should trust God to meet that challenge and help them, despite what is lacking in their family life. But it is clear from the beginning, just as God intended marriage to be a lifelong commitment between a man and a woman, He intended children to be the fruit of that lifelong commitment. Not every person will get married and not every marriage will produce children, but there is a normativity to these realities.

From the very beginning, God ordained multiplication and fruitfulness to take place within the context of marriage. The Christian view of sex starts with its creational goodness; it is not evil or defiling in its essence. The Scriptures show us sex is a gift from God, within the context of the covenant of marriage between one man and woman for life (Heb. 13:4). God's design is that in the covenant of marriage, there is a oneness between husband and wife, such that "they shall become one flesh" (Gen. 2:24). While the Scripture warns about sex outside of marriage, it celebrates the goodness of sex within marriage (e.g., Prov. 5:19ff). If the husband is an icon of Christ and the wife an icon of the church, the children they have are icons of their shared love. If marriage is patterned after the economic Trinity in some way (1 Cor. 11:3), then children complete the picture, as the product of their shared love and life, even as the Holy Spirit is the shared love of the Father and Son.[74]

Malachi 2:15 tells us that one of God's purposes for marriage is that He seeks godly offspring. Why did God join a Christian man and woman together in the covenant of marriage? He makes them one so that they can become many. Children are not tacked onto marriage, but are integral to God's design for marriage. He wants to fill the world with His children.

---

74. The family is designed to image the economic Trinity, but only in a very limited, circumscribed sense, so we must be very careful about pressing the analogy too far.

In the old covenant, infertility was a curse in part because Israel's purpose was to bring the promised seed into the world. Now that the promised seed has come in Jesus Christ, the mission of the church does not depend upon biological children, at least not in the same way. It is a trial and burden for a Christian couple to be infertile, but not a curse. It may be a part of living in a fallen world, but it does not have to frustrate God's kingdom purposes since there are other ways to grow the kingdom. Singles and Christian couples without children can participate in expanding the kingdom of God and being fruitful through evangelism and discipleship. Biological reproduction is not the only way to expand the kingdom. If it were, Jesus did not fulfill the commission given in Genesis 1:27-28. But indeed, Jesus does fulfill the commission as He grows His church.

It is not just that God seeks offspring. He seeks godly and faithful offspring. He wants children who grow up to be mature, faithful, and loyal disciples of Christ. The point isn't just to raise up another generation to carry on your family name, but to raise up another generation who will carry forward the name of Christ. The whole process of parenting, from beginning to end, is in the Lord. Martin Luther said:

> Children are the sweetest fruits of marriage. They tie and strengthen the bonds of love. The greatest good in married life, that which makes all suffering and labor worthwhile, is that God grants offspring and commands that they be brought up to worship and serve Him. In all the world, this is the noblest and most precious work because to God there can

be nothing dearer than the salvation of souls. This, at least, all married people should know: They can do no better work and do nothing more valuable either for God, for Christendom, for all the world, for themselves, and for their children than to bring them up well.[75]

In marriage, husbands and wives not only stand face to face to build up one another. They also stand side by side, as allies, working to advance God's kingdom in missional marriages. Christian marriage is a partnership for the sake of the gospel, to renew and transform the world in Christ's way. The single largest lifetime project that a husband and wife undertake for the sake of the kingdom is raising up godly offspring. Those children continue the warfare of the kingdom into the next generation (cf. Ps. 127).

Conclusion: Culture of Life vs. Culture of Death

The sexual revolution opened Pandora's box of chaos and confusion in our culture. We have been on a sexual slide for quite some time now. From destigmatizing fornication and childbirth out of wedlock to no-fault divorce, widespread fatherlessness, the taking of innocent life in the womb, widespread role confusion and role reversal for men and women, homosexuality and now transgenderism—we have created a disaster of epic proportions by rebelling against God's Word and God's design. Our technology—the birth control pill in particular—has given us the illusion that sex can be separated from procreation. This in turn has created

---

75. Martin Luther, *A Sermon on the Estate of Marriage* (1519).

the illusion that we can have an androgynous society (since it is somewhat possible to hide or minimize male and female differences in modern society, at least to some degree until children come along, at which point the differences reassert themselves). The idea that sex can be kept sterile also has the effect of making people think the act of sex has no intrinsic meaning, that sex can be meaningless or casual. Of course, this is false. Sex is always supercharged with meaning whether we intend it to be so or not. The package of lies that stands at the heart of the sexual revolution is slowly being exposed, as the horrific and dehumanizing fruit of the sexual revolution becomes more and more obvious.

The health of any society can be measured by the strength of its marriages and families. Judged by this standard, our society is quite sick. Falling marriage rates and birth rates suggest that with the collapse of sexual ethics, our culture is beginning to unravel. The loss of sexual discipline, seen in widespread fornication, pornography use, and other vices, dissipate the very energy needed to keep civilization advancing. A culture that hates God will also hate life and love death. The sexual revolution has become a death wish throughout our civilization. Those who do not value life will not create new life. Our record-low marriage rates and birth rates are a sign something is deeply wrong with us. The only way to reverse this course is through the gospel.

At the most foundational level, marriage (including sexual union) is a metaphor for the oneness of Christ and the church (Eph. 5:22-33). Marriage was designed to serve as a parable of the gospel, to be a replica of Christ's relationship to the church. Marriage is a sign, pointing to the everlasting marriage between God's Son and God's people. The husband's calling in marriage is to portray Christ to his wife. The calling of the wife is to portray the church to her husband. When a man and a woman get married, the man is saying to the woman, "You are worth dying for, even as Christ died for the church." And the woman is saying to the man, "You are worth following the way the church follows Christ." When this happens, people look at their lives together in this one-flesh union of marriage and see a living embodiment of the gospel and a living enactment of the kingdom of God.

Marriage images the kingdom of God, but more than that, marriage exists to grow and advance the kingdom of God in the world. A strong marriage is full of covenantal love between the spouses, but it is not a self-enclosed entity. Strong marriages produce a love that spills over to children, friends, and to those in need. It flows out into the world, to bring transformation, in the shape of hospitality and ministry. Leo Tolstoy said:

> The goal of our life should not be to find joy in marriage, but to bring more love and truth into the world. We marry to assist each other in this larger task. Though we should indeed love our spouse with true satisfaction, the most selfish and hateful life of all is that of two beings who unite merely in order to enjoy pleasures. The highest calling is that of a man who has dedicated his life to serving God

and doing good and he unites with a woman in order to happily further that purpose.[76]

Marriage only works the way it should when tied to some larger purpose than just making one another happy. Making marriage about nothing more than personal fulfillment makes marriage a brittle thing. In such cases, a lack of fulfillment becomes grounds for divorce or a justification for adultery. Marriage must be grounded in God's purposes, God's kingdom, God's glory. God aims to make us holy through our marriages—and while holiness is not at odds with happiness in the long run, it might sometimes be in the short run. Marriage must be connected to a vision of seeking the kingdom first (Matt. 6:33). This is a focus which Christian couples and Christian singles have in common. At the most foundational level, we all share a common commitment to building and growing the kingdom of God.

A Christian's marital status, whether married or single, is in service of this larger goal of furthering God's kingdom on earth. Through marriage, not only do husbands and wives transform one another with their love, but they increase the flow of love, truth, and joy out into the world at large. Of course, this vision will not fully be achieved until human marriage falls away and the only marriage left is that of Christ and His people. This is what Christian marriage is all about: gospel symbolism.

---

76. Henri Troyat, *Tolstoy*, trans. Nancy Amphoux (New York: Grove Press, 1967), 467.

A culture that is completely confused about gender will be unable to understand the gospel because the gospel comes to us as a love story between a man and a woman. The gospel is a gendered narrative: The Father sent his Son to die for, fight for a bride, and thus redeem her, so they can live together as husband and wife happily ever after. Any deviation from the male/female marital pattern God set up in the creation renders the gospel unintelligible. The gospel is marital: marriage was designed to reveal the gospel. This is yet one more reason why it is of the utmost importance that the church proclaim the whole truth of God, including His revealed truth about male and female who are created in His image.

Chapter 16

Parenting from the Promises

It has been said that married couples are really just on a long date until that first child arrives. In some ways, that is true. There is no point in pretending that it is easy to raise children in a fallen world. Children cut into a couple's social life, sleep time, and budget. Raising children together is the most difficult task most couples undertake. With all the sacrifices that come with having children, some people today ask, "Why even have children?"

Our culture is hostile to children because it focuses solely on the burden, viewing children as a curse and a form of bondage. The biblical view is different: in spite of the reality that children require sacrifice, children are fundamentally a blessing from God (Ps. 127:3). Even in a fallen world, we can insist that children are a blessing. But why is that? It is because the children of Christians come with promises attached. Our children are really God's children. When God gives children to Christian parents, He is giving a gift, a heritage, a legacy. But parents are really just stewards who are entrusted with caring for God's children. Every Christian parent is a foster parent or babysitter. Our children belong to God. This is the good news about parenting. We are raising *His* children.

The foundation of covenantal parenting is the covenantal promise which means that we are to parent by grace through faith. In the Christian life, everything is to be through faith from first to last, including the way we bring up our children. We are to entrust our children to God, relying on His grace and resting in His covenant promises. The contrast is between raising children in the flesh or raising them by faith. Faithful parenting is not just a matter of trying hard. Parental good works, like all other good works, flow out of trusting God. Parents must start their task by trusting God's covenantal promise. God says, "I am your God and the God of your children" (cf. Acts 2:39, Gen. 17:7). This is the starting point for parents and the touchstone parents turn to when concerned about their calling to rear children. Christian parenting, from start to finish, is by faith.

Election, Parenting, and Mission

In Genesis 12:2-3, God promised to Abram, "I will make you a great nation; I will bless you and make your name great; and you shall be a blessing. I will bless those who bless you, and I will curse him who curses you; and in you all the families of the earth shall be blessed." Abram was chosen, not just for his own benefit, but as the means to a global end: to bless all the families of the earth.

In the Scriptures, these three things are tied together: election, parenting, and mission. Parenting is the hinge between election and mission. God graciously chose Abraham to initiate the formation of a people through whom His mission to the nations would be fulfilled. This mission will be fulfilled (at least in part) through faithful parenting: as Abraham trains his household in the way of the Lord, teaching them to practice righteousness and justice, the promises come to fruition. Righteousness and justice will flow from Abraham to his children and through his children out into the world. And his household after him, one generation after another, will repeat this pattern in covenant succession.

We tend to think of mission and parenting as being at odds with one another. Mission is outward-facing, going out into the world with the gospel. Parenting is an inward-facing task, protecting and nurturing our children until they are ready to go out into the world. Many churches focus on one or the other, mission or parenting. In the Scriptures, however, parenting that leads to covenant succession and God's mission to the world go together. You cannot have one without the other.

What good is it if we gain the hearts of the world but lose our children to the world? This is not going to grow the kingdom. And what good does it do to raise up children who practice a personal and private piety but are so separated from the world that they cannot do anything to carry the mission forward and reach the nations?

Biblically, there is a vital link between raising children and fulfilling the Great Commission. Parenting is not an end in itself, it is for the sake of the mission. Missional parenting is needed to raise up missional children who can go out and bring about righteousness and justice in the earth (Gen. 18:17-19). Parenting is not just about building a hedge of protection between our children and the world, in a defensive posture. Rather, it is about raising up children who will be part of the church that knocks down the gates of hell (Matt. 16:18). We must train our children so that they will learn how to engage the world in order to transform it in the name of Christ. We need multiple generations of Christians who inherit a godly culture from their parents and build upon it, standing upon the shoulders of their parents and reaching higher to develop and mature the godly culture they inherited.

Kingdom Identity of Covenant Children

Like Abraham, Christian parents know their children are part of God's covenant. In Matthew 19:13-15, Jesus gives us a biblical theology of children and parenting:

> Then little children were brought to Him that He might put His hands on them and pray, but the disciples rebuked them. But Jesus said, "Let the little children come to Me, and do not forbid them; for of such is the kingdom of heaven." And He laid His hands on them and departed from there.

On a large scale, Jesus's words do not factor enough into what we believe and do with our children in the church. The children of believers belong to the kingdom of God. The children that are brought to Jesus are covenant children, the children of believers. Jesus says, "of such is the kingdom of heaven." This is a statement about the identity of our children. Above all, our children need to know this about themselves: they belong to the kingdom of God.

God does not want our children growing up guessing or confused about who they are. Jesus identifies our children as kingdom members, not because they are innately good or pure, nor because they inherit some kind of spiritual DNA from their parents. Speaking of the covenant children brought to Him, Jesus says, "of such is the kingdom of heaven" because God designed His covenant to run in lines of generations (Gen. 17:7).

God's family is not purely biological, as if children of God can be born of the flesh, nor is it purely spiritual, disconnected from the structures of creation, as if it had no connection to marriage. Rather, God's family is covenantal. It is created and sustained by God's covenant promises and these promises embrace the next generation. God's covenant promises are about the restoration and fulfillment of His original purpose for the creation.

If Adam and Eve had not sinned and had begun having children, would their children have been loved by God and had a relationship with God? Would their children have grown up knowing God every day of their lives? The obvious answer to these questions is "Yes." Adam and Eve's children, apart from the Fall, would have grown up as members of God's kingdom.

The covenant promises given to us in Scripture show us God's intention to repair and restore the fallenness of the family. In order to do that, God's promises must cut across generations. The children of believers are members of God's kingdom and covenant and thus have a gracious relationship with God. We are to raise them up and train them in accordance with this relationship. We are to nurture this relationship so that our children mature and bear fruit. It is true that some might grow up and fall away from the faith, breaking covenant with God. They become like olive branches broken out of the covenant tree (Rom. 11). But the children of believers should be treated as believers, as fellow covenant members, until and unless they prove otherwise.

Jesus delights in the children of His people. Through baptism, He makes them members of His family and part of His covenant community. Some Christian parents do not believe their children are Christian in any sense. Sometimes, well-meaning but misguided Christian parents have an implicit double standard. They are much harder on their children than they are on themselves. They will say things like, "I know my child can't be a Christian because he told a lie." But when we sin, must we doubt our salvation? We are Christians who are saved by grace and are struggling with sin in our lives. Our children can certainly struggle with sin, too.

It is not at all inconsistent to say, "My children belong to Jesus and my children are sinners who need to grow in grace and their relationship with God." Our children belong to Jesus and our children are sinners, just like their Christian parents. In Psalm 22:10, David said, "I was cast upon You from birth. From My mother's womb You have been My God." Yet in Psalm 51:5, David said, "I was brought forth in iniquity, and in sin my mother conceived me." In Psalm 22 and in Psalm 51, it is the same David speaking. Was David counted righteous from the womb or was he a sinner, brought forth in iniquity? The answer is that he was both. That answer applies to all believers at any age: we are sinner-saints.

The same spiritual dynamics are at work in Christian parents and Christian children. We are sinners saved by grace and believers journeying toward maturity. Our job as Christian parents is to disciple our children so that we are moving them toward Christian maturity. Just as we deal with our children's sin and need for growth, we also have to deal with their theology. We need to make sure that our children are growing in their understanding of who Jesus is. If we were to gather together four-year-olds and start asking them questions about the Trinity, they would likely not have precise doctrinal answers. But this does not mean that we say that our children are heretics. They are immature and need to grow in their doctrinal knowledge. Our children need to not only be growing in their obedience, but also in their understanding. There must be diligent teaching in an age-appropriate manner to strengthen our children's identity as sons and daughters of God.

Parents tend to make one of two mistakes regarding the identity of their children. Some view children as innocent repositories of virtue and wisdom. They do not recognize the fallenness that comes through original sin, passed down since Adam. The other extreme are Christians who claim that their children are just as depraved as the world's children, with no difference between them. They refer to their children as "vipers in diapers." Biblically, the child of even one believing parent has a covenant relationship with God and is called holy (1 Cor. 7:14). If you treat your children as if they are not Christian at all, you are essentially training your children in doubt. You are training your children to doubt God and doubt their identity. Instead we should train them to embrace and rejoice in their covenant privilege.

Nurture that Leads to Maturity

Parenting is a specialized form of discipleship. Parents, not the state or even the church, have the primary responsibility for rearing children. The goal in view for parents is to bring their children to maturity. Parents have about eighteen to twenty years to train up their children, before they release them like arrows, ready to strike the enemy (Ps. 127). The days are long, but the years are short. The long-range goal when we bring a child into this world is to prepare him to go out into the world and serve God. Our aim is to make our children mature enough so that by the time they leave our house, they no longer must depend upon us. We want to raise children who know what to do with the responsibilities and freedoms that come with adulthood. If we nurture them in an age-appropriate way all along, the end result will be maturity.

In Ephesians 6:4, the apostle Paul said, "And you, fathers, do not provoke your children to wrath, but bring them up in the training (nurture) and admonition of the Lord." The word used for "nurture" is the Greek term *paideia*. The term *paideia* refers to the process of shaping someone in a way that affects all of life. Consider someone who moves from one country to another country: to assimilate to the new ethnic group requires a process of inculturation, or *paideia*. Nurture is not merely imparting information but the formation of the whole person.

The nurture that is the *paideia* of the Lord ultimately means impressing upon our children the Christian way of life, training them to take their place in a Christian culture. It is training them to live as faithful Christians, as citizens of God's kingdom. They have been taken out of Adam's kingdom and placed in Christ's kingdom and now we train them in the way of life that comes with that status. They learn the Christian "language" in the confessions and creeds. They learn the Christian story, including who the heroes and villains are. They learn the Christian songs and chants, especially the Psalter. They learn Christian symbols and rituals in the liturgy. They learn the Christian way of life.

Nurture by Loving Your Children

Nurture leads to maturity. The fundamental way we nurture our children is to love them, love them, love them, and keep on loving them. When John Calvin explained what Paul meant by "nurture," he said the point is that children should be fondly cherished by their fathers. We are to love our children as God loves His children. The best model for parents is God Himself (Heb. 12:5-9). God is our Father and He defines fatherhood. Ephesians 3:14-15 says, "For this reason I bow my knees to the Father of our Lord Jesus Christ from whom the whole family in heaven and earth is named." The family itself is derived from God's Fatherhood. Loving our children as God loves His own means that we love them with a compassionate love. Psalm 103:13

says, "As a father pities his children, so the LORD pities those who fear Him." God has a tender love for His children that we ought to have for our children as well. God's love is multi-faceted. It is a tough love, unearned love, demanding love, a love that both praises and critiques. We are to immerse our children in an environment of secure, God-like love.

It is important to understand that mothers and fathers do not love their children in identical ways. In fact, it has been rightly suggested that we should not speak of "parenting" in general but "mothering" and "fathering" because mothers and fathers pour into their children in such different ways (cf. 1 Thess. 2). Fathers love us by exhorting and encouraging children, and they challenge kids to grow, mature, stretch, and become the best they can be. Mothers love in a nurturing and affectionate way. While there is obviously some overlap, we could say a father's love builds strength and a mother's love brings security.

Nurture through the Gospel

We nurture our children by giving them the gospel. We give them the gospel, not as something that we hope they someday will embrace (as if they were outsiders) but as something that presently belongs to them because, by their baptisms, they are currently part of the covenant community. They are part of the people that Jesus died for and part of the people who have received the Spirit. We nurture them with the gospel, teaching them God's ways at every opportunity (Deut. 6:7). We teach our children the kingdom story of creation, mankind's ruinous fall into sin, and God's mighty acts of redemption culminating in Christ's death on the cross and His resurrection on the third day. We build them up within the context of the covenant community, including them in weekly worship, instilling the truth that they are part of God's people and God's story in the world. We also teach them there is no neutrality (Matt. 12:30), and thus everything in life must be connected to the resurrected and ascended Christ's reign. We teach them to embrace the gospel and live by the Gospel in all they do.

Nurture through Discipline

We nurture and admonish our children, discipling them through discipline. Discipline is a significant theme in the Bible, especially in the book of Proverbs. Proverbs 13:24 says, "He who spares his rod hates his son, but he who loves him disciplines him promptly." This is counterintuitive for modern people, who think that if you love your child you won't use the rod. But the Word of God says that if you love your son, you will discipline him with the rod promptly. One of the great parental sins of our age is the sin of parental softness—being too indulgent. If children are constantly entertained and coddled, they never learn key lessons. Children should be taught to fear God from their earliest days. They should be taught to submit to their parents as representatives of divine authority. They should learn the meaning of the word "no," as this lesson becomes the basis of all self-control later in life. The rod is a helpful tool—not the only tool but an effective one when used properly.

Why does the Bible talk so much about the rod? It is not because the Bible is barbaric. It is because the Bible was written by the inspiration of the Holy Spirit, and God knows who we are and what we need. He made us and He knows that we are bodily creatures. He knows there is a deep connection between the body and the soul and that discipline with the rod is a means for parents to shape the heart of the child. The child's backside is connected to his heart. This outward form of discipline is useful for molding the inner man because we are integrated, body and soul.

It is true that some parents are cruel and abusive. The rod gets a bad rap because some parents have misused it. We must acknowledge that. But when used in love, with consistency, to enforce a few clear rules, the rod is helpful. One illustration of misusing the rod is waiting until anger sets in. All too often parents let Junior get away with a particular sin, giving mild rebukes, until the sin gets so annoying, the parent flies off the handle and uses the rod in anger. Had the rod been employed at the very first sight of sin, it could have been applied in a kindhearted and non-emotional way. Instead the rod was used to vent parental anger rather than shape the child in righteousness. Another example of misusing the rod is simply spanking the child before returning to whatever it is you were doing before without providing sufficient context. The best use of the rod will be surrounded with prayer, a clear explanation of the sin (when the child is old enough), reminders of forgiveness, and so on. The rod should not be used in isolation.

Just as the Lord's service combines the Word with various physical rituals, so it is in parenting. The physical use of the rod needs to be accompanied by teaching. Parents should instruct, exhort, and admonish. Wise parents will seek a balance between nurturing and cherishing their children, and rebuking and correcting their children. The discipline that Christian parents give their covenant children is always to be within the context of a loving relationship and is itself a form of love. This biblical discipline is to build up your child, not berate or crush him. The Bible specifically warns against being overly harsh and abusive, and especially reminds fathers to "not provoke your children, lest they become discouraged" (Col. 3:21).

Obviously, the rod is not the only tool in the parental toolbox. And the rod should always be used in age-appropriate ways, surrounded by love. But if we reject the rod altogether, we are abandoning the teaching of Scripture. God's Word is clear that the rod is a necessary aspect of parenting. Yes, the rod can be used in abusive ways. But the abuse of something does not negate its proper use. Use the rod in love and wisdom for the good of your children.

In our age, many people say any form of discipline is at best discouraging to your children and at worst abusive. At a young age, it may seem that discipline is unnecessary because parents can control and manipulate the child's environment in order to get them to do what the parents want. This seems like the easy way out. But what happens when children get older and into their teenage years or beyond? What happens when you can no longer control the variables in their environment and they can get on drugs, engage in premarital sex, or rebel in myriad other ways?

If Christian parents have not disciplined their children from a young age, it becomes too late very quickly. It is hard to play catch up. It is much better to begin disciplining your children from their earliest days. Some parents say that they will delay discipline until the child can understand cause and effect. But if the child does not understand cause and effect, why is he whining to get what he wants? We should not underestimate our children's ability to absorb truth and correction, even at a very young age.

God is gracious and meets us where we are and not where we should have been. He can change anyone from a sinner into His saint. But it is a much more difficult path for both parents and children when parents refrain from godly discipline of their children. The principle can be seen in 1 Samuel 2-3, with the story of the sons of Eli. First Samuel 3:13 says of Eli, "For I have told him that I will judge his house forever for the iniquity which he knows, because his sons made themselves vile, and he did not restrain them."

Faithful discipline yields the fruit of faithful children. Consistently disciplining our children is hard, but it is hard work that pays off. Like everything else in the Christian life, it must be done by grace through faith. There may be no immediate results. It may take days, weeks, months, or even years of consistent faithful nurture and admonition before we see the fruit we desire. But we must take God at His Word, and trust Him with the results.

Conclusion

Scripture teaches a doctrine of covenant succession. God's covenantal intention is to pass along the faith from parents to children. True, sometimes this chain is broken. Sometimes parental failure is the reason. But on the whole, parents who seek to raise their children in the ways of the Lord should expect their children to grow up and walk in those ways. God's design includes using procreation to populate

His kingdom. He does not give children to believing parents to fill hell but because He seeks holy offspring (Mal. 2:15).

Biblically, there is a connection between faithful parenting and faithful children. Faithful teaching, instruction, discipline, and prayer within the home and in the church are the ordinary means that God uses to raise up faithful children. Parents should remember God ordains the ends and the means. The responsibilities that parents have are weighty, but as they rely on God's grace they can raise their children free of fear and worry. Even the best of parents are going to make countless mistakes in the eighteen to twenty years during which they raise their children. But God is gracious.

It is really important to keep the big picture in view, namely that God loves our children even more than we love them. He says to them, "I will be a God to your children even as I am a God to you." Parenting starts with what God says to us as parents, and the gracious promises He makes to us about our children. God gives us multigenerational promises that He will give His Spirit to the next generation and the next generation after that. Psalm 103:17 says, "But the mercy of the LORD is from everlasting to everlasting on those who fear Him, and His righteousness to children's children." Parental mistakes do not negate or overthrow God's promises. He made these promises, not to perfect parents, but to fallen parents. Faithful parenting is a huge responsibility and undertaking, but God is with us in it.

Faithful parenting is not just a matter of parents submitting to what God requires but is fundamentally a matter of believing God's covenant promises. It has been rightly said: *The essence of covenant keeping is promise believing.* The covenant is God's grace given to us and our proper response is to trust in Him. We must believe those promises and declarations that God has made to us in His Word concerning our children. Christian parents, empowered by the Holy Spirit, should make every effort to raise their children to be faithful and fruitful servants in God's kingdom so that the promise to Abraham—a world full of believers—will become reality.

Chapter 17

Kingdom Work:
Your Labor is Not in Vain

When God created our first parents, He gave them a task: "Be fruitful and multiply; fill the earth and subdue it" (Gen. 1:27). Being made in the image of the Creator, Adam and Eve were to have dominion as God's vice-regents, cultivating and creating through their labors. Being fruitful and multiplying, humanity would reflect God's glory back to Him throughout all the earth. God established work at creation as part of His good design for mankind and for the world.

Work is God's gift, not a necessary evil or a result of the Fall of man into sin. The Fall of man into sin deformed work, just as it deformed everything else, and our work is now frustrated by the curse (Gen. 3:17-19). But Jesus came to reverse the curse and restore the creation which fell in Adam's rebellion. When Adam subjected creation to futility, God promised a redeemer. In Him, God's purposes for the created order are going to be fulfilled, as Christ works through His redeemed people. While we still struggle with the effects of the Fall (and all too often sin ourselves), the reality is that, by grace, we can experience God's blessing in our work once again.

Martin Luther communicated the holiness of work performed by Christians:

> If you ask an insignificant maidservant why she scours a dish or milks a cow, she can say, "I know that the thing I do pleases God, for I have God's work and commandment. God does not look at the insignificance of the acts but at the heart that serves Him in such little things."[77]

Elsewhere Luther wrote that if we viewed work aright, the entire world would be full of service to God, not only in churches, but also the home, the kitchen, the cellar, the workshop, and the field of the townsfolk and farmers. He goes on to say, "What you do in your house is worth as much as if you did it in heaven for our Lord God." Luther caught sight of this biblical truth that our work is a form of priestly service. Our work is a form of prayer when offered up in faith and done with a zeal for the glory of God.

Obviously, we must work to live. Scripture is clear that the man who does not work should not eat. Man was made to be a worker. But the prime value of work lies not

---

77. Quoted in Leland Ryken, *Redeeming the Time: A Christian Approach to Work and Leisure* (Grand Rapids: Baker Books, 1995), 131.

in its paycheck nor the notoriety that we can gain from it but in its worth to God and the service that is offered to our neighbors (Eph. 4:24; Phil. 2:4). Christians are to use their talents and gifts not to make a name for themselves but for the glory of God (Ps. 115:1). When asked by fathers about how to instruct their sons to select a profession, John Calvin gave this counsel:

> When a man comes to consider by what trade his son may best earn his living and provide for himself and his family after marriage, at the same time let him also see to it that he serves his neighbors and that the use of his skill and occupation redound to the common profit of all men.[78]

Luther also said any work that is done only for God and not also for neighbor is not really a good work: "If you find yourself in a work by which you accomplish something good for God, or the holy, or yourself, but not for your neighbor as well, then you should know that that work is not a good work." This is the Christian criteria we must use to evaluate our work: Does it glorify God *and* serve my neighbor? Paul gets at the social good of work in Ephesians 4:28, when he sets down a pattern: Stop stealing and start working so that you can give to others instead of taking from them.

---

78. John Calvin, *Sermons*, Ephesians 4:28.

Kingdom Work for the Common Good

God works through our work in order to fulfill His purposes. In the same breath that we pray for God's kingdom to come, we also pray for our daily bread. How does God answer that prayer? Usually, He does not drop down manna from heaven. God usually answers this prayer for daily bread through farmers, bakers, truck drivers, grocery stores, good roads, and good government: All to get one loaf of bread from the field to our table. Society is a kind of body in which each member serves the good of the whole when it is functioning as it should. When we have the freedom to serve in ways that suit our gifts and talents, we benefit one another. In the Eucharist, this whole social network and economy is gathered up into the kingdom of God and offered to us as the body of Christ, showing us that God is redeeming creation itself. Redemption is not an escape from this world but the transformation of it.

This simple example of God answering our need for a loaf of bread can be multiplied thousands and thousands of times over as various people work in their vocations throughout society. Behind a vast array of ordinary social structures, there is the extraordinary work of God. And within this array of social structures, God places Christians to be the leaven of the kingdom, working its way through the whole lump of dough that is human society, transforming the world (Matt. 13:33).

The kingdom of God comes about in the here and now as God works through our work to make His promised future a present reality. God is not merely interested in redeeming individuals or even families but redeeming whole societies, cultures, and nations across the world.

Therefore, we do not work merely for private, selfish ends but for the common good of the world that God has committed Himself to saving. We not only work for our own ends, but for God's ends. In *An Open Letter to The Christian Nobility*, Martin Luther wrote:

> A cobbler, a smith, a farmer, each has the work and office of his trade, and yet they are all alike consecrated as priests and bishops. And everyone by means of his own work or office must benefit and serve every other, that in this way, many kinds of work may be done for the bodily and spiritual welfare of the community, even as all the members of the body serve one another.

In our various callings, we each serve one another, for the common good, rightly understood. The Puritans, known for their work ethic, captured this concept of serving God by serving neighbors for the common good. Cotton Mather said, "God made man a social creature. We ought to expect to benefit from human society. It is but equal that human society should receive benefits from us."[79] Richard Steele said, "God doth call every man and woman…to serve him in some peculiar employment in this world, both for their own and the common good."[80]

If we think only in terms of jobs that can make us money, rather than as vocations through which we have

---

79. Cotton Mather, *A Christian at His Calling*, 1701.

80. Quoted in Leland Ryken, *Worldly Saints: The Puritans as They Really Were* (Grand Rapids, Michigan: Zondervan Publishing, 1990).

been called by God to serve society, we will end up with a society that is built on nothing more than envy and greed. The free market is a great blessing but the market is not autonomous. A free market needs to operate within the moral framework of God's law. Money matters, to be sure. We need money to live and there is nothing wrong with making money, even a lot of it. The Bible does not demonize the wealthy as such. But the true value of work is not solely monetary. It must be tied to virtue, service, and the kingdom of Christ. For example, one key indicator as to whether you are working for yourself or for the kingdom of God is tithing in the Lord's service. In the tribute offering, we offer up ourselves and our work to the Lord for the furthering of His kingdom.

God's purposes for society, the common good, and our work all converge together in the way God has designed the world to work. In Jesus's name, our work has a certain breadth. As we co-labor to build His kingdom through loving service on behalf of others, our work fits into the cosmic plan of God as described in Colossians 1:19-20:

> For it pleased the Father that in Him all the fullness should dwell, and by Him to reconcile all things to Himself, by Him, whether things on earth or things in heaven, having made peace through the blood of His cross.

God is reconciling all things to Himself through the Lord Jesus Christ. Through Christ, our work can become part of the great project of the kingdom of God, building the kind of society and civilization that God intended from the beginning.

Work Heartily Unto the Lord

Whatever God has called us to do, we must do it *Christianly*. We are not merely Christians who happen to be artists, doctors, lawyers, or businessmen, but we are Christian artists and Christian doctors and Christian lawyers and Christian businessmen. We begin to do our work in a distinctively Christian way, rather than just coating it over with a layer of Christian varnish.

The gospel must become more and more intrinsic to the way we do our work. John Cotton said: "A true believing Christian lives in his vocation by faith. Not only my spiritual life, but even my civil life [his whole social and cultural life] and all the life I live is lived by faith in the Son of God."[81] In other words, the gospel is as big as life. The Gospel is not just private truth, it is public truth that is to touch and transform every aspect of human life. We are to turn our whole lives over to Jesus Christ, to look at our place in society and all our relationships in the light of the gospel. We are to take our faith with us wherever we go so that our lives are holistically shaped and formed by God's Word. And when we live out our faith in public as well as in private, society will begin to take on the shape of the gospel, reflecting the realities of God's kingdom.

In Colossians 3:23, the apostle Paul said, "And whatever you do, do it heartily, as to the Lord and not to men." Why does God want us to pursue excellence, to do whatev-

---

81. Quoted in Ryken, *Worldly Saints,* 26.

er we do heartily unto the Lord? One reason it is important for Christians to do their work well is so we might attract people to the Lord Jesus Christ. First Peter 2:12 captures this logic: "Having your conduct honorable among the Gentiles, that when they speak against you as evildoers, they may, by your good works which they observe, glorify God in the day of visitation." If we do our work with excellence, not only does that in itself become an act of glorifying God, but others are drawn to praise God as well (cf. Tit. 2:9-10). Our work as Christians represents God in society and to society. Therefore, our ditches should be dug straight, our pipe fittings should not leak, our term papers should be well-researched, our surgical cuts should be clean and precise, our business deals should be honest, our artwork should be beautiful, and so on. Whatever God has called us to do, He has called us to do it with excellence. When we work this way, we reveal that we serve the God of beauty, order, love, and wisdom.

The pursuit of excellence is not to be confused with perfectionism. Someone with a perfectionistic mentality will become prideful if they do well but crushed when they fail. For them, success means self-glory, and failure means self-destruction. His idol has let him down and his god has failed him. When you are driven to pursue excellence as a way of serving Christ, you are always humble even when you accomplish something great because you know that Christ has worked His work in you. And when you fail, you are not crushed by it because you know that in the end, your worth is not tied to what you can accomplish, but what Christ has accomplished for you. Your self-worth is not tied to your job but to the cross. You must always look at yourself in light of what Jesus has done for you. The gospel sets us free from slavery to perfectionism in order to pursue excellence for the right reasons. Because we know that our work is offered up to God in the Lord Jesus Christ and through Him, it is really His work in us.

However, excellence is not our only aim. There is no doubt that work will be frustrating in a fallen world. Thus, we are called to serve *with contentment*. In 1 Corinthians 7, Paul instructs us to be content in whatever situation God has called us. He sums everything up in 1 Corinthians 7:24, "let each one remain with God in that state in which he was called." This is not a rule against changing jobs or seeking better employment since Jesus Himself changed jobs from being a carpenter to a preacher. But Paul is showing us how we should view our place in society. We must view it as God's gift and vocation. That is why Paul says "remain with God" where you are.

Whatever circumstances you are in, God is with you. No matter how difficult it may be, you can have peace, contentment, and even pleasure in what God has called you to do because He is with you in the midst of it. When the world sees us pursuing excellence and being content, the world sees the difference that God makes in the way we live our lives.

We should also remember that pursuing excellence does not mean overworking, or working for the wrong reasons. Overwork can be just as damaging as a lack of work. And working out of improper motivation can lead to burnout. Proverbs 23:4-5 calls us to proper balance in life, and proper motivation in work:

Do not overwork to be rich; because of your own understanding, cease! Will you set your eyes on that which is not? For riches certainly make themselves wings; they fly away like an eagle toward heaven.

We should be motivated by a desire to glorify God and serve others, lest our lives get out of balance.

We also should remember that God must establish our work if it is to have any lasting value. No matter how talented we might be or how much effort we put forth, without God's grace, it all amounts to nothing. Unless God establishes the work, it is all in vain. Psalm 127 shows us that because the Lord builds the house, we can get to work. It also shows us that because the Lord builds the house, we can sleep at night. We do not have to spend the night tossing and turning about what we did not get done. If productivity, efficiency, or success is your god, this god will never be satisfied with you and will break you. Everything you do for that god will be in vain and will be futile.

We do not have to live in anxiety about whether or not the Lord will provide for us. The daily rhythm in Scripture is to work hard during the day and sleep soundly at night, entrusting ourselves to God at all times. Jonathan Edwards wrote, "Oh how good it is to work for God in the daytime and at night to lie down under His smile." The weekly rhythm in Scripture was established by God in the creation week. He labored six days, created all that is, and on the seventh day He rested. Even God rests and delights in what He has done. As finite creatures, how much more do we need to do the same!

Work in the New Creation

The creation account is foundational to our understanding of work, but this is amplified in the new creation. The reality of the resurrection of Jesus and our future resurrection also becomes a source of understanding the ultimate meaning of work. In 1 Corinthians 15, after spending fifty-seven verses on the subject of the resurrection, Paul says, "Therefore, my beloved brethren, be steadfast, immovable, always abounding in the work of the Lord, knowing that your labor is not in vain in the Lord." What does Paul mean by "your labor…in the Lord"? Some would say it must be preaching or helping the poor. In this view, only pastors and missionaries really do the Lord's work, and this text does not apply to the rest of us. But limiting the scope of the Lord's work in that way would contradict everything Paul has been saying in 1 Corinthians. When we look at the Scriptures as a whole, all legitimate work is the work of the Lord. Whatever our calling, we are to excel in the Lord's work.

Paul is saying in 1 Corinthians 15:58 that because our bodily resurrection is coming in the future, we should stand firm in the truth of the gospel and work hard in the Lord, knowing our labor is not in vain. Deep down, we want our lives to make a lasting difference. Yet, if we look at our daily existence, what we do does not seem to have a big impact. It appears that our lives are lived in vain. We go about our routine, day after day, and week after week, just going in circles, not really getting anywhere. Leo Tolstoy raises a profound question in his book, *A Confession*:

My question, the one that brought me to the point of suicide when I was fifty years old, was a most simple one that lies in the soul of every person, from a silly child to a wise old man. It is the question without which life is impossible, as I had learnt from experience. It is this: what will come of what I do today or tomorrow? What will come of my entire life? Expressed another way the question can be put like this: why do I live? Why do I wish for anything, or do anything? Or expressed another way: is there any meaning in my life that will not be annihilated by the inevitability of death which awaits me?[82]

The atheist philosopher Bertrand Russell answers Tolstoy's question with an emphatic, "No!" concluding that nothing we do survives death. In Russell's view, the death of the universe will wipe everything away that human beings have ever accomplished, so it is all in vain. Russell said,

all the labours of the ages, all the devotion, all the inspiration, all the noonday brightness of human genius, are destined to extinction in the vast death of the solar system, and that the whole temple of Man's achievement must inevitably be buried beneath the debris of a universe in ruins.[83]

---

82. Leo Tolstoy, *A Confession and Other Religious Writings*, trans. Jane Kentish (London: Penguin Books, 1988), 34.

83. Bertrand Russell, *Why I Am Not a Christian* (1927, repr. New York: Simon and Schuster, 1957), 107.

Russell is simply being honest as someone who does not believe in the resurrection. If there is no resurrection of Jesus leading to the future resurrection at the end of history, this present life is meaningless. We can contrast the sentiments of Russell with the certainty of Paul in 1 Corinthians 15:58, "Your labor is not in vain." The future resurrection and the promise of the new creation make your work in the present meaningful.

Christ is the new Adam, the founder of a new creation. As the new Adam, He is taking dominion over the whole of creation. He is doing this through His people, making our work part of His new creation project. We cannot build the kingdom of God on our own, but when we do our labor in the Lord, He works through us to build His kingdom. If you are in Christ Jesus, you will be raised up at the last day *and* your work will be raised up.

As Revelation 14:13 says, "Blessed are the dead who die in the Lord…that they may rest from their labors, and their works follow them." Our works do not end up in some cosmic incinerator. They follow us into God's new world. Isaiah 60 speaks of the nations of the earth bringing their treasures, their achievements, into the kingdom of God, into the new Jerusalem to be transformed and perfected. The fruit of all their cultural tasks will be brought into the new creation. John sees the same thing in Revelation 21:26 where "they shall bring the glory and the honor of the nations into" the new Jerusalem. Just as our bodies will be transformed in the resurrection, so will our labors and achievements. This means that our work, no matter how mundane or insignificant, truly has eternal significance.

In some form or fashion, work will continue, even in the resurrected new world. We will do our work in a matured and perfected way. Eternal life is not going to be what Huck Finn thought it would be: just strumming harps sitting on a cloud, playing boring music forever. We will have bodies and will be working in and with God's new creation. Victor Hugo captures this so well:

> I feel in myself the future life.... For half a century I have been writing my thoughts in prose, verse, history, philosophy, drama, romance, tradition, satire, ode, song—I have tried all. But I feel that I have not said the thousandth part of what lies in me. When I go down to the grave I can say, like so many others, "I have finished my day's work," but I cannot say, "I have finished my life." My day's work will begin again the next morning. The tomb is not a blind alley; it is a thoroughfare. It closes in the twilight to open with the dawn.[84]

When we see our life's work in light of the future world to come, we start to look for ways to make our work an instrument for making this present world look like that future world in appropriate ways. Our work, in the quality of it and how we treat people, becomes a new creation preview. When we labor in light of the resurrection, our work is transformed.

---

84. Victor Hugo, "Victor Hugo on Immortality," *Sacramento Daily Union*, Volume 15, Number 20, 16 March 1882.

On the resurrection at the end of history, the prayer of Moses in Psalm 90 will be answered by Christ: "And let the beauty of the LORD our God be upon us, and establish the work of our hands for us; yes, establish the work of our hands." It is God's pleasure to bless and delight in His children and the work of our hands. The gospel restores us as workers made in the image of God, to our true purpose in God's world. We were made to give the world beauty, order, and design that reflects God's own truth and beauty. As we learn to work for the glory of God and the good of our neighbor, we are giving to the world a vision of what the kingdom of God looks like, offering a glimpse of the beautiful picture of God's intention for human society.

Epilogue

Into the Public Square

Since the Enlightenment of the eighteenth and nineteenth centuries, or the modern period, the world has been cut in half. In the "upstairs" realm, "god" is allowed to exist and do his thing. But he has been banished from the earthly, social, historical realm "downstairs." The Enlightenment project was simple: relegate the deity to the sphere of the private and spiritual, making room for human autonomy in the realm of the public and political. The strategy adopted was clever, clear, and effective. Its rhetoric has now woven its way deep into the consciousness of the Western mind. Secularization is seen as an inescapable political reality for Western democracies, with the public square a supposedly religiously neutral zone. Frankly, the state does not care what crazy beliefs people have so long as they keep them private. We only get a culture war when people insist on bringing those convictions into the public square. But, of course, that is exactly what we must do. *The gospel is public truth.* We do not just believe in our hearts and confess with our mouths that God raised Jesus from the dead. We believe He is currently reigning over heaven and earth and this public fact has inescapable consequences for human society and politics, not just our private lives.

As John Milbank has written, "Once there was no 'secular'"[85] —at least in the sense of secular space within culture. Secular space had to be imagined and made from scratch to create a sphere of human life which would be governed by "pure reason," free from the dogmatic prejudices of "religion." Or to put it another way, a "private religion" had to be invented in which the religious life was fully severed from public and political life. Milbank's profound thesis is that sociology—which separated out the "social" from the "religious" as distinct factors in human life—in effect became a counterfeit theology and ecclesiology.

The problem, of course, is that "religion" is not just one factor among many and cannot be factored out of any aspect of human life. Nor, for that matter, can religion be brought into some human endeavor at a secondary or tertiary level. In reality, religion is always already there because God is always already there and religion is simply our way of interfacing with and interacting with God in our moment-by-moment existence. But the Enlightenment sought to carve out a sector of life which was free from any kind of religious influence, a realm where God is neither active nor relevant. This is the Enlightenment myth.

---

85. John Milbank, *Theology and Social Theory: Beyond Secular Reason* (Oxford: Blackwell, 1990), 9. These are the opening words to Milbank's profoundly insightful and difficult work.

The impact of the Enlightenment shift would be hard to overstate. This movement inverted the worldview that had gripped the West for the previous millennia and a half. Previously, the church had thought in terms of "Christendom," a Christian civilization, in which Christ's preeminence extended beyond the human mind and heart to every nook and cranny of public life. Christ was lord of body as well as soul, of the political sphere as well as the domestic.

Christendom had its flaws, of course, because even the best of Christian societies (like the best of Christian individuals and Christian families) remain sinful. We should not overlook those flaws or brush them away. But we should learn from what Christendom got right. The notion that "Christ" and "culture" should be—or even could be—separated was unthinkable. The gospel was not a layer added to religiously neutral human life. Rather, biblical faith constituted a new way of living life in its entirety, a new way of being human. Nothing was "secular," for everything belonged to Christ and came within the scope of His lordship and redeeming grace. Pre-modern expressions of biblical religion acknowledged no dividing line between the public and private realms. Christ's lordship could not be placed in a box.

The post-Enlightenment view treated religion as an "aspect" of one's existence. It came to be regarded as one of many social factors that shaped a person's way of living. Other personal features, such as socioeconomic class, nationality, race, and gender were considered just as determinative. Religion could be stripped away and public life remain unaltered because religion was seen as private business. Political life would remain unchanged, no matter what god, gods, or goddesses happen to exist—or not exist—in the belief of the people.

In the modern period, evangelical Christianity shifted from being a public-facing church to a private system of beliefs and experiences for individuals. It was not a total way of life and it had no vision for the broader culture. The biblical reality is that God's work of redemption takes place in the time-space arena (Ps. 98:1-3), and not just inside the minds or hearts of individuals. God did not just give us a set of ideas to master. He gave us Himself in the person of His incarnate Son. The Son of God became embodied in the man Jesus. And Jesus formed a community around Himself—a community that shares in His very life and mission (John 20:21).

When reduced to some disembodied set of principles, "Christianity" is a perverse distortion of God's holistic work of salvation. The church is God's new creation, the restoration and reconstruction of our shattered humanity in and through Christ (2 Cor. 5:17-19). God's redemptive target is not isolated, fallen individuals but the entirety of creation (Rom. 8:19-25), represented by a new human race formed through union with Christ, the new Adam (Rom. 6:5-14).

The church is the firstfruits of God's saving work in the world (Jas. 1:18). Thus, the church models, in principle, human life the way God intended it to be lived. We are God's renewed humanity. In a fundamental way, we live the life of the future in the present, the life of the kingdom of God in the midst of the world. As the church, we are a new city set upon a hill and therefore distinct yet existing within the cities of the world. We are an alternative society, rivaling and subverting the idolatrous societies of the world. We are a counter-culture, called to reform and transform the cultures of the peoples around us. We are a kingdom, transcending the kingdoms of earth. And we are a new Israel, a new nation, dwelling amid the nations of the earth, with our own defining story, rituals, songs, celebrations, and way of life marking us out as a unique people. We are a contrast society—specifically contrasting the light of a gospel-shaped life with the darkness of the old fallen world order.

The church is our true family, city, nation, and kingdom, and none of these designations denigrates or destroys our participation in earthly families, cities, nations, and kingdoms. Those realities continue to exist in the present era, quite obviously, and should be discipled by the church. This is why Paul tells Christian fathers how to raise their children in the nurture and admonition of the Lord; while the church is our ultimate family, it does not cancel out the natural family, and the hope is that our natural families will be absorbed into God's eternal family. Likewise, this explains why and how Paul utilized his rights as a Roman citizen. His citizenship in the kingdom of heaven did not lead him to renounce his earthly citizenship, but he began to use his earthly citizenship in ways that furthered his work for the kingdom of God. In a similar way, we should use whatever political means we can to advance an agenda that is friendly to the kingdom of God.

Though much of the church has an under-realized eschatology, we must also beware of an over-realized eschatology that would lead us to a kind of (im)practical Gnosticism, cutting us off from participation in familial and cultural life. Rather, the point is that the church, as the body and bride of Christ, as the family and household of the heavenly Father, as the temple of the Holy Spirit, is our true and eternal home. Joining the church does not normally eradicate our membership in earthly institutions, but it does transform how we live in those this-worldly structures. Becoming a Christian does not mean you cease to be a member of your family—though in some cases, your family may cut off a new convert, and in those cases a Christian experiences in a real way what it means to have the church as your true family. Becoming a Christian does not mean one ceases to be an American or a Brazilian, but it does mean we will begin to work to disciple America or Brazil. A Christian American is a different kind of American and, if enough Americans are Christian, it will produce a different kind of America than the one we see today. The church is an international, global, multi-ethnic community, and this is what we mean when we call the church "catholic." But the goal of the church is not to replace or dissolve the nations of the earth. Rather the church in every nation seeks to transform that particular nation. When enough nations have been discipled and transformed in this way, living in fellowship with one another, we call the result "Christendom" (a Christian civilization).

Suppose we were to ask, "What would our community or city look like if everyone here wanted to serve Christ and give him preeminence in everything?" The church should be the answer to that question in a microcosm. The church is to place kingdom life on display. Just as car manufacturers release prototype models ahead of time to show in the present what we will be driving in the future, so the church is God's prototype of the life of the world to come in the present age. In the church, we hold up a picture of heaven to display resurrection life to those around us. We show the cities of man what the city of God looks like.

Sadly, many modern Christians do not share this view of the church because we have a bankrupt ecclesiology. Any concept of the church is grafted onto a "personal relationship with Jesus." Such a privatized connection with Jesus is considered the essence of true religion, rather than participating in new life and community in the body of Christ. For Enlightenment devotees as well as modern evangelicals, "religion" is a slice of life, not the overall slant of one's life. It is an isolated dimension of life rather than the totalizing direction of one's life. We have severed salvation from the church, and in doing so we have ripped apart what God intended as a whole package. We have individualized the communal and privatized the public. We split apart religion and politics, and comfort ourselves by reading that split back in the text of Scripture. But we cannot read Scripture through the lens of the Enlightenment, but must read the Enlightenment through the lens of Scripture.

If "Christianity" is essentially privatized in this way, it is no surprise that modern Christians do not desire a distinctively Christian culture. When bankrupt ecclesiology is coupled with pessimistic eschatology, modern evangelicals do not even think that Christian culture is possible.

An Enlightenment Gospel?

We have touched on how the Enlightenment pressed the church into a new mold, creating a new, highly truncated ecclesiology that would barely be recognized by the likes of

John Calvin and Martin Luther, much less medieval Christians. Now we need to explore this shift a bit further, especially as it relates to the emergence of the modern "state."

Over the course of a few centuries, the church went from a public institution, representing Christ on earth in the social matrix, to a privatized club for those with an interest in a personal relationship with Jesus. Enlightenment principles required that "reason" govern the public square because supposedly "reason" is religiously neutral and equally accessible to all. In this view, reason is universal and unites, whereas faith is particular and divides. Because the church speaks the dogmatic word of a particular faith, rather than the universal language of reason, the church must be left out of political discourse. The older, church-centered pattern of society, shaped by the story of the kingdom of God, had to give way to a newly-crafted secularism. The plot of this Enlightenment-generated story centers on ever-increasing autonomy for the individual, played out on a field of secularism, fenced by the (supposedly) religiously uncommitted state.

Individuals might still pursue a transcendent purpose, but society as a whole would be limited to this-worldly, immanent goals. No one "common good" could be used to structure the society. Previously the story of the kingdom of God gave society its purpose, goal, and structure. The vision of society's "common good" was formed and molded by the Bible. Now, in the wake of rising modernity, "goods" could only be chosen by individuals and pursued in private. Insofar as society itself could still have a common goal, the goal had to be religiously neutral. In reality, there would no longer be a "common good" because there was no longer a common faith. Thus, the church's social role would be largely diminished, unless the church simply acted to underwrite the emerging story of secularism.

We can understand the shift that took place in politics by looking at how religious liberty came to be redefined in the wake of secularism's rise to supremacy. Enlightenment philosophy and politics put a squeeze on the church by shifting the focus of religious liberty away from the church as a publicly visible, corporate entity—an institution—to the individual's conscience. Many U. S. state constitutions speak of the liberty of the individual's conscience: a person is "free" because he is permitted to follow the dictates of his conscience in religious matters.

For example, the Georgia State Constitution includes a Bill of Rights that defines religious liberty in the following way:

> Each person has the natural and inalienable right to worship God, each according to the dictates of that person's own conscience; and no human authority should, in any case, control or interfere with such right of conscience.

However, if the location of religious liberty is the individual's conscience, rather than the institutional church in the public square, "religion" has already been defined in Enlightenment terms, rather than biblical terms. This type of "religion" is free from the state's control because it is a matter of disembodied ideas and emotional experiences. It is not "incarnated" in the public square (where, no doubt, it might very well impinge upon the state's agenda).

While we should certainly appreciate what the framers of the Georgia Bill of Rights bequeathed to the citizens of that state (individual religious liberty is better than no religious liberty), we should not be satisfied with it.

Only religions that are defined according to the Enlightenment's model are truly "free." Religions that have "absolutizing" visions—that would desire to reshape and remold all of social life according to some ideal—are not free. To put it another way, the Enlightenment essentially outlawed the Great Commission. Instead we have the invisible, subversive religion of secularism pervading public life, "discipling" the nation in the secular worldview. Secularism is just cleverly disguised idolatry. It goes unnoticed because modern people have not been trained to detect its fundamentally religious nature.

Under the reigning modernity model, the church is still free to disciple individuals, but not nations. The present social structure does not allow Christians to embody their beliefs in American public life, at least not without great risk and social ostracism. In that sense, one might say that pre-Enlightenment forms of faith are illegal in America. Privatized Christianity is tolerated because it does not interfere with the secular agenda, but Christendom, or Christocracy, is not tolerated.

By contrast, the first point of the thirteenth century *Magna Carta* concerned the liberty of the church as an institution over and against the king (the state): "The English Church shall be free, and shall have its rights undiminished, and its liberties unimpaired." In the *Magna Carta*, "religious freedom" means the freedom of the church from state interference, not the freedom of the state from church interference, nor the freedom of the individual from all external authorities. Religious liberty is the freedom of the church to disciple (and discipline) her members, including those who hold public roles, and to even act as an institution in the social sphere.

The point here is *not* that the *Magna Carta* established a better system of civil liberties than the American nation and American states. The wide expansion of individual liberties that accompanied the Reformation and American War for Independence have been a positive good, and may even be seen as the legitimate outworking of the *Magna Carta* tradition (which is a tradition very much shaped by the church and the gospel). Furthermore, the Reformation's respect for personal conscience was a tremendous advancement in human rights. Rather, the point here is simply that the church's freedom, as an institution, to act in and shape the public square, has been radically diminished in the last few centuries. In its place we have religiously free individuals and, as the myth runs, a religiously neutral public arena.

The church's role in society has become virtually invisible. Most Christians have accepted the premise that Christian influence in the public arena can only be exerted by Christian individuals, and not by the church in any form or fashion. The church that subscribes to the Enlightenment model is most certainly not a political entity—which is to say, she really is not the city of God, the new Israel, or the kingdom of Jesus Christ. Those political images and metaphors for the church have been muted. She is a voluntary organization that serves the private needs and desires of her members.

None of us have escaped the influence of this Enlightenment shift. If modern Christians hear the words "freedom of religion," they instinctively think not of the freedom of the church to be the church but of the freedom of any individual to adopt whatever belief system, ideology, or religious opinions he wants. Ironically, he may not be free to live out those principles in practice because that might involve "imposing" his beliefs on others. "Freedom of religion" is really freedom for Gnosticism and not much else.[86] Mormons are not allowed to practice polygamy; Native Americans are not allowed to use intoxicating drugs in their religious services as their ancestors did; and Christians are not allowed to press the crown rights of King Jesus in political discourse. Enlightenment "religion" has lost its corporate, public dimension.

It should be noted that when we understand the public, political, totalizing nature of religion, we find that no religious neutrality is really possible. Secularism has dominated the field by pretending to be neutral. But it is not. It is a rival to the gospel. We must be at war with it, using the spiritual weapons Christ has given us.

We should be aware that this is not the first time in history that privatized religious pluralism in the public square has been exploited for political ends. Indeed, the strategy of the Enlightenment philosophers is one that has been adopted through the corridors of history.

The book of Daniel is instructive. King Nebuchadnezzar did not mind various expressions of "private piety" in his empire, provided people were willing to bow down to

---

86. Lee, *Against the Protestant Gnostics*

his statue. This civic religion was a public way of gluing together the various competing religions and keeping peace. Worship who or what you want in private, but pledge loyalty to the empire in public or else be accused of treason. Daniel's three friends refused to privatize their faith, and the end result (after passing through a fiery trial!) was Nebuchadnezzar's conversion and public recognition of the God of Israel (Dan. 3-4).

Similarly, the Roman Empire tolerated a wide range of religious diversity, provided citizens gave ultimate public allegiance to Caesar. A religion could be licensed so long as it agreed to Rome's privatization plan. Because the early Christians refused to comply and would not allow the church to become a pawn of the state, they were regarded as atheists![87] The empire offered at one point to give Jesus a place in the pantheon of their gods (that is, a "place at the table" in Rome's civil discourse) but the church rejected the offer. They knew Jesus was not one deity among many. He was the lord and conqueror of the pagan idols. His truth and lordship were every bit as public and totalizing as Caesar's. Indeed, even more so. They could not purchase peace for themselves or the empire at the price of fidelity to their king and savior.

87. See R. J. Rushdoony, *The "Atheism" of the Early Church*. Rushdoony quotes Justin Martyr: "We confess we are atheists so far as gods of this sort are concerned, but not with respect to the most true God, the Father of righteousness and temperance and the other virtues, who is free from all impurity."

The Gospel is Political

In the wake of the Enlightenment, faithful Christians lost sight of the intrinsically political nature of their faith. Politics and faith became separate, parallel pursuits, never intersecting. Modern politics was totally immersed in human culture, with no transcendent reference point. The modernized faith was formulated in such an extreme transcendent way, that it was of little cultural value. The old cliché, "he's so heavenly minded, he's of no earthly good," has proved true in the case of the modern church.

Biblically, we can say that *the political is always religious and the religious always political.*[88] "Politics" is being used here in the broad, classical sense. The political is not merely the organization and administration of civil power (what Paul called "the sword" in Romans 13), but the structure and ethos of human communities (the *polis*) as a whole. Thus the "political" is roughly synonymous with the "public" or "societal."

The gospel is an intrinsically political message. This is not to say the gospel consists of particular pieces of legislation, nor is it to promote one particular candidate or party from the left or the right. The left and right are both constructs within modern Enlightenment political philosophy. Rather than coming from the left or right, Jesus's kingdom

---

88. The New Testament is, in fact, shot through with political language. This political vocabulary has been lost for a long time, though it is being regained today by a wide swath of scholars such as Stanley Hauerwas, Rodney Clapp, N. T. Wright, Peter Leithart, John Milbank, Barry Harvey, Oliver O'Donovan, Rodney Stark, Richard Horsley, George Lindbeck, and William Cavanaugh, to name a few.

comes from above. His kingdom does not fit into the Enlightenment's box.

To say that the gospel is intrinsically political is to acknowledge that the gospel announces that the world has a new king—Jesus Christ. The Greek term *evangelion* was used in the ancient world to announce decisive political events of a public nature, such as the ascension of a new emperor, a great military victory, the birth of a royal heir, and so forth. Some have suggested that "gospel" should be translated as "political tidings." The term was decidedly public in nature in the first century context. It did not announce a new religious experience on offer. It announced a new state of affairs, the dawning of a new phase in the imperial narrative.

To the extent that Christians have lost sight of the intrinsically political dimension of the gospel, they have lost touch with the apostolic teaching. The gospel is the announcement that a new world order has been established through the death and resurrection of Jesus Christ. It is God's public service announcement that things are now going to be put right on earth as they are in heaven.

Moreover, the gospel is politically charged because it has everything to do with the way we structure communal life in society. The biblical story reveals that God originally intended humanity to live in harmonious community. The Fall of man into sin wrecked that unity and turned diversity into division. The gospel is God's work in Christ to restore creation and rebuild human community.

Think how much time politicians spend trying to find ways to get people to live side by side in peace, without killing one another. Think how much time politicians spend trying to achieve compromises between competing racial, social, and economic groups. And yet those contrived solutions are equivalent to treating tumors with band-aids. All the king's horses and all the king's men cannot put humanity back together again. Only the gospel of Christ can mend the ripped fabric of human society. The gospel is the answer to all the public and political ills of the modern world (cf. Isa. 2).

To go one step further, we must avoid thinking of the relationship of gospel and politics in a "two-step" fashion. The gospel does not merely have political *implications* which come in at some secondary level. It is not as if the gospel is apolitical at its core but intrudes upon political matters when one moves out to the periphery. Instead, we must say that politics is internal to the gospel, all along the way. Politics cannot be "brought into" the sphere of the gospel because the gospel was never separated from politics in the first place.

The core declaration of the gospel, "Jesus is Lord" is as political a statement as one can make (Acts 2:36; Rom. 10:9; 1 Cor. 12:3). It cannot be translated into non-particular, universal categories that meet the requirements of Enlightenment political philosophy. The announcement that Jesus is Lord demands that human society be structured in a certain way. It demands that we not exploit each other, that we turn the other cheek, that we cross over all kinds of lines between the races and classes, that we pursue justice and truth in all our relationships, and so forth. "Jesus is Lord" is the seedbed of a far greater social revolution than "Liberty or death" or "Peace, liberty, and the pursuit of happiness" or "Liberty, fraternity, and equality."

Those other slogans are supercharged political declarations, to be sure, but none of them are as radically subversive and transformative as the declaration of Acts 2:36. Thus, we do not need to add politics to the gospel. Rather, we need to understand the political shape the biblical gospel has had all along and restructure our own lives and agendas accordingly.

Early opponents of the church understood these issues. Pagans knew the declaration of Christ's lordship was a threat to the status quo of the Roman Empire. In Acts 17, Christians were accused of treason against Caesar because they were preaching "another king—Jesus" (Acts 17:7). Here, an ordinary, mundane Christian practice (preaching the gospel) was seen to be a directly *political* action. Indeed, it turned the entire existing social order "upside down" (Acts 17:6)—or more accurately, from the perspective of the gospel itself—right side up. If our evangelism does not lead people to believe we are proclaiming an alternative king and kingdom, we have fallen short of the biblical message.

First-century Jews also had an acute sense of the politics of the gospel. The gospel-wrought reconciliation of Jew and Gentile believers in Christ (cf. Eph. 2:11ff) is thoroughly *political*. It restructures the ethics and makeup of human community, transforming the old world order into something new. Jews understood very clearly that the gospel turned their political order upside down. The gospel caused just as much chaos in Jewish contexts as it did in pagan ones (cf. Acts 19:21ff; 21:26ff).

Every culture and political order ultimately has to settle the issue of authority. Who is Lord? By what standard?

Every culture is founded on certain religious commitments. It is not *whether* but *which*, as many are fond of saying—it is not a matter of *whether* a society will be religious, but *which* religion will be foundational. The god of any society is revealed by asking, "Who is protected? Who are we not allowed to criticize?" Every society has blasphemy laws to protect its god(s). Cancel culture reveals our blasphemy laws.

In a Christian society, the state still has authority, but it is not absolute. Christ is Lord, which means Caesar is not. Instead, the scope of Caesar's power will be limited. Caesar will conform his own law-system to those aspects of God's law that are appropriate to the state. Likewise, in a Christian social order, husbands and fathers still have authority in the home. But such familial authority will be restrained and its exercise will be shaped by gospel principles.

The Wrongs of the Religious Right

Modern Christians are often more modern than they are Christian. The Religious Right is a case in point. While the Religious Right has largely died out as a movement, the way of thinking that animated the movement is all too common in traditionalist and conservative Christian circles.

The Religious Right's mentality is the creation of American evangelicalism, as an attempt to "apply" the gospel to American politics. But the movement is deeply flawed because it follows the Enlightenment in defining politics too narrowly (as a civil power game) and never calls into question the basic assumptions of modernity (e.g., the nature of "religion" as a private belief system or ideology).

It plays by modernity's rules instead of the gospel's rules. It does not make the declaration of Christ's lordship the center of its political agenda. Indeed, the Religious Right is usually far more modest, asking only for a "place at the table" of American public discourse. But Christ did not tell us to get Him a place at the table of religious pluralism, He told us to make the nations His disciples (Matt. 28:18-20).

The Religious Right operates in terms of the religious freedom of the individual rather than the freedom of the church to be the church. It is based on the same mistaken ecclesiology as the Enlightenment, not considering the church a player in the public arena. There is still a lingering tendency on the part of some politically active evangelicals to view politics, narrowly defined as a civil power game, as the source of cultural transformation. In this respect, not only has the movement lost sight of the social role of the church, but the Religious Right has not come to grips with the end of Christendom, and still looks rather naively to the civil government and other cultural institutions (e.g., Disney, WalMart) to uphold vaguely Christian moral standards.

It is ironic that many involved in the Religious Right are quicker to "discipline" (via boycotts) major corporations like Disney or Netflix for failing to uphold traditional moral values, even though the same people generally fail to discipline members of their own congregations for moral failings. They are looking to extra-ecclesiastical structures to do their disciplining for them. They must learn that the world is the world, and the job of the church is to provide a contrast to worldly society by being holy (distinct, different) at precisely those points where the world is most fully rebelling against Christ's lordship.

Because the Religious Right divorces politics from the church's mission and fails to reckon with the intrinsically political character of the gospel, it can offer no sustained challenge to the Enlightenment's program of privatization. Indeed, the Religious Right has been too quick to comply with post-Enlightenment political philosophy.

The political program of the Religious Right is not really explicitly Christian and does not grow out of the church's mission or ministries. Instead it tends to promote a bland platform of "traditional values." The movement does not view the church as intrinsically political, especially in her liturgy, sacraments, preaching, discipline, and hospitality. It does not view the Bible as a political, covenantal book. Rather, for the Religious Right, the only way to act "politically" in the world is to lobby, organize voters, promote candidates, march on Washington, write letters to the editor, and so on. In this model, politics has to be "tacked on" to preaching, baptism, and the Eucharist since the church's rituals are viewed as intrinsically private acts rather than public. The only "political weapons" in the Religious Right's arsenal are identical to those used by the secularists.

The Church's Political Practices

We have just noted above that the New Testament's "gospel" language functions not merely at the level of personal salvation, but also at the level of the political and the public as well. Evangelism is a political activity. The claim "Jesus is Lord" was a direct assault on Caesar's idolatrous pretensions. Because Jesus is the world's true king, Caesar's kingship can be nothing more than a shallow parody. We have not preached the gospel to an unbeliever unless he says back to us, "You're preaching another king—Jesus!" Evangelism is not just about offering "personal" salvation or a new religious experience. It is about announcing the world's new king and calling people to faithful submission.

As we declare this gospel, and summon people into the kingdom, we find that God does marvelous and miraculous things. When we announce the crucified one is now lord of all, history shoots off in new directions. Culture is transformed. Society is recreated. The mere preaching of the gospel—if we really got it right—would be enough to cast down the strongholds of secularism (2 Cor. 10:4-11). Preaching is thoroughly *political*. Through preaching, God shapes and reshapes the world, directing the course of history. Herman Melville recognized this when he called the pulpit the "prow" of the world. But other Christian practices are political as well. Indeed the entire life of the church has a political texture to it.

Take prayer as another example. We do not need to "add" politics to prayer. Instead we need to realize how politically potent prayer already is. Biblically speaking, prayer is the primary way God brings radical change in the public square. If we want to change our society, we should not first march on Washington. Instead we should fervently pray—and then watch what God does. Prayer is intensely *political* because it is supplication offered before the throne of grace.

We may be excluded from places of political power on earth. We may not hold prominent positions in government. We may not be cabinet members, with access to the Oval Office. But we have something better than all these things. We are the bride of Christ. And if Jesus is King of Kings and Lord of Lords, that makes the church Queen of Queens. We have power in the world because our divine husband, the one who rules over all things in heaven and earth, consults us and hears us in corporate prayer in the Lord's service. As a good husband, He listens to His bride. Thus, prayer directs the course of history. Through the prayers of the saints, God causes empires to rise and fall, battles to be won and lost, rulers to come and go, pieces of legislation to pass and fail, Supreme Court rulings to come and go.

Likewise, the weekly partaking of the Eucharist not only fills our hearts with gratitude, it also is the basis of our leaning into the world in a Christian manner. Ancient Roman cities like Corinth organized their public life in terms of religious festivals and rituals. The citizens of the city would gather together to eat an animal that had been sacrificed to the god of the city. The table arrangements were highly segregated. If you had a higher rank in the city, you got a better seat at the table, a better cut of meat to eat, and a better cup of wine to drink.

The ancient city was centered around its table fellowship, and we can say the same of the church, the city of God. When the church moved into a city, the first thing she did, along with proclaiming the gospel, was to set up a new feast with new table arrangements and table manners. Paul says that at the Lord's table, we have fellowship with the Lord and with one another (1 Cor. 10:16). Christ's giving of Himself becomes the pattern of our relationships with one another. The Eucharist creates unity, but also requires unity from us.

Coming to the table rightly is coming in unity and love. In the ancient Roman festivals, there was no shared table. There was no mixing of citizen and non-citizen or rich and poor together. But at the Lord's table, there is a communing together that breaks through all of the social divisions. Do you know of any corporation where the CEO and the janitor have lunch together on a regular basis? At the Lord's table, these class divisions are broken down. It does not matter your rank in society or what color your skin is. If you are in Christ, you come and eat with the rest of Christ's family. This is the politics and economics of the kingdom of Christ.

The early Christians are a good example of the church's "alternative politics" at work. They had no direct political leverage in the sense that they were highly marginalized socially and culturally. Yet, they were still able to act as a subversive, transforming presence within the Roman empire, ultimately bringing it to its knees before Jesus. They accomplished this astounding (political) coup simply by being the church—preaching and confessing Jesus is Lord, being united to Christ through public baptism, regularly manifesting the church as the new and true humanity at the Lord's table, dying for the life of the world in mercy ministry, showing hospitality, binding and loosing in church discipline to maintain the integrity of the community, and so forth. This is the church's "political agenda" properly conceived.

Conclusion

In the beginning, God assigned a task to Adam and Eve: "Be fruitful and multiply; fill the earth and subdue it"

(Gen. 1:28). His intent was that His image bearers would spread throughout all the earth, building a civilization that would reflect His glory back to Himself. This same task has been re-issued to the church through Jesus, in the Great Commission (Matt. 28:18-20). For the modern church to get onto the path of cultural transformation, rather than cultural retreat, the ministry of the church must get back to the biblical record.

The church must preach the gospel of the kingdom, proclaimed by Christ. We must recover the entire kingdom story, beginning with creation, through the Fall of man, with the centrality of Christ's death and resurrection, His ascension, and sending of the Holy Spirit at Pentecost. The church must acknowledge her central role within the kingdom of God, and take seriously her mission to disciple the nations, with the Lord's service fueling that mission through biblically prescribed practices of worship. The church must go out into the world, loving God and neighbor through service in various vocations.

We cannot accept the modern dualism that privatizes the church and the gospel. We must keep Christian civilization in view as the goal. God will be satisfied with nothing less than a saved, glorified world, and neither can we. The Bible gives us hope, through its eschatological promises, and it gives us direction, through its blueprint for life in the covenant community. It is high time we claimed the promises and enacted the vision.

Appendix A

The Culture War and the Spiritual War

I sometimes get asked why my sermons so frequently engage so-called "culture war" issues. The same question could be asked of this book. Here are some reasons why I think pastors need to be address the culture's trends.

One

What if the culture war is actually much more than a culture war? What if the culture war is really a proxy for the kind of spiritual war Paul describes in Ephesians 6? What if the culture war is really a battle over spiritual allegiances? Obviously, not every divisive issue in our culture rises to that level. But many do. For example, abortion is not just a cultural or social or political issue. It is ultimately a spiritual and even liturgical issue. Abortion is nothing less than child sacrifice, offering up innocent little ones to Molech on the altar of convenience, comfort, and career. In opposing abortion, we are waging war against the principalities and powers, evil forces of darkness in high places. But abortion is not the only issue that works this way. Many issues that get framed as cultural, social, political, or economic are actually spiritual, liturgical, and theological. The reality is that the culture war and the spiritual war are almost indistinguishable at this point in our history. To opt out of the culture war is actually an act of cowardly surrender to the principalities and powers. It is to retreat precisely when our Lord has commanded us to advance, to charge the enemy, to take the battering ram of the gospel to the gates of hell. The ironic thing is that while many on the left are starting to recognize the religious nature of the culture war, many Christians still naively deny it.

Two

In 1 Timothy 4, Paul warns Timothy about demonic doctrines infiltrating the church. What are these demonic doctrines? The false teachers were forbidding people to marry and to eat certain foods. But if Paul could see false teaching about such mundane realities as marriage and diet to be aspects of spiritual warfare, surely many of the so-called culture war issues in our day fall into the same category. We must recognize that gender ideology, critical race theory, feminism, socialism, and so on, are all doctrines of demons. They frustrate God's design for humanity in the same way the false teachers in 1 Timothy 4 were doing. We must fight against these satanic teachings from the pulpit as well as out of the pulpit. And, yes, this means we should view progressivism/leftism as demonic doctrine. This does not mean everyone advocating these doctrines is demon possessed or any such thing (though some undoubtedly are), but it does mean these views arise from an anti-God spirit. Take gender ideology as an example. Some gender fluid persons use plural pronouns, reminiscent of the legion of demons that inhabited the man in Mark 5. The bodily mutilation that transgenderism requires is significantly similar to pagan rituals. And some transgenders have been very explicit about the connection between witchcraft, Satan worship, and leftwing politics. Of course, our ministry cannot be characterized only by what we are against. As has been said, to fight a culture war, you have to have a culture. And so it is just as important that we build a positive vision of what we are for—namely, the next Christendom. But note that when our civilization finally collapses into rubble, those who best understood what caused the rot will be in the best position to rebuild it.

Three

In terms of preaching and teaching on these issues, the faithful pastor has an obligation to do so because Scripture does. Many so-called culture war issues are directly addressed by biblical teaching (marriage, sex, and gender issues; racism/partiality; the role of the state and the way to care for the poor; etc.). Most modern evangelical and Reformed preaching is very therapeutic. It focuses on the individual—his needs, his experiences, his sins, his challenges, his life. Certainly, faithful biblical preaching will address the individual heart, and call on individuals to trust Christ, repent from sin, etc. But the overall message of the Bible is far greater than this. The Bible gives us an overarching view of the cosmos and history. It gives us broad redemptive-historical categories. It tells the true story of the world. It is just as concerned with national experiences as individual experiences. Pick up a Bible and read virtually any of the prophets: You will find the prophets continually talking about the nations, their sins, their idols, and their need to repent, just as much as (if not more than) you find them talking about the individual heart. It is the same with the Psalms. Calvin rightly called the psalter an "anatomy of the human soul." But it is also an anatomy of kingdoms and empires. If the Psalms were only concerned with individual experiences, there would be no need for imprecatory psalms. Those psalms are about enemies, but their spiritual enmity manifests itself in political and cultural ways. The prayers and songs of the psalter blend personal piety with political and cultural piety. Thus, any sharp divide between the culture war and the spiritual war is unbiblical. The culture is a spiritual reality. The culture is shot through with theological issues. Ultimately, culture is formed by what we worship. So culture wars are always about much more than just the culture, narrowly considered. Our cultural divides are deep divides, rooted in what we worship and what we love.

Churches that are under the influence of liberalism and progressivism (if they can still be called churches) preach about political issues, but disregard the Bible as they do so. They have no spiritual message to preach, and their social message is completely dominated with the agenda of the anti-God, anti-Biblical American left. But churches on the right often preach only a message of individual salvation. While that is much better, it is still not fully adequate. We need to preach the whole counsel of God, which necessarily means preaching on cultural and political topics.

Four

Preaching about culture war issues is critical to doing cultural apologetics. Cultural apologetics is an important aspect of discipleship. It makes church members into sons of Issachar, who understand the times and therefore know what the people of God should do. Preaching biblically and boldly on these issues grows people in understanding and wisdom.

A significant aspect of wisdom is foresight—not that the wise can foresee the future in detail, but they can discern where current trajectories will lead. In the year 2023, it has become painfully obvious that many conservative evangelicals in the 1980s and 1990s were exactly right about where our culture was headed. (Perhaps many of us owe them an apology for thinking they were overreacting?) One by one, things that were once unthinkable have become realities. And if you question the new morality, expect to be canceled. Truths everyone accepted as common sense fifteen minutes ago are now disdained as barbaric.

Because wisdom gives foresight, it is preemptive. Preaching about cultural issues, showing where the current cultural trajectories will lead, helps the church exercise a role of cultural leadership. To put it in Edwin Friedman's terms, a church that has been trained to understand the trends and direction of culture can be anticipatory and preemptive, rather than just reactive. It took the church well over a decade to really understand what the *Roe* ruling of 1973 meant. Many in the church were much quicker to understand what the *Obergefell* ruling would mean and were able to predict it before it even happened.

Five

We must distinguish the way in which we critique and oppose positions in a sermon from the way we treat people who advocate those same positions we are preaching against. While numerous issues have been politicized, that does not mean we have to politicize all our relationships. We can distinguish cultural movements and forces from the persons who are caught up in them. We can distinguish how we respond to a movement institutionally from how we respond to it at a personal level.

Thus, I can oppose same sex "marriage" even while loving a gay couple that lives next door. Disagreeing with someone is not the same as hating them. If they are enemies in the culture war, remember, Jesus commanded us to love our enemies. I can oppose the transgender movement, with all its political and cultural implications, while still having compassion toward those who suffer from gender dysphoria. I can point out the wretched results of feminism, or the welfare state, or critical race theory, while showing kindness to those who hold to these very positions in my neighborhood or workplace. Just as disagreeing with someone's positions or lifestyle does not mean I hate them, loving my neighbor does not mean I approve of everything he believes or does.

At the same time, it is important to not be naive. Just because we show kindness to those we disagree with, or just because we are winsome (to use a favorite evangelical buzz word) in how we speak truth to them, does not mean we will escape their ire. At one point in our history (during what Aaron Renn calls the "neutral world," which ended about 2014), Christians could expect relatively fair treatment in most situations in our culture. That is no longer the case. It is simply impossible for Christians to gain acceptance or preserve respectability while holding to biblical positions on sexuality, among other things. So we must be prepared for pushback. It will come.

Six

Evangelicals did not invent the culture war in the last thirty years. Christians, at least mature Christians, have always understood that the Christian faith is an embodied, and therefore culturally incarnate, faith, and that the kingdom of God's conflict with the kingdom of Satan can be manifest in historical, political, and cultural ways. Consider a brief historical survey of the culture war.

Jesus established the culture war in new covenant form when He gave the Great Commission. Discipling the nations means doing battle with the false gods of the nations. It means converting nations and teaching people how God's Word applies to all of life. To back away from the culture war in order to save souls is to truncate the Great Commission, robbing it of its greatness. It fails to do justice to the authority over heaven and earth that has been granted to Jesus. Why engage in the culture war? Because Jesus is Lord. And because He told us to. A culture war is the inevitable result of the church undertaking the Great Commission.

The apostles involved themselves in a culture war by directly challenging the pretentious claims of Caesar. Their announcement, "Jesus is Lord," was a direct threat to Caesar's claim to lordship. This is why they were accused of treason against the empire (cf. Acts 17). When Peter declared in Acts 4:12, "Neither is there salvation in any other, for there is no other name under heaven given among men whereby we may be saved," he was actually paraphrasing the decree of Augustus Caesar, who declared in 17 BC, "Salvation is to be found in no other but Augustus, and there is no other name given to men in which they can be saved." Peter obviously substituted Jesus' name for Augustus' name. And no doubt, Peter had a different understanding of the kind of salvation in view. But Peter's announcement makes no sense unless he understood that Jesus is Lord over all. And precisely because He is Lord over all, all of culture and all nations are to be discipled in terms of His Word. You could say Peter was firing some of the first shots in the culture war between God's kingdom and Satan's kingdom, a war that continues down to the very present. If you were to ask Peter if his message was religious or political, he would not have understood the question; the religious was totally intertwined with the social, cultural, and political.

The early Christians in the post-apostolic era were persecuted because they would not burn a pinch of incense to Caesar. They did not conform to the customs and ways of the Roman Empire, particularly when it came to sex and money, which made them easy targets. But had they wanted to avoid persecution, they could have done so by downplaying those issues that made them stand out. They could have avoided persecution by becoming culturally invisible. They were not persecuted because they worshiped Jesus; the Romans cared little about which gods were worshipped in their empire. They were persecuted because they were against worshiping the state. In other words, they were early Christian culture warriors and stood firm on the issues of the day, even if it cost them their lives.

Augustine's *City of God* is one of the greatest works of cultural apologetics and cultural warfare in the history of the church. Augustine wrote to expose the moral corruption of Rome, rooted in its idolatry, and to defend Christians against the charge that they were to blame for the collapse of the empire. Augustine wrote as a critic of Rome, starting with its founding myth, showing that a society built upon fratricide could never be stable, or serve as a source of peace and justice. It is interesting to consider the balance of Augustine. He wrote *Confessions* to tap into the heart of Christian experience at the personal level. In *City of God*, he complemented *Confessions* by looking at the big, historical, cultural, and political picture, examining how God has worked across the generations to establish His "city" over and against man's "city" (which is really Satan's city). Every society is based on a common good, and a common good requires a common love. Augustine explains Rome is fraying because the empire is divided against itself. As Augustine explains, the city of man is organized around the loves of fallen man. The city of man seeks to satisfy man's disordered lusts. By contrast, the city of God is rooted in love for God, and a desire to satisfy His will. Augustine believes men will always "become what they love." Thus, the conflict of the ages is a conflict of loves. Augustine sees the two cities as locked in a comprehensive battle—a totalizing culture war—that will endure until the last day. Augustine's work undoubtedly marks him out as one of the greatest culture warriors in church history. His work gives us a paradigm for understanding all cultural conflict.

The Reformers were culture warriors. They were wrestling for the soul of Christendom. But their battles were not just theological or liturgical. They were cultural and political and social as well. For example, Martin Luther very clearly saw his marriage to Katie as an act of spiritual warfare. When the former monk married the former nun, Luther said he gave "a roundhouse kick to the devil in the snout." John Calvin addressed his *Institutes* to the King of France. He was not only writing a systematic handbook of theology; he was writing a work of political theology with wide-ranging cultural ramifications. The heirs of his project in the new world implemented his principles in the War for American Independence. The formation of America happened largely because Christians were willing to turn a culture war into a hot war, with real fighting and real bloodshed. They understood that the Christian faith cultivates a love for freedom and a hatred of tyranny.

By historic standards, American evangelicals of the late twentieth and early twenty-first centuries have been pretty tame culture warriors.

Seven

I preach on culture war issues for the sake of the children. In fact, one thing I have noticed over the years is that those with children are usually (though not always) much more concerned with culture war issues than those without children. And those who have older children (teenagers) are much more concerned than those with younger children. Wise parents will realize that the world they are preparing their children to enter is hostile to them and their faith. And they will want their children thoroughly equipped. I pity the covenant child who is sent off to college without a firm understanding of how feminism has helped wreck the family, or how critical race theory is actually a deeply racist ideology. I have seen many kids left unprepared who have fallen away from the faith the first time they experienced a real challenge.

It is important to understand the culture war is largely a war about who will disciple the next generation. Secularists hardly have any children. Between abortion, homosexuality, and a burgeoning anti-natalism movement (based largely on terrible "climate science"), non-Christians have very few children. But that means if they are going to have a future, they must take our children. Why did the San Francisco Gay Men's Chorus sing "we're coming for your children"? Whatever they might claim after the fact, it was not a joke. Why is Disney so intent on sexualizing children with their content? Why do Florida's progressive public school teachers react so strongly to a bill that would forbid exposing very young school children to sexual matters? Why have so many public school boards across the country exploded over the teaching of critical race theory in the classroom? It's because, with the birth rate dropping to record lows, children have become a scarce commodity. We fight over children because children represent the future. Whoever disciples the children will win the future.

The fact that conservative Christians have more children than most other groups in the culture is a hopeful sign, but it only matters if we actually keep our children in the fold of the faith. If the world captures them, they will fight on the wrong side of the great battle of history. We can only win by "outbreeding" the enemy if our children are truly straight and sharp arrows in the quiver of their fathers (Psalm 127). In the long run, the only hope progressives have of winning the culture war is to capture and corrupt our children, which is why the public school system and universities are so important to them. Of course, they can also count on Hollywood, the pop music industry, and social media to aid their cause. Christian father, are you awake to what is happening to the world your child is going into? Christian mother, do you realize what the world is seeking to do with your children? You may be uninterested in the culture war, but the culture war is interested in your children. Even if you have become wary and weary of the culture wars, fight them for the sake of your children. Your children will be culture warriors; the only question is which side they will be fighting on.

We need to understand that Satan counterfeits everything good. The left has its own version of theonomy (they want the will of their god to be legislated), postmillennialism (they fight the culture war to win it, with optimism and a sense of inevitability about their cause), and covenantalism (they claim the next generation as their own, and aim to indoctrinate kids into their perverted worldview). We can only fight back with the weapons of true theonomy, postmillennialism, and covenantalism. We fight the culture war by obeying God's law in every area of life, trusting in God's plan of kingdom growth, and claiming God's promises to and about our children.

Many of us have wondered what lurks under the "+" sign in the LGBTQ+ movement. Many of us have suspected pedophilia would be the next domino of perversion to fall. There are now signs that the legitimizing of pedophilia is on the agenda. For our part, we must do all we can to protect children from sexual predators. That should include calling for the death penalty for child molesters. Jesus seemed to think those who abused children should have a millstone tied around their necks and be cast into a deep sea (Matt. 18:6). I agree.

Eight

All that being said, some conservatives do fight the culture war in dumb ways. Having Donald Trump in the pulpit is a good example of what not to do. But that's obviously not what we are advocating. We are seeking to fight the culture war with the spiritual weapons God has given us—preaching, prayer, worship, psalms, and hymns. We will suffer and serve our way to victory. The sword that will slay the enemy comes from the mouth of the Messiah (Rev. 19).

Nine

If we are not supposed to preach on so-called culture war issues, what is left to preach? There are very few issues in our culture that have not been politicized. There are very few issues that are not connected to the culture war in some way.

If we are not supposed to preach on culture war issues, then marriage and sex cannot be preached because every aspect of marriage and sex have been swept up into the culture war. Obviously it is ridiculous to say these issues should not be taught from the pulpit. A pastor who does not address marriage and sex is not a faithful pastor. But take something that might seem to be more distant from the culture wars, like anxiety. Preaching about anxiety might seem to be insulated from the culture war, but it's really not. As soon as we start preaching about anxiety, we are going to touch on issues of mental health, medication, and the causes of anxiety. Each one of these will get into culture war issues. We live in a culture that once stigmatized mental illness but now glorifies mental illness; surely the church must say something about that. The issue of medicating away anxiety and other emotional problems has been a hot topic in the culture since the Rolling Stones sang about it in their 1966 song, "Mother's Little Helper." The church has to say something about it. There are many reasons for increased anxiety in the culture today, ranging from family breakdown to social media use to incompetent leadership at virtually every level of government and society, and so it is impossible to separate the causes of anxiety from the wider problems facing our world. If we are going to cast our cares on the Lord who cares for us, we have to identify those cares, and that will undoubtedly run us into culture war territory.

Or take another example that may seem far removed from the culture wars but really isn't: Love of neighbor. It might seem like a pastor could preach about love of neighbor without getting entangled in the culture war. But for the last couple years, we have had leading evangelicals and many politicians from both sides of the aisle tell us that loving our neighbor requires shuttering the economy, canceling public worship services, socially distancing, not visiting the sick in hospitals or the elderly in retirement communities, receiving an experimental vaccine, and wearing a mask in public. Either love of neighbor requires these things or it does not, but it is impossible to remain neutral. The church will either meet or not. The church will either require masks or not. There's no way to avoid these issues.

That's really the bottom line: It is simply impossible to avoid the culture war. It is all pervasive. It has seeped into almost everything. There is no way a church's leadership or a pastor in his preaching can somehow avoid being a player in the culture war. The calling of the church is not to somehow transcend the culture war (that would likely turn us into Gnostics) but to fight the culture war faithfully.

Ten

I've had a number of people thank me for occasionally addressing these issues, basically telling me, "It's good to be reminded from time to time that I am not crazy!" The world is going insane. It's good to have regular reminders from the pulpit of what sanity looks like. Preaching should put people in touch with reality, especially in an age that has detached from it almost completely.

Appendix B

A Brief Overview
of Ecclesiocentrism

This book has presupposed ecclesiocentrism but has not spelled out what that means. Ecclesiocentrism is incredibly simple to understand and absolutely ubiquitous in Scripture.

The church is the central and most important thing in the world and in history.

That's it. That's the fundamental claim.

Ecclesiocentrism can be found on almost every page of the Bible. Some examples:

- Nations are blessed or cursed according to how they treat the church (Gen. 12)

- God rules all things for the sake of his church (Eph. 1)

- Grace restores nature, but where is that grace found? In the means given to the church (e.g., in Psalm 128 the blessed man's blessing comes from Zion, which is the church according to Hebrews 12)

- As the church goes, so the world goes (e.g., in Matthew 5 where the church is salt and light)

- Ecclesiastical reformation drives cultural transformation (the lesson of Haggai 1)

- Judgment and reformation begin with the household of God (1 Pet. 4)

- The discipleship of the nations and of every sphere of life begins in the church (Matt. 28)

- The church is the leading institution in society and church history is the core of world history (this is evident from the prophets, Acts, etc.)

- The Lord's service on the Lord's Day with the Lord's people in the Lord's sanctuary is the most important thing we do (the Fall took place with a forbidden meal in the sanctuary; restoration is manifested through a meal in the sanctuary)

- God created the world for the sake of the church (as Luther said) so that his Son might have a bride (as Edwards said)

- The storyline of the Bible is basically the storyline of the church (e.g., when the prophets and Acts deal with history, they present the church as central to world events)

The basic point: the world won't change until the church changes. The church leads the way.

Ecclesiocentrists strongly resist dualisms that would marginalize or privatize the church. We believe the church has a public, even political character, as God's holy nation. So, for example, in many "two kingdom" approaches, it is claimed that the church should deal only with "heavenly" or "spiritual things." The church helps people reach their heavenly *telos*, but has little to do with man's earthly *telos*. Some "two kingdom" advocates claim that Christians do not learn about earthly citizenship in the church; presumably the magistrate does not learn how to be a Christian magistrate from the church as well. The church should not teach on manhood and womanhood because those are earthly, not heavenly, concerns. And so on.

The problem with such thinking is that the Bible teaches about all those things and the church is entrusted with teaching the Bible. That does not mean the church's teaching is exhaustive in these areas or that church is the only place that people learn about these things. But the church does have responsibility to disciple the other spheres.

If we think of society in a Kuyperian, "sphere sovereignty" way, Christ rules over all spheres, but the church has a kind of centrality among the spheres. And because the church is responsible for teaching the Word of God, it is responsible for providing basic discipleship to each of the spheres.

That being said, some ecclesiocentrists go too far and make claims that go beyond what is warranted. The other spheres matter too and they have their unique roles to play; the church must not usurp them or swallow them up. Worship and prayer should never be treated as a substitute for other forms of action and dominion-taking in the world, but rather as their foundation.

Ecclesiocentrism is not ecclesiocracy, as if the church ruled the other spheres. But it does connect all the other spheres to the church in some way since every sphere is not only bound by God's natural revelation but also by His special revelation.

Basically, ecclesiocentrism is Book 4 of Calvin's *Institutes*. The church is the mother of believers and we need to be under her care for the whole of our lives. Ecclesiocentrism is basically just Westminster Confession 25.2. The church is "the kingdom of the Lord Jesus Christ, the house and family of God, out of which there is no ordinary possibility of salvation."

Some fear that an ecclesiocentric program will lead Christians to substitute prayer and worship for cultural and political action. I tend to think the problem in much of American evangelicalism is the opposite—divorcing political activism from worship. But I will grant that both can be an issue. Here is the solution: It's not worship *instead of* cultural action, but worship as the *foundation* of cultural action. Worship is the basis of dominion. To seek to take dominion apart from a foundation of worship is idolatry. And, of course, the goal of dominion is worship as well since the nations are to bring their treasures into the kingdom (Isa. 60).

Ecclesiocentrism slices through the dualisms of many "two kingdom" approaches which separate man's heavenly end from his earthly end. Where is the Christian citizen going to learn how to be a Christian citizen? Where is the magistrate going to learn about his basic duty to "kiss the Son"? The church needs to exegete what Romans 13 means for ruler and ruled alike. We need to sing Psalm 2 so loud that our rulers down at the capitol building can hear us. There is no way we will ever have discipled nations unless the church teaches and preaches on these topics.

When this kind of transformation has happened in the past, it's because Christians, especially pastors, informed Caesar of his duty to God. There were Election Day sermons. Calvin addressed his *Institutes* to the king of France. Lactantius discipled Constantine about how to govern as a Christian. Ambrose excommunicated Emperor Theodosius until he repented of evil actions and policies. The church has a political power that the American church has completely ignored, which is one reason why our political activism has been so thin and weak.

Appendix C

Two Kinds of
Christian Nationalism

It seems there are two primary alternative forms of Christian nationalism in play, vying for the loyalty of politically engaged Christians: Ecclesiocentric Christian nationalism versus Ethnocentric Christian nationalism. I want to advocate for the former but with a few key qualifications.

Perhaps there are shades in between these two basic positions depending on how much ethnic homogeneity someone thinks is required to have a stable, coherent nation. The church has both nationalist and internationalist aspects to her identity. While I can have a spiritual bond with Christians in Mongolia, there is very little opportunity for us to worship and work together because of language and cultural barriers. We are one in Spirit, but in practice there is little we can do together unless one of us assimilates the language and customs of the other. Scripture has no trouble linking a subsection of the catholic church to a geographic area. Nevertheless, it must also be stressed that all Christians, from whatever ethnicity or nationality, form one holy nation (1 Pet. 2:9) and will live together in perfect and glorious fellowship for all eternity. Scripture repeatedly celebrates the global scope of God's salvation (e.g., Rev. 7). So we must never lose sight of the true global catholicity of the church, spanning across lines of nations-states and linguistic barriers.

An extreme ecclesiocentrism (really, a pietistic or gnostic form of ecclesiocentrism) runs aground against God's creational ordinances that are still in effect. But such extremism is not inherent in the ecclesiocentric position. The church does not *replace* the nation or the family, even if we claim the church is our first and ultimate nation and family. To seek first the kingdom does not mean we *only* seek the kingdom. And it is not a gnostic pursuit either, as if seeking the kingdom is somehow separable from membership in an earthly nation, family, etc. We fulfill our kingdom responsibilities precisely *within* these earthly spheres.

Further, ecclesiocentrism does not mean we have to ignore or bracket out natural/providential realities, e.g., real differences that exist between different nations, different races, and so on. The point of ecclesiocentrism is not to replace or displace the nation, but to disciple the nation. The idea that ecclesiocentrism somehow leads to the godless globalism we see rising in our day, or that it somehow aids and abets hatred of America or "whiteness," is, frankly, absurd. Confessing the centrality of the catholic church in history and society does none of those things.

That being said, I grant that an extreme form of ecclesiocentrism can go too far in relativizing the roles and importance of family and nation.

But an extreme ethnocentric nationalism also runs into problems. It is simply impossible to make a Christian case for racial or ethnic segregation. Even in the old covenant we see all kinds of ethnic and racial intermixing, fully approved by God. Nations are real, but permeable and contingent; thus they come and go from the stage of history. Israel was a mixed multitude from the time they came out of Egypt. Many Gentiles were incorporated into Israel via conversion/circumcision or marriage. Still others became Gentile God-fearers, and no doubt adopted many aspects of the Jewish way of life, though without becoming full Jews. God gave laws to Israel in the Torah regulating and limiting immigration, but made it very clear they were to love the alien and stranger in their midst. Hospitality—literally "love of stranger"—is a prized virtue in Scripture. The ethnocentric concerns of Jonah were roundly rebuked. And so on. Of course, with the arrival of the new covenant, on this side of Pentecost, we know the blessings of Abraham are flowing out to all nations and families. A huge swath of the New Testament, especially Paul's epistles, is taken up with helping Jew and Gentile Christians learn to get along in local congregations. The answer to their problems is never for these groups to segregate, to retreat into their own ecclesiastical or political enclaves. The point is for them to become a new humanity, united together in Christ Jesus, by a common love and faith. It seems that many advocates of an ethnocentric Christian nationalism prioritize national and civil unity over any kind of ecclesial unity. Do they believe there is really one holy catholic and apostolic church? How do they understand the oneness and catholicity of the church? Do they grant that membership in and loyalty to the church transcends and trumps loyalty to the family and nation?

If the "Christian nationalism" discussion is to go forward, it will have to avoid the extremes. If some ecclesiocentrists are guilty of denying the ongoing importance of natural/creational realities like the family, some on the other side are guilty of clinging to the natural to the exclusion of the Spiritual. If extreme ecclesiocentrists are wrong to deny the ongoing importance of creational ordinances like marriage and family, and what we can learn about them from God's design embedded in nature, the ethnocentrists are wrong to deny the clear gospel principle of ethnic and racial integration brought about by the work of Christ and the outpouring of the Holy Spirit.

Take a couple examples of the kinds of statements we ought to avoid. In James B. Jordan's otherwise helpful "Letter on Paedocommunion," he wrote, "The new family is the church. The parents are not the biological parents, but the elders of the church, who act for Christ." In context, Jordan is arguing against certain mistakes made by hyper-patriarchalists, especially in the context of public worship, e.g., the view that fathers rather than church elders hold the keys to the kingdom and can incommunicate and excommunicate their children. He is stressing the church as the new and ultimate family—the household of God, as Paul and the Westminster Confession put it. But it is worded in an extreme way, and thus easily provokes misunderstanding. The church does not displace the natural family, and elders do not take the place of biological parents. The elders of the church are not going to brush your kids' teeth at night, tuck them into bed, or pay their college tuition. The statement goes too far and becomes unhelpful. The church disciples the natural family, but it does not replace the natural family.

But consider another extreme statement. In Stephen Wolfe's book, *The Case for Christian Nationalism*, he says, "The instinct to love the familiar more than the foreign is good and remains operative in all spiritual states of man."[89] But this is simply wrong—or at least wildly overstated. The point is not that we stop loving the familiar—our families, our nations, our customs. The point is that if love of the familiar is raised to a principle that cannot be corrected or transformed in any way, it leads quickly to idolatry. It is contrary to the gospel. It was precisely love for the familiar over the foreign that led Peter to abandon fellowship with believing Gentiles (Gal. 2). The Jerusalem Council had to be called to help Jewish Christians in the apostolic era understand that "foreign" Gentiles were to be welcomed into the family and kingdom of God as fellow heirs and citizens. The water of baptism is thicker than the blood of genetic kinship. If the apostles had followed the instinct Wolfe describes, it would have disastrous for the church; the union of Jewish and Gentile believers in Christ would never have happened. We would be left with a "nationalism of the flesh" rather than a distinctively "Christian nationalism." The gospel does not leave our natural affections

---

89. Stephen Wolfe, *The Case for Christian Nationalism* (Moscow, ID: Canon Press, 2022), 118.

unchanged. It transforms and expands them. Becoming a Christian does not mean I love my family or nation less. But it does reprioritize and expand my loves. It transforms and reshapes my loves. I now love my Chinese Christian next door neighbor in a way that I would not have before; indeed, I have a deeper love for him than I do a neo-pagan white neighbor, even though I more genetic commonality (and perhaps cultural familiarity) with the latter than the former. Further, I hate my own nation for countenancing the slaughter of babies and "gay marriage"—and this hatred is not incompatible with a genuine patriotism, but it indicates that my love and affection for America is not controlled by merely natural considerations but ultimately by Spiritual ones.

Wolfe's nationalism is, in a very crucial way, a nationalism of the flesh. It is a natural nationalism, not a Spiritual or properly Christian nationalism. It will not do to say that whenever various ethnic groups have tried to live in close proximity, it has led to disaster. The early church disproves that. The unity of medieval Europe disproves that (e.g., arguably the fusion of the Normans and Saxons into a new nation/people created the most advanced civilization and most impressive empire in history). The best periods of American history disprove that. From the colonial era onward, America was a melting pot of various European people groups; an "American" was a new kind of person with a distinct cultural heritage, that incorporated many of the best features of a variety of European peoples. Further, up until the Obama presidency, America was largely becoming a post-racial nation in a healthy sense; sadly, since the early 2000s, old racial hatreds have been artificially stoked.

This is the bottom line: We need to have more confidence in the work of the gospel. Wolfe's principle of "like likes like" is simply bad ecclesiology and bad missiology. Our love for the familiar and the foreign cannot remain a merely natural love, but must become a Spiritual love, guided and shaped by the Spirit's work and the revelation of Scripture. Wolfe has constructed a speculative doctrine about how unfallen humans would gather in ethnically and racially segregated/homogenous groups and declared these natural impulses (even post-Fall) are immune to gospel critique. But this does not seem any different from those who justify same-sex attraction by claiming it is "natural" to them. Wolfe has built a speculative doctrine and refused to let clear biblical texts correct it. This is mistaken.

Ecclesiocentrists need to guard against denials of nature/natural revelation and the creation ordinances; grace does not destroy or override nature, but rather restores and perfects nature, rightly understood. Ethnocentrists need to guard against denials of the transformative power of the gospel and the weight of new covenant catholicity; while families and nations continue to exist, they are secondary to the family and nation that is the church catholic. Perhaps if both sides avoid extremes, they can at least find substantial common ground.

Recommended Reading

Creation in Six Days: A Defense of the Traditional Reading of Genesis One by James B. Jordan

Through New Eyes by James B. Jordan

The Kingdom and the Power: Rediscovering the Centrality of the Church by Peter J. Leithart

The Lord's Service: The Grace of Covenant Renewal Worship by Jeffrey J. Meyers

The Puritan Hope by Iain H. Murray

How Christianity Changed the World by Alvin J. Schmidt

Heaven Misplaced: Christ's Kingdom on Earth by Douglas Wilson

Angels in the Architecture: A Protestant Vision for Middle Earth by Douglas Jones and Douglas Wilson

Surprised by Hope by N.T. Wright

God at Work by Gene Veith

www.ingramcontent.com/pod-product-compliance
Lightning Source LLC
Chambersburg PA
CBHW070900120626
46546CB00001B/82